Into the Transcendent Light

Into the Transcendent Light

Awakening Through Plato's *Republic*

JACK CRITTENDEN

CASCADE Books • Eugene, Oregon

INTO THE TRANSCENDENT LIGHT
Awakening Through Plato's *Republic*

Copyright © 2025 Jack Crittenden. All rights reserved. Except for brief quotations in critical publications or reviews, no part of this book may be reproduced in any manner without prior written permission from the publisher. Write: Permissions, Wipf and Stock Publishers, 199 W. 8th Ave., Suite 3, Eugene, OR 97401.

Cascade Books
An Imprint of Wipf and Stock Publishers
199 W. 8th Ave., Suite 3
Eugene, OR 97401

www.wipfandstock.com

PAPERBACK ISBN: 979-8-3852-3590-2
HARDCOVER ISBN: 979-8-3852-3591-9
EBOOK ISBN: 979-8-3852-3592-6

Cataloguing-in-Publication data:

Names: Crittenden, Jack [author].

Title: Into the transcendent light : awakening through Plato's *Republic* / by Jack Crittenden.

Description: Eugene, OR: Cascade Books, 2025 | Includes bibliographical references.

Identifiers: ISBN 979-8-3852-3590-2 (paperback) | ISBN 979-8-3852-3591-9 (hardcover) | ISBN 979-8-3852-3592-6 (ebook)

Subjects: LCSH: Plato. Republic. | Form (Philosophy). | Plato—Ethics. | Self-realization—Philosophy. | Self-actualization (Psychology)—Philosophy. | Well-being—Philosophy.

Classification: JC71.P6 C758 2025 (paperback) | JC71.P6 (ebook)

01/15/26

Hackett Publishing Company has granted Jack Crittenden permission in *Into the Transcendent Light: Awakening Through Plato's* Republic to quote extensively from *Plato Complete Works*, Hackett, 1997.
All images used are in the public domain and are reproduced under Creative Commons license

"God's language is silence; all else is poor translation."
—Rumi

"Behind your image, below your words, above your thoughts, the silence of another world waits. A world lives within you. No one else can bring you news of this inner world."
—John O'Donohue
Anam Cara

Contents

Acknowledgments | ix

Introduction | 1

1. The Settings | 15
2. The Ring of Gyges and the Rise of Cities | 25
3. Philosophical Dogs | 44
4. Education of the Guardians | 54
5. The Noble Lie | 69
6. The Good City | 88
7. The Tripartite Soul | 99
8. The Good | 111
9. The Forms and the *Tao* | 131
10. Up the Divided Line and Out of the Cave | 145
11. Returning to the Cave | 165
12. Are the Forms a Noble Lie? | 182
13. Political Character and the Nature of the Soul | 202
14. Imitation and the Myth of Er | 218
15. Inner Harmony Through the Transcendent Light | 234

Bibliography | 255

Acknowledgments

Over the years, as part of a survey course in ancient and medieval political thought, I taught Plato's *Republic* to graduate students and undergraduates alike. Later on in my career, I offered on two occasions a special-topics graduate seminar on Plato. Later still, I offered graduate seminars exclusively on the *Republic* and permitted talented undergraduates to enroll in them.

These seminars were highlights of my thirty years of collegiate teaching. Students seemed to enjoy them as well. In one of the *Republic* seminars, I had as many drop-in students attending as I had students formally registered for the course. Every one of those drop-in students had taken the seminar with me before. There can be no greater compliment, it seems to me, for any teacher.

The quality of all of these seminars depended solely on the participation of the students. Their active, creative, and trenchant discussions enabled me to remove myself and allowed me to remain, as Nicole Mayberry (one of those students and now a friend) phrased it, "infuriatingly Socratic." I was a mere footnote to their full texts. I would have it no other way.

Now, I count many of those seminar students as dear friends. I do the minimum here by simply listing their names and thereby fail utterly to convey to the readers of this book how much I value each of them and how much they have contributed to my thinking about Plato's *Republic*.

Thank you all for your willingness to risk your reputations by voicing and writing half-baked ideas and arguments that with input from your colleagues and with your own revisions became significant contributions to my own thinking and thus to this book. And thank you all for using your intellectual machetes to hack your way through my copious marginal notes on drafts of your seminar papers.

But that hacking in no way cancels the debt you owe to me. At the very least, at our next coffee or lunch, it is your turn to pay. This includes you, Eyal Bar, Dana Bersch, Debi Campbell, Stefan Dolgert, Sean Hays, Bobby (Borislav) Iovtchek, Alisa Kessel, Toby Lacarra, Jentry Lanza, Matt Lucky, Nicole Mayberry, Tyler Olsen, Daniel Pout, Jenny Reich, and Rory Varrato.

Introduction

On the upper level of the Metropolitan Museum of Art in New York hangs Jacques-Louis David's painting *The Death of Socrates* (1787). In the painting Socrates, seated on a bed, expostulates as he gestures with the forefinger of his left hand up toward the ceiling, the sky, the Empyrean. With his right hand, Socrates reaches out for the cup of hemlock with which he will end his life. He seems little bothered that soon he will be dead.

Socrates is little bothered, because he always lived life true to his word. He announced during his trial that death did not trouble him. Indeed, he said in the dialogue the *Apology* that death is a blessing: Either it is "like a dreamless sleep and [thus] a great advantage, . . . for all eternity would then seem no more than a single night," or death is "a change and a relocating for the soul from here to another place . . . [where] we keep company with [the likes of] Orpheus and Musaeus, Hesiod and Homer . . . [and] I could spend my time testing and examining people there."[1]

Surrounding Socrates in the painting are several of his students and friends, many of whom, on the other hand, seem truly bothered by what is to come. One of them is Plato, sitting at the foot of the bed, with his back toward Socrates, his head bent downward, his eyes closed, a pen and scroll beside him on the floor.

At the time of Socrates's death Plato would have been twenty-nine years old. Yet David portrays him as quite old, seemingly even older than Socrates. Why? One reason might be that in his depiction David imagines Plato in his old age reliving the scene of his mentor's death, as if Plato had been writing about it, but then overcome by the recollection dropped the pen and scroll and sank into melancholy or reverie or trance. Plato looks composed and relaxed. He might well be sleeping, dreaming of Socrates at the end, aged seventy-one but with the body of a muscular middle-aged man and the senescent pate of the wisest man in Greece.

Another possibility is that David realized that even at twenty-nine Plato was an old soul, one who relished in, understood, and lived by Socrates's teachings about wisdom and the transcendent. Plato's wisdom far exceeded his earthly years, and if that wisdom, beyond human and into the divine, were to be animated or depicted as human, it would take the form of an ancient wise one. That is Plato seated at the foot of his mentor's bed.

Socrates's pointing skyward may be one indication that this is Plato's recollection or dream. Over 250 years earlier, Raphael had depicted the same clue in his fresco *The School of Athens*, which decorates one of the walls in the Room of the Signatura in the Vatican. In the fresco Plato walks with Aristotle, deep in conversation, Aristotle laying his hand out

---

1. Plato, *Apology*, 40c4–41b5. In addition to the *Republic*, titles in the footnotes and in the text that appear like this, unless otherwise explained, refer to one of Plato's other dialogues—for example, the *Crito* or the *Theaetetus*. All citations from the *Republic* and Plato's other dialogues, unless otherwise noted, are taken from Plato, *Plato Complete Works*.

The numbers and letters following the dialogue title above refer to the numerical system known as "Stephanus numbers." Toward the end of the sixteenth century, a French classical scholar and printer, Henri Estienne (also known as Henricus Stephanus), numbered sections of all of Plato's dialogues. This numerical system, as I show in this footnote and use in parentheses throughout my text, makes it easier to locate passages in the dialogues and for scholars to cite Plato's works. The numbers are uniform across all translations and editions of the dialogues.

flat, attuned to the earth's surface, while Plato points the forefinger of his right hand skyward, as Socrates does in David's painting. Though David's Plato is in repose, wrapped and almost hidden in his robe, Raphael depicts Plato as old but thick and robust, keeping pace with the much younger Aristotle.

We know that it is Aristotle and Plato at the center of the fresco, because the younger man carries a copy of the *Ethics*, while the older man is carrying the *Timaeus*, a dialogue of Plato's that discusses the origin and nature of the universe. But it is the pointing that connects these two Platos, as Plato replicates with his student Aristotle the orientation that he himself learned from his teacher, Socrates. It is the Forms to which both Socrates and Plato point, and the Forms are the central focus of my meditation on the *Republic*.[2]

What exactly are the Forms? To answer that will take up much of this volume. Please don't lose patience just yet, but the very short answer

---

2. In her review of Pritchard's *Plato's Philosophy of Mathematics*, Verity Harte concludes with the suspicion "that few Plato scholars are card-carrying believers in Forms" (Harte, "Review," 227). Given my emphasis on the Forms, about which you shall read much in this volume, I can state that I am one such card-carrier. Yet I am not a card-carrying scholar of Plato; that much to all is evidently true. This fact excludes me, therefore, from Harte's category. But a believer I remain.

is that the Forms are the realm of perfection, true reality, Being, what Is. Again, don't lose patience yet.

Equally important to understanding the Forms is seeing how knowing them—and we can know them—affects our lives, especially our moral outlook and behavior. Knowing the Forms is a way to create a robust, moral, and happy life.

Answering the question "Why be moral?" is the focus of Plato's *Republic* and, of course, is the focus of this book. The Greek term *dikaiosunē* is central to both. Most often *dikaiosunē* is translated as "justice." In my text, however, I follow the translator Robin Waterfield and use "morality" rather than "justice." *Dikaiosunē* is a broad, abstract term encompassing justice, but also its moral underpinnings. My concern, then, is that by using "justice" alone, we miss some aspects of *dikaiosunē*. In Book IV of the *Republic*, for example, Socrates declares the city he is describing as "completely good," and therefore it contains the four cardinal virtues: wisdom, temperance, courage, and justice. But there are more virtues than these four. To be "completely good," should not that city reflect other virtues as well? By following Waterfield and using "morality," there is a better chance, I think, of capturing some other virtues.

I think so for this reason: The virtue of justice is outward looking, whereas other virtues, such as temperance or moderation, tell us something about the character and internal life of a person, but do not necessarily have much to do with others.

"Morality" encompasses both inward and outward virtues. Plus, "morality" can also comprise virtues not mentioned in the *Republic*, but that might also be important in how individuals conduct themselves with others. Here we could include Aristotle's virtues of friendliness and magnanimity, for example.

Therefore, for me, the idea of morality encapsulates the many virtues of the city, which every good city and every good person need. Granted, any of the virtues can lead us to the Forms; all of the virtues are, in and of themselves, reflections of the highest Form, the Form beyond form—the Good. One's life, then, is an expression of the Good in what each says and does.

I have a final reason for preferring the term "morality" over the use of the term "justice." A focus on justice can mislead readers, even close readers, of the *Republic* into emphasizing the creation of an ideal city, the beautiful city (*kallipolis*), ruled over by philosopher kings. This distorts our perspective, as I argue throughout the text, by taking us away from the creation of moral souls. There is very little, I think, in Plato's city of three classes that constitutes anything that we might think is moral, let alone beautiful.

The city stands in as a metaphor for the structure of an ordered and integrated soul. The possible attainment of that soul is, for me, the point of the *Republic*. The way to that attainment is up the path out of the Piraeus, the setting of the *Republic*, and out of the cave of shadows that constitute so much of earthly life. Plato, therefore, offers lessons for all of us, especially today as our politics and our cultures—our "city" or civilization—pull us deeper into materialism, consumerism, expediency, and status, as they simultaneously push us away from morality and virtue. Reading Plato, and I hope reading this book, can provide some insight into and arguments for the value of attaining a soul reoriented toward the Good, the True, and the Beautiful.

The *Republic* is a sprawling work, moving as conversations do from topic to topic, sometimes in ways that might seem random. It is also a big book, both in length and in the array of ideas. And it is a great piece of literature. When Alfred North Whitehead commented that Western philosophy was little but a series of footnotes to Plato, he might not have been far off even if he had excluded consideration of any work of Plato's other than the *Republic*.[3]

I've taught the *Republic* at least a dozen times. Over the course of that teaching, in facing undergraduates and graduate students alike, I've established one firm conclusion drawn from my professional colleagues: most of them have gotten it wrong. To be frank, I now question the conventional reading of the *Republic*, that it is a text about justice and Plato's ideal state. That is the position of many academics and general readers.

I am not alone in this assessment. Despite my long list of disagreements with Jean-Jacques Rousseau, I agree with his observation that the *Republic* "is not at all a political work, as think those who judge books only by their titles. It is the most beautiful educational treatise ever written."[4]

While accepting his observation, I don't agree with all of it. Of course, the *Republic* is in part a political work. There is much beyond

---

3. Here is the exact quotation from Whitehead: "The safest general characterization of the [Western] philosophical tradition is that it consists in a series of footnotes to Plato" (Whitehead, *Process*, 39).

4 Rousseau, *Emile*, (trans. Bloom), 40. Rousseau's is also a comparison noted by Bloom, who translated the *Republic* as well: "*Emile* is the canvas on which Rousseau tried to paint all of the soul's acquired passions and learning . . . a book comparable to Plato's *Republic* . . ." (Bloom, "Democratic Man," 135).

the title that can lead readers—academic and general—to the view that Plato is creating the ideal just society. But that society is not the focus of the work. Here I fully accept Rousseau's judgment and repeat my own: Readers who think that the *Republic* is about the ideal polis have gotten it wrong.

How or why do they? They overlook, I think, two fundamental orientations that alter our understanding of the dialogue.

First, Plato and Socrates were *teachers*. Using the dialectical method of questions-and-answers, both let their students and interlocutors guide the conversations. Neither Socrates nor Plato was on a mission to provide ready answers in their conversations. Instead, they were probing their students' thinking to bring them to deeper and greater insights and understanding.

Today, we often refer to this process as the "Socratic method." It is dialectical in operation, using questions, answers, and further questions based on those answers to excite further thought. With this method in mind, we can see in the *Republic*, just as Rousseau commented, that above all else Plato is creating a philosophy of education built on dialectic. That philosophy of education is both philosophical and psychological education.

The second orientation often missed by readers is that Plato and Socrates were *mystics*. Both might well have been participants in the Eleusinian Mysteries, but we cannot know for certain, since the word "mystery" derives from the Greek word *muo*, which means "to keep one's eyes shut." "Mystic" derives as well from *muo*, and so participants at Eleusis kept their mouths shut as well. About which one cannot speak, one must remain silent.

Nevertheless, we do have the record of what Plato wrote and Socrates spoke in the dialogue the *Phaedo*:

> *For as they say in the* [Eleusinian] *mysteries, "the thyrsus-bearers are many, but the mystics are few"; and these mystics are, I believe, those who have been true philosophers. And I in my life, so far as I could, left nothing undone, and have striven in every way to make myself one of them.* (69c–d)

"Making himself one of them" might well have involved initiation into the Mysteries, as well as imbibing an elixir known as *kukeon*, a psychedelic brew made with the natural-growing fungus ergot.[5] How-

---

5. Muraresku, *Immortality Key*.

ever the ceremony proceeded and however the elixir worked, Plato and Socrates developed their philosophy of education in conjunction with their mysticism, introducing readers of the *Republic* to the importance of the transcendental through the theory of the Forms.

So, Plato and Socrates were teachers and mystics. Without those two perspectives readers will struggle to understand why in the *Republic* Plato has Socrates, proclaimed by the Delphic Oracle as the wisest man in all of Greece, use so many bad arguments.[6] Chief among those bad arguments is the use of the Noble Lie, the idea that each soul is born as either gold or silver or bronze. If the *Republic* is a dialogue about the construction of the just or moral city, how can such a city be founded on a lie?

But, as said, the *Republic* is not really about such a city. It is about the growth and perpetuation of a moral soul—harmonious, ordered, and happy. As Plato shows us, any person is potentially a soul of gold, able to rise through philosophical education and dialectic to the Forms—to knowledge of the transcendent, the realm of true Reality and Being.

To me the dialogue is chiefly about the Forms, how to know them, and what follows in life once one has known them.[7] Holding that perspective in mind, the reader will therefore find that I move quickly (some will think too quickly; others, not quickly enough) to a discussion of the Forms, while stopping along the way at various "lookout spots" to ponder for a time certain images, ideas, or puzzles that catch my eye.

So, this book is not a thorough philosophical study of the entire dialogue. That doesn't interest me, nor am I fully capable of such a study. Instead, this book is a reflection of—a meditation on—what I hold to be centrally and profoundly significant about the dialogue: principally but not exclusively a discussion of Platonic Forms and how to know them.

Some critics—my friend Dave Yount is one[8]—argue that the Forms may be important but only in a limited way. There isn't enough consistent

---

6. As many readers will know, Plato uses Socrates as his mouthpiece in most of his dialogues. Whether Plato is reciting in the *Republic* and in other dialogues what Socrates actually taught or whether Plato is placing in Socrates's mouth Plato's own thoughts and arguments is incidental to me.

7. The conventional translation of the title, the "Republic," derives from the Greek term *Politéia*, which I prefer translating as "Constitution." This preference follows from my view that the dialogue is not as much about political matters and governmental organization as it is about the "organization," "setting in order," or "making firm" of one's own character and soul—that is, one's own "constitution."

8. See his books *Plotinus the Platonist* and *Plato and Plotinus on Mysticism, Epistemology, and Ethics*.

discussion of the Forms throughout all of the dialogues for this to be a central concern of Plato's. Plus, Aristotle's criticism of Platonic Forms hasn't helped.

But, of course, I read Plato differently, which in part explains why you, my reader, will find this book a combination of philosophical meditation and fiction. You see, I imagine that Plato used his dialogues as many of us have used them in class; that is, as teaching tools for focusing our students' thinking and discussions on an important moral, social, or political concept, e.g., love or piety or justice. In his Academy—a school, but also perhaps the greatest intellectual salon ever—I imagine that whenever Plato wished to introduce a topic for discussion, he would use a dialogue, as I have done here with the *Republic* in my own imaginary pedagogical setting.

Plato used his dialogues as teaching tools because every dialogue is itself a dialectic, the Platonic and Socratic method of moving back-and-forth between a preceptor—most often Socrates—and his interlocutors. The back-and-forth often took the form of question-and-answer, another teaching tool we instructors use.[9] Its frequent Socratic use or method was that of exclusion—namely, to undercut and thereby eliminate inadequate understandings or definitions of important concepts or ideas. This overall method of philosophical discourse is known as "dialectic," though its nuances far exceed this simple rendering of the term.[10]

The dialogical or dialectical method is significant not only because the back-and-forth uncovers hidden and faulty assumptions that the interlocutors hold and use, but also because it stimulates, if not drives, the students' thinking to greater and deeper insights into, conclusions about, or understanding of the topic under discussion. This is so because dialectic is a method of discovery; it is not an instrument of imposition.

---

9. "Someone who knows how to ask and to answer questions," Plato, *Cratylus*, 390c9–10.

10. The method is sometimes also referred to as *elenchus* (from the Greek *elengchein* meaning "to refute"), which is the formal name for the Socratic technique of using the question-and-answer format (or cross-examination) to point out, if not highlight, the inconsistencies in the fundamental assumptions and positions held by the discussants. In many of Plato's dialogues, Socrates's use of *elenchus* results in irritating his interlocutors. In some instances the result is the interlocutors' stupefaction or silence. This is the bloodless way to describe that result. In this silence, I think, the interlocutors arrive before the beginning, before the birth or the moment of thought; that is, they arrive at the infinite silence and stillness of pure awareness without any object (Plato, *Republic*, 511). I discuss this in the text.

As I see it, in a pedagogical setting the dialogues were discrete, designed for specific concepts or ideas. Naturally, for continuity and also because themes overlapped or led from one into another, there would be carry-over of themes across dialogues. Yet, from this perspective, we should no more expect repetition of the same themes from dialogue to dialogue than we would expect to see such repetition in every score by Mozart or every painting by Picasso, especially if they were using their work to teach fundamental lessons. This is my position on the theme of Platonic Forms.

So, my use of fictional characters and of a fictionalized setting attempts to animate my idea of how Plato used the dialogues in the Academy. Since there is no evidence of how Plato actually taught, I created two fictional students of Plato's and also offer two imaginatively rendered versions of the historical figures of Hermias, the former slave, from Atarneus and of Plato himself. The setting of my work is an evening in the olive groves of the Academy where Plato introduces the *Republic*, or parts of it, for the first time. The lesson that he pursues is as much about the Forms as it is about justice and morality.

In using this approach, you will also see that I have created a dialogue about the dialogue. What could be more fitting for delving into different aspects of Plato's most famous dialogue than using a form of dialectic itself?

A dialogue is not, and is not meant to be seen as, a definitive statement on any issue. When we enter into a Platonic dialogue, we are in the midst of a conversation in which characters try out positions. The dialogue opens up questions and leaves them open, once the dialogue proper has ended. In short, the point of a dialogue is to open up the reader to the questions and positions discussed within it. The dialogue stimulates the reader's thinking and imagination.[11] Imagination is as important to Platonic dialogues as is philosophizing, for Plato has given us a dramatic structure for the presentation of philosophical ideas.

As a representative example of dialectic, the discussion in the *Republic* moves and turns depending on what the interlocutors say in response to Socrates's statements or questions. This approach is in keeping with what Socrates himself says in the *Republic*: "I myself don't really know yet, but whatever direction the argument blows us, that's where we must go" (394d7–9). Much of the blowing will come from the students, his

---

11. *Dialegesthai*, our "dialogue," is the Greek term for "sorting things out" by "talking things through" with others. Literally it means "speaking across or between."

interlocutors. So, it is they who set the course of the dialogue.[12] Socrates simply goes where the interlocutors point or direct him. Their positions, reactions, queries, and objections lead him. Socrates extrapolates from or examines what they offer.

Sometimes the arguments that Socrates proffers, as I pointed out earlier, are bad arguments, even cringe-worthy. He seems to be testing his interlocutors to see where and whether they might object. In the *Republic*, as my own students often reported aghast, there are several such bad arguments. But Socrates fulfills his role, as if he is saying, "Well, if you'll accept this position and won't argue back, let's see where the position leads us." I take it that Socrates's (and Plato's) stance is always to tease out the nature, scope, and ramifications of the arguments that students accept or let slip by.[13]

Thus, in the *Republic* Glaucon and Adeimantus—two principal interlocutors and also, playfully, Plato's brothers—help set the tone for and devise the course of the conversation. In my own text, my interlocutors—Kydes, Hermias, and Demetra—are integral to uncovering aspects of the *Republic* often unexamined and unseen.

My characters don't really steer the conversation as much as they offer commentary on the dialogue. They react as students in my classes reacted: pondering, analyzing, challenging, and toying with the text. That is, in my rendering Plato is testing out how certain parts of the *Republic* play with three of his most promising though young students. There is less room for them, therefore, to redirect the discussion, since Plato in my text wants to cover certain specific arguments and topics. My text, then, is my opportunity to explore and discover aspects of the *Republic*.

Nevertheless, there remains ample room for real dialectic to proceed. That dialectic is what occurs within you, the reader. This makes you

---

12. In the *Theaetetus*, Socrates says much the same thing: "The arguments never come from me; they always come from the person I am talking to. All I know, such as it is, is how to take an argument from someone else . . . and give it a fair reception." Plato, *Theaetetus*, 161b2–5.

13. Stanley Rosen comments on bad arguments this way: "No competent reader of . . . the *Republic* . . . can miss the fact that Socrates employs an unusual number of faulty arguments. This presents us with two choices. Either Socrates is himself incompetent, or he has no hesitation in making use of unpersuasive arguments in order to obtain what he no doubt regards as salutary arguments" (Rosen, *Plato's Republic*, 233). But there is a third option that Rosen overlooks. Socrates intends those faulty arguments as tests of his interlocutors, who are both friends and students. That is the position that I am taking in this book. Whether the arguments are good or bad, Socrates will present them and see what his interlocutors do with them and where the arguments lead.

a participant, willing or otherwise, in Plato's philosophy of education, because it is your reaction to and interaction with my dialogue that is the real dialectical or educational experience. A reader of the dialogues who is only interested in what Socrates and his interlocutors have to say has missed the point. The point is to intervene in the dialogue, to raise your questions, and to announce your disagreements and complaints. We readers most often do this in the margins of the texts. I hope you find some way to record your reactions. As Plato himself might have asked of his readers, is there anything in this dialogue that helps you think about how to live a better, more fulfilled, more compassionate, more beautiful, or more moral life? In this way, you yourself exercise dialectic.

There is a final element of dialectic important to point out. In Plato's dialogue the *Meno*, the main interlocutor, Meno, is in conversation with Socrates. Meno claims that he has heard that Socrates is "always in a state of perplexity" (*aporia*) and that through his conversations (dialectic) he brings others to the same state of perplexity. Indeed, Meno continues, "you seem, in appearance and in every other way, to be like the broad torpedo fish [*narke*], for it too makes anyone who comes close and touches it feel numb."[14]

On the surface, being rendered numb can hardly be construed as something beneficial. Yet, it is the key, I think, of dialectic. As so often happens in the dialogues, Socrates's interlocutors are left numb, speechless, and perplexed. They are rendered silent. Within the context of esoteric, mystical, and meditative traditions, silence is just where one needs to be to experience the transcendent, the ethereal, the divine. Through his pedagogical approach, through probing questions and responses, Socrates brings his interlocutors to the very edge of their reasoning capabilities and then often gives them a little shove. By doing so, he leaves them frozen or suspended in the moment, outside of time, and open in their internal perplexity to states of insight not available through language and logic.

This, I think, is the height of dialectic: to move discussants beyond language and logic to knowledge available only through other avenues or means. To achieve this state requires the silencing of the logical and chattering mind; to take reasoning to its pinnacle, only to find that reasoning itself must be transcended: "For both my mind and my tongue are numb,

---

14. Plato, *Meno*, 80a1–7.

and I have no answer to give you."[15] At that moment, insights from and about the Forms can rush in, like a fire arising from a spark from an adjacent fire. The fire metaphor will come up again in a couple of forms in my text, as my characters will find themselves "aporetic." My hope is that you, too, may find yourself reduced to a silence found through perplexity.

That silence is significant when reading the *Republic*, for one of the most important messages in this as in other Platonic dialogues is not really a message at all: It is to show dialectic, the method for exploring the foundations of concepts central to our lives—justice, beauty, love, piety, courage, friendship—as a way to the transcendent that is the ground of those foundations.

Speaking of transcendental states was not foreign to Plato or, therefore, to my text, as you shall see. To that end, I have also set the exploration of the Forms in the context of the "Axial Age," German philosopher Karl Jaspers's term (from the German *Achsenzeit*) for the explosion of new philosophical and spiritual ideas and institutions that sprang up in, energized, and transformed several civilizations between 900 to 200 BCE. This was the time of the Buddha, Confucius, Lao Tzu, Zoroaster, and, of course, Socrates. S. N. Eisenstadt, the editor of and one of the contributors to *The Origins and Diversity of Axial Age Civilizations*, comments that this age spawned "a new type of intellectual elite [who] became aware of the necessity to actively construct the world according to some transcendental vision."[16]

When reading this statement, one might place an emphasis on the idea of an "intellectual elite ... actively constructing" the internal mechanisms of society according to this vision, which is one conventional way of reading the *Republic*. On the other hand, I focus on the metaphysical experience or the "transcendental vision" that initiated the awareness to reorder society.

In particular I wish to show that the realm of Plato's Forms, his transcendental vision, is related to insights found in the *Tao Te Ching* and in the *Māndūkya* Upanishad.[17] The *Tao Te Ching*, compiled by and attrib-

---

15. Plato, *Meno*, 80b2.

16 Eisenstadt, *Origins and Diversity*, 1.

17. Although the dates and authorship of the *Tao Te Ching* are unconfirmed, scholars have been able to narrow the dates of its composition to around the sixth century BCE and probably no later than the fourth century BCE. The dates of the composition of the Upanishads are also unconfirmed, but the range of their production is thought to be between the ninth and the fourth centuries BCE.

uted to Lao Tzu, is the heart of the Chinese philosophical and religious school known as Taoism. The Upanishads are part of the Indian Vedic tradition. Commonly referred to as *Vedānta* or "the end of the Vedas," the Upanishads are mystical texts that, along with all of the Vedas, became a foundational part of the Hindu religion.

Because Athens was a seafaring city and traded throughout the Mediterranean, I find it plausible that Athenians, especially those curious about the goods and ways of life of other societies, could have traveled to India and even China, just as merchants, teachers, and philosophers from the Far East could have visited and did visit Athens. The exchange of transcendental insights might have been one of the most significant transactions among all of the trading going on in and through the Piraeus, the seaport setting of the *Republic*. After all, it is the installation of Bendis, a goddess foreign to Athens, that brings Socrates and his mates down to the Piraeus.

So, students of both Socrates and Plato might well have traveled far from Greece to see how others lived or, perhaps more ambitiously, how they might influence others to live according to dialectic. These students might well have encountered fellow philosophers studying the transcendental insights indigenous to their regions and independently derived from their own experiences and foreign texts that they would be happy to share with the visitors from Athens. These visiting peripatetic "Platonic" philosophers might be eager to return to Athens to share with Plato scrolls that they have discovered or that they themselves created that reflect different but simpatico insights. From these scrolls the Plato of my imagination will share with his three charges portions of the teachings of two seemingly quite different schools: Taoism and Vedānta. As I stated earlier in this introduction, for me the point of the *Republic* is to show us how to order and harmonize the soul. The attainment of that soul, moving from individual soul to universal Soul, is the same, I think, for these and other schools from the Far East.

But is this attainment, this reorientation from material life to the life of the soul, really better? Always better? To put the point more crassly, "What's in it for me?" Plato, through Socrates, tells us, but much of it might be opaque, even murky. Thus, I think, the need for this book.

The short answer to those questions is this: When we harm others, we also harm ourselves; when we help others, we also help ourselves. So, a good life, a happy life, is one in which we maximize helping others and minimize harming them.

If you are attracted to this short answer, then you might next want to know how to attain such a moral constitution and a happy life. That, too, is covered in this book, but here is a clue:

In the Louvre hangs Rembrandt's painting *Philosopher in Meditation* that is reflective of this Platonic attainment. In Rembrandt's painting the philosopher sits in repose as if in meditation or contemplative prayer, not unlike Plato in David's painting. The light coming in through a set of windows illuminates him. This light contrasts with the darkness of the room in which the philosopher sits. A small arched wooden door lies behind the philosopher; a short distance away is a set of many curved wooden steps spiraling up in and through the darkness. Next to the stairs and opposite the philosopher a murky figure pokes tongs into a fire.

This painting reminds me of Plato's allegory of the cave. I'll save the detailed discussion of the allegory for the text, so here it will suffice, I think, only to point out that the sources of light and fire in the painting connect to the fire in the cave, the sun outside it, and the long climb out of the cave to the light. The point of this is to say that all of us in life, and not just philosophers, are looking for the light. We cannot remain satisfied with small fires and need those small fires only to light our way out of the dark and into the transcendent light.

1

The Settings

PLATO'S ACADEMY

Plato stood in the olive grove, a sacred site dedicated to Athena, at the far end of the Academy, one of his finest creations. The shroud of branches and leaves protected his broad shoulders and wide forehead from the sun. He awaited the arrival of three of his most advanced "friends," not students as many might call them, but friends, since to Plato all in the Academy, regardless of age or station, were engaged equally in the same educating endeavor. This friendship was holy to all but the most jaded.

So, Plato awaited Hermias, the ex-slave from Atarneus; Demetra, the granddaughter of Pericles and Aspasia; and Kydes, from the family of Plato's friend and colleague Eudoxus. They were coming from Athens, a mile walk to the Academy from the Dipylon Gate, the largest and most significant of the fifteen gates into and out of the city.

Soon he saw the three, shoulder to shoulder, crowding the pathway, walking toward him. Hermias was on the far left, already with a full beard, his face sharp and angular, matching his tall, thin body, though his movements were languid, as if walking through water. In the middle came Demetra, who had inherited her grandmother's beauty—large, blue eyes framed by long, dark lashes, her nose a small cliff sheltering the full pool of her lips, her thick, dark hair pulled off her face and tied, unbraided, in the back, her womanly curves accentuated by the wrap of her *peplos*, which lay snug against her body. That left Kydes, whose clean-shaven, boyish face belied the compact musculature below that propelled him along the path with the direct, purposeful prowl of the boxer or wrestler.

They jostled one another, as friends do, and this playfulness revealed the mix of youthful frolic and burgeoning sexuality typical of late adolescence. There were many students older than these three, more experienced than these three, even better schooled; none, however, as elastic intellectually or as curious and open-minded. None, either, with the experiences of this trio.

The three saw Plato, his *himation* and his beard moving in unison with the light wind. The gown accented his wrestler's body, still muscular at his late age, and yet he was renowned for his broad outlook and learning more than his reputation for past physical exploits.

The three bounded toward their teacher like trusting hounds, tails wagging, waiting for whatever treat the master would bestow. Any observer could see the affection with which they greeted Plato and the eagerness with which they awaited any explanation for this gathering. He had brought them into adolescence and into their awareness of life inside and outside of Athens. They owed much to this philosopher, who could not walk through the Agora, the bustling Athenian marketplace, without being stopped and engaged at least a dozen times. He was gracious to all, never denying anyone of any age some time and his attention. No one in Athens—indeed, no one within all of Greece—was more admired for his insight, no one in the courts, no one in the Assembly, and no one in the military.

This reputation animated the Academy. Whatever Plato judged suitable for his students and for his colleagues—from math to astronomy, from poetry to wrestling—became the curriculum. Plato and his colleagues taught whatever moved and pleased them, lessons that in turn moved and pleased their students.

Plato's pedagogical style, mimicked by colleagues and students alike, was the Socratic method, developed entirely by Socrates's example of deliberating with and interrogating citizens in and around Athens. Socrates was to Plato as Plato was to these students. Kydes and Hermias thought that they would gladly die for him; Demetra, that she would gladly bear his children. She, unlike the boys, who announced their bravura at every turn, would never admit this, seeing with ease its scandalous side, though she had fantasized about it since first coming to the Academy.

During his lessons, Plato lectured from time to time, in a voice slightly above a whisper, but mostly he posed questions and problems and then sat or stood back as his students, in collaboration and combat, tore the questions and problems to bits, trying to figure them out.

The Settings

Standing now before their teacher, Demetra asked, "Where is Aristotle? Shouldn't he be here?"

Plato said, "Aristotle went to the mountains to collect plant samples. This is not an evening for him."

Kydes added impishly, "He's really missing out," to which Plato with a quiet smile responded, "Perhaps."

The trio of students, bemused, snuck sideward glances at one another. Then, for the first time, they gazed around the grove. They scanned the *kline* or couches arrayed in a tight semi-circle. The servants were bringing and laying out the food for this evening. The boys focused on the food, while Demetra admired some of the wine urns.

Plato watched his star pupils, each shining with intelligence like the sun's first light. Hermias, a slave from Atarneus, a commercial town on the Troad coastline of Asia Minor, just north of the island of Lesbos, had been sent to the Academy by Eubulus, Hermias's owner. Eubulus could not deny the slave's intellectual promise. Because of his experiences in the streets of Atarneus, Hermias had a practical side to his intellect that might well help him later in business and especially in politics.

Kydes, from the family of Arrichion, the greatest pankratiast[1] in the history of the Olympic Games and one of Athens's greatest athletes, possessed the body and attitude of an athlete, which Plato openly admired, given his own background. Yet Kydes was also a cousin of Plato's close friend and fellow "Academic" Eudoxus from whom Kydes may well have inherited his reflective and, when unguarded, sensitive side. In Kydes Plato saw the makings of a teacher, if Kydes, like a wrestler emboldened by his skill, could restrain his penchant for the quick move, too often leading to unnecessary risks.

Demetra had her own royal background, a more obvious one. She was the daughter of Pericles the Younger, himself the son of Pericles, the great statesman of Athens, and was the granddaughter of Aspasia, the controversial consort of Pericles and later his second wife. Of all the senior students at the Academy Demetra was the most gifted intellectually. She had the fire of philosophy, embodying both the heat of insight and the danger of burning herself out early with her dogged determination to master whatever topic caught her gaze.

---

1. A pankratiast was one who participated in the sport *pankration*. This was a mixture of boxing, wrestling, and submission holds and thus is a precursor to the modern form known as MMA or mixed-martial arts.

The three had strong urges and prodigious appetites . . . for all life. The quiet smile returned to Plato's mouth, as he thought about how those appetites might later play tonight in the depiction of the tripartite soul. "Come," he said to the trio, "let us walk in the sunlight while it lasts."

"Shouldn't we eat first?" Kydes asked, still surveying the food arrayed across two tables—delicacies like *artos*, a white bread made from wheat, along with cheeses, honey, and olive oil to eat with it; fresh fish, including eels; roasted meats; an assortment of vegetables, including cabbage, asparagus, carrots, onions, radishes, and cucumbers; a variety of nuts: almonds, walnuts, hazelnuts, and chestnuts; and a tray of grapes, figs, dates, apples, and pears. "It's been a long day, and now we're late into the afternoon."

Had he been close enough, Plato would have run his hand, a patient stroke of affection, over Kydes's curly hair. Adolescents, Plato knew from long experience, were often hungry, so many hormones thrashing in their bodies; but too often they ate simply out of habit, not out of genuine hunger. He knew that once he fed their constant hunger for real discussion, then they would have to be reminded to eat. For now, Plato simply said, "Let us walk in the remaining sunlight. I need to get my blood flowing before our evening's conversation." For the three that was enough.

Walking at the Academy was not a novel suggestion. Indeed, every teacher incorporated it into his lessons, though, unlike the other teachers, Plato never talked as he walked. Instead, he asked his students to walk in silence and gather their thoughts about whatever the topic of the day's lesson might be. Sometimes he would ask them to pay attention as they walked to something as simple as their breathing or the fall of each foot along the ground or path.

Today, however, he gave no instruction or topic at all. The group simply set out. With Demetra next to Plato and the boys side-by-side close behind, they walked from the grove along the shady avenues and then through the meadow, occasionally passing a knot of students tight in conversation, some with, but most without, a teacher. All acknowledged Plato with a wave or short-shouted salutation. Plato dipped his head slightly in response to each incident. Soon, the four came to the small stream, the Cephisuss, that ran along the north boundary of the Academy and that Cimon had used to irrigate the Academy. They stopped at its edge and watched the flowing water, so vital for a city in the hot southern plains of Attica.

Plato gazed for several minutes at the flowing stream. The three students squatted down—the boys on their knees, Demetra on her haunches—and dipped their hands in the water, cool like an autumn night. They cupped their hands and brought the water to their lips.

Plato intoned over them: "Life is like water." He paused for a few seconds and then continued. "That which is most yielding overcomes that which is most hard." He looked up into the trees, their leaves caught in the wind. Then he returned his gaze to the stream. The students rose. Several minutes passed. The three, like their teacher, watched the water glide over rocks, around branches, under outcroppings. Plato watched each student out of the corner of his eye. None said a word, nor moved, nor fidgeted. He smiled, waited another few minutes as they stood attentive in silence, and then said, "I want to share with you a story that Socrates shared with me. This is not a story that I have told before and thus have never told here at the Academy."

The trio, transfixed, waited for Plato's next words, like waiting for the thunder after a lightning strike, for they knew that anything of this magnitude, any story never heard by any students and perhaps not by any teacher either, could be as important as anything they had heretofore learned at the Academy. Such stories, which Plato called "dialogues," washed over the students; day after day, year in and year out, the stories worked their insidious seduction, until one day the students awoke to the power, the effortlessness, the flow of their thinking brought forth by the dialogues.

Plato's examples and parables grew in complexity as the students matured. He used his dialogues as teaching tools to challenge, befuddle, and even amuse his students. "Place yourselves in the place of the interlocutors," he would urge them. "What would you have responded to Socrates?"

If no one had heard this story before, then there had been no time, or maybe no appropriate setting, for sharing it. Whatever its lessons, this story was worth paying attention to. All three sensed this without sharing a word or a look, not even a quick glance, with one another. They stared only at Plato.

"This is a long story," Plato continued, "and I have asked you to come now, when night is falling, because we shall be virtually alone, and thus without interruption, to spend all night and into the morning discussing this tale."

"Plato," Demetra said, facing her teacher, "we could have met instead at your house. It's such a lovely home."

Plato looked at each of his students, destined, he thought, for philosophy. "The Academy is the best place for you to hear this story. You are accustomed in this environment to hearing and discussing didactic tales, without being distracted, however innocently, by persons or places outside this . . . atmosphere. So, there is no better setting for our discussion than here, no better place in all of Athens or in all of Greece." He extended his arm and with a sweep motioned the way back across the meadow. "Let us return to the grove. I shall begin this story when we arrive."

As they walked, Plato remained silent. The three tyros were restless, even with the walking, edgy in anticipation of the tale, any thoughts of couches and savory delicacies vaporized by the challenges offered in all of Plato's stories. Finally, having arrived at the couches, but before they were settled, Plato announced to the group: "Let us eat freely before we talk, and after the tables of food have been cleared away, we shall pass the time in conversation as we share the wine."

Plato watched his brood eat and cajole. They served themselves again and again, as youth were wont to do.

When they were finished and the tables and food were cleared from the area, Plato poured a small amount of pure wine in a cup and drank a toast in honor of the *Agathos Daimon* or Good Spirit. The master then instructed his servants on the proportion of water to wine that he wished to have for the night.

With that task completed, Plato offered the remaining food to his servants, wished them a good night, and sent them off. Then surveying the Academy and the group and finding that all tension and pangs were now released, Plato announced: "This dialogue is longer than many, even if I am sharing with you only portions of the entire dialogue. For that reason, we shall take occasional breaks to stretch, to amble, and to 'freshen' ourselves. And please be sure to take a trowel to bury the 'fresh' remnants." The trio laughed to hear the solemn Plato expostulating on excretions. Then, with the laughter subsiding, Plato began.

THE PIRAEUS

PLATO: One morning, just as the sun rose, Socrates came home for a change of clothes before heading to the public baths. Waiting for him, blocking the doorway, her hands resting on her hips, stood Xanthippe, his wife. In no mood for amusement, and perhaps perturbed at having to rise before dawn, Xanthippe said, "Where in the name of Hades have you been all night?"

Socrates smirked, which didn't help to defuse the tension. "As you know, last night *I went down to the Piraeus with Glaucon, son of Ariston*" (327a1) . . . .[2] Xanthippe snapped at him, a chill in her voice: "I know whose son he is. I don't need any explanation from you."

The three students giggled at the rebuke.

KYDES: Of course, she doesn't, Plato! He's your brother. Even we know that. (The other two giggled.) What was he thinking? And where was Adeimantus, your other brother? Off to the mountains with Aristotle to collect plant specimens? (More laughter from the other two and a smile from Plato.)

HERMIAS: And down to the Piraeus? Plato, Socrates is corrupting your brother, taking him at night down to the docks, to the land of brothels and taverns, where petty thieves and predators lie in wait for drunken residents and befuddled visitors.

KYDES: You never know what is lurking down there in the shadows.

HERMIAS: I have a pretty good idea. I lived there when I first arrived in Athens.

DEMETRA: One group you'll find in and out of the shadows is the rowers of our triremes, loaded with drink and looking for mischief.

HERMIAS: Rowers aren't alone in that.

---

2. Aside from individual terms and titles; foreign words; and passages from the *Tao Te Ching*, the Upanishads, and Sophocles's play *Antigone*, text in italics indicates a quotation from one of Plato's dialogues. Unless specified otherwise, the text is the *Republic*. Stephanus numbers accompany any such references. When Plato quotes something from the *Republic*, but also interjects his own words or phrases in the quotation, I use regular type rather than italics to indicate the distinction.

DEMETRA: Certainly not. But after days of intense training, this group, above all others, wants to relax, which they do by drinking to excess, whoring too much, and brawling all the time.

KYDES: And this you know from your vast experience in the Piraeus?

DEMETRA (smiling): Don't underestimate what I know and how I know it, Kydes.

KYDES: Never, princess, never!

Remember what Socrates said in the *Gorgias*: The great rulers of Athens, and I guess he meant men like Themistocles and Pericles, "*with no regard for temperance and justice have stuffed the city with harbors and arsenals and walls and tribute and suchlike trash.*"[3] That's a description of the Piraeus.[4]

HERMIAS: As you all have already suggested, life there can be like the bottom of the well. Visit any of the three harbors—Mounychia, Zea, and Kantharos—and you'll find any sort of activity that pleases you.

KYDES (as all three laugh): That's right, Hermias. At Kantharos you can buy anything, find anything—and I mean *anything*—to excite you.

DEMETRA: And you know this from your experience, Kydes?

KYDES (winks at her): I never said that.

HERMIAS: If Socrates wanted a test of virtue and morality, that would be a very good place to go.

KYDES (laughing): Hermias is right. The Piraeus is the bottom of the well. The very bottom. One is always looking up from there. Going "down to the Piraeus" is the proper way to phrase it.

PLATO (smiling): If I may continue with Socrates and his story . . .

---

3. Plato, *Gorgias*, 519a.

4. Because the Piraeus was Athens's principal port, foreigners of all kinds entered the city here and largely stayed. The port was the home of merchants, doctors, shipbuilders, craftsmen of all sorts—the working class, but also the lower class *Thetes* who were freemen. So, the Piraeus was a section of the city with great diversity. Those living there wanted a say in how the affairs of Athens were conducted, and so, as Aristotle observed in the *Politics*, the Piraeus was more democratic than any other part of the city (Aristotle, *Politics*, 1303b10–12).

The Settings

> "I wanted to say a prayer to Bendis, the newly installed Thracian goddess, and to see how they would manage the festival. (327a2–3) As we headed back to Athens, our prayers complete, we were caught up by Polemarchus, Niceratus, and Adeimantus, all of whom convinced us to stay. 'Don't you know,' Adeimantus said, 'that there is to be a torch race on horseback for the goddess tonight?'
>
> 'On horseback?' I said. 'That's something new. Are they going to race on horseback and hand the torches on in relays, or what?'
>
> 'In relays,' Polemarchus said, 'and there will be an all-night festival that will be well worth seeing.'" (328a1–6)

KYDES (winking at Hermias and Demetra): I'm so glad to hear that Adeimantus won't miss out.

PLATO: You need not worry about my brothers, Kydes. Not yet, anyway.

Then Socrates agreed with Glaucon that they should stay. So, they went to Polemarchus's house, and there, among others, they found Polemarchus's father, Cephalus, as well as the sophist Thrasymachus. Cephalus, who seemed quite old, had just finished offering a sacrifice in the courtyard. He said:

> "'Socrates, you don't come down to the Piraeus to see us as often as you should. If it were easy for me to walk up to town, you wouldn't have to come here.'
>
> I said, 'I should, Cephalus. You are right. I enjoy talking with the very old, for we should ask them, as we might ask those who have traveled a road that we too will probably have to follow, what kind of road it is, whether rough and difficult or smooth and easy.'
>
> 'By god, Socrates,' he replied, 'I'll tell you exactly what I think. A number of us, who are more or less the same age, often get together. We complain about the lost pleasures—sex, drinking parties, feasts, and the other things that go with them. For me, old age brings peace and freedom from such things. On the other hand, when someone thinks his end is near, he becomes frightened and concerned about things he didn't fear before. It is then that the stories we're told about Hades, about how people who've been unjust here must pay a penalty there.'" (330d3–6)

So, Socrates said, "it is of morality, then, that you speak of Cephalus. We should attend, therefore, precisely to what morality is." Thus ensued a lively discussion about morality. Thrasymachus threw himself into the debate, like a coiled beast about to chase down game. He wanted Socrates to prove to him that morality is always more profitable than immorality. They went back-and-forth, Socrates and Thrasymachus, until, as he tells it, Socrates had to admit that they had diverted, because of Thrasymachus, from the initial focus of the discussion on the nature of morality. Socrates then had to confess:

> *"I know nothing, for when I don't know what morality is, I can hardly know whether it is a kind of virtue or not, or whether a person who has it is happy or unhappy."* (354c)

Plato surveyed the faces of his three charges. Soon he resumed speaking:

PLATO: At this point, Socrates thought that the conversation might well be over. Or did he? Is not the confession of not knowing what morality is, of not knowing whether morality is even a virtue, the very kind of Socratic lure that would invite interlocutors such as my brothers to push further?

Moving on: Thrasymachus argued that immorality brings rewards and advantages to the strong and is therefore better than morality. The weak would also be immoral if they thought that they could get away with it and escape punishment. So, not yet having an adequate definition of morality, Glaucon and Adeimantus, as we might have suspected, demand that Socrates argue against the Thrasymachian view and demonstrate to them that the moral life is always better than an immoral one.

And so our conversation begins here, with Glaucon and Adeimantus taking up the claim that since immorality brings us whatever we want without any punishment, then it must be better than morality.

2

The Ring of Gyges and the Rise of Cities

PLATO: Not surprisingly, then, Glaucon and Adeimantus were not satisfied with where the discussion had ended. Not knowing what morality is, they thought, is precisely where the conversation should head. "Yes, yes," said Glaucon, "maybe morality can't be equated with force, as Thrasymachus argued. But can you argue that morality is better than immorality in all circumstances? More important, can you convince us of that?"

HERMIAS: I like that your brother, Plato, is persistent here. After all, Socrates isn't a sophist like Thrasymachus. He can't be satisfied with merely winning the argument. He needs to persuade by defining and explaining the concept.

PLATO: Not by accident was Glaucon called "the courageous." And you're quite right, Hermias. Socrates would not and cannot stop at that point. He accepts Glaucon's challenge and resumes the discussion.
  Glaucon said,

> "I want to know what morality and immorality are and what power each itself has when it's by itself in the soul. . . . I have yet to hear anyone defend morality in the way I want, proving that it is better than immorality. I want to hear it praised by itself. (358b4–5, 358c8–d1) Now, I don't believe any of what I'm about to say. I'm going to play Thrasymachus's role, and I am going to speak at length in praise of the immoral life, and in doing so I'll

> *show you the way I want to hear you praising morality and denouncing immorality."* (358b4–5, 358c8–d1)

"Well, I agreed," said Socrates. Then Glaucon laid out his basic argument: Those who practice morality do so unwillingly, because the immoral life is better. The origins of morality arise through a social contract. Glaucon continued:

> *"Those, for example, who suffer injustice but lack the power to do unjust acts themselves decide that it is profitable to come to an agreement with each other neither to do injustice nor to suffer it. As a result, they begin to make laws and covenants, and what the law commands they call lawful and moral."* (358e6–359a3)

So, morality is intermediate between the best—to do immoral acts without paying a penalty—and the worst—to suffer immorality without being able to take revenge (359a5–7).

DEMETRA: Wait, now, Plato. Glaucon is making morality the mean between two extremes, but the entire scale is based on immorality. Morality, then, is not a good. It's not something anyone wants. People settle for morality, only because they are too weak to commit immoral acts with impunity. If they could get away with immoral acts, they would. And anyone with the power to commit such acts and get away with them would never accept the laws and covenants. Why would he?

HERMIAS: Remember, Deme; Glaucon is simply recapitulating earlier arguments. He told us that he doesn't believe what he's saying.

DEMETRA: Even so, the premises are ridiculous. I might concede that any strong or authoritarian man might resist making any kind of social contract, because he doesn't need to. But would a virtuous man? This seems to rule out the right and the good from the outset. It means that the weak "invent" morality to thwart the strong, not because there is anything good in and of itself called "morality."

PLATO (Plato smiled.): If you accept the premises, Demetra, as Glaucon had done, then would you not find yourself arguing as Glaucon did? Certainly you can see how someone using these premises would conclude that those who practice moral acts do so unwillingly because they lack the power to do immoral ones.

DEMETRA: Okay, I agree. The argument is that people act morally simply because they lack the power to exercise immorality. (Heads nod all around.) But this also means that what's good is reduced to getting as much as you can any way you can.

KYDES: Isn't the point, Deme, to stretch the position so that immorality looks like the best life, which leaves Socrates needing to make the best case for why morality is better?

DEMETRA: I understand that, Kydes, but is the best case for being immoral that you can gather and have more . . . things?

HERMIAS: Immorality doesn't have to be that. It's the freedom to do whatever you want—gather things, sell things, gain more freedom, whatever—whenever you want without fear of punishment.

PLATO: Let us see where Socrates goes next.

THE RING OF GYGES

Glaucon then said,

> "We can follow a moral man and an immoral man to see where their desires lead. We'll catch the moral person red-handed travelling the same road as the immoral. Because when they have freedom to do whatever they like, the overarching goal is the desire to get more and more. This is what anyone's nature naturally pursues as good." (359c2–6)

Glaucon continued: To catch both the moral and the immoral red-handed, let's give both the power they say that Gyges of Lydia had.[1] As the story goes, he was a shepherd, and during

> "a violent thunderstorm, an earthquake broke open the ground and created a chasm. . . . He went down into it . . . and there he saw a hollow bronze horse. There were window-like openings in it, and, peeping in, he saw a corpse, which seemed to be of more than human size, wearing nothing but a gold ring on its finger. He took the ring and came out. (359d2–8)

---

1. At this point in the *Republic*, Socrates attributes the power to "an ancestor of Gyges," rather than to Gyges himself (539c10). But later in the dialogue, Socrates refers to the power as derived from "the ring of Gyges" (612b3), the ancestor somehow dropping out. I'm dropping him out here as well.

> "He wore the ring at the usual monthly meeting that reported to the king [of Lydia] on the state of the flocks. And as he was sitting among the others, he happened to turn the setting of the ring towards himself to the inside of his hand. When he did this, he became invisible to those sitting near him, and they went on talking as if he had gone. He wondered at this, and, fingering the ring, he turned the setting outwards again and became visible. (359e2–7)
>
> "So he experimented with the ring to test whether it indeed had this power—and it did. If he turned the setting inward, he became invisible; if he turned it outward, he became visible again. When he realized this, he at once arranged to become one of the messengers sent to report to the king. And when he arrived there, he seduced the king's wife, attacked the king with her help, killed him, and took over the kingdom." (360a3–b1)

Having conveyed the story, Glaucon moved on to his central point:

> "Let us suppose, then, that there were two such rings, one worn by a moral and the other by an immoral person. Now, no one, it seems, would be so incorruptible that he would stay on the path of morality or stay away from other people's property, when he could take whatever he wanted from the marketplace with impunity, go into people's houses and have sex with anyone he wished, kill or release from prison anyone he wished, and do all the other things that would make him a god among humans." (360b2–8)

So, now we can see Glaucon's conclusion: Both the moral and the immoral person would act in the same way. Whenever a man thinks he can get away with immoral acts, he will do them. That is so, because immorality is far more profitable than morality.

HERMIAS: Maybe so, Plato; maybe immorality is more profitable than morality when one has the power of Gyges's ring. But profit is not the sole reason why a moral person is moral. Glaucon assumes that it is the sole reason. Virtue would hold a moral man back. This is Deme's point.

KYDES: Also, Glaucon seems to think that circumstances drive every wish and action. If I can do something, whatever it is, and get away with it, then I'll do it. But we also have character. We aren't compelled by every circumstance to act a certain way, any more than we must be compelled to act morally. So, I'm with Hermias on this one, Plato.

DEMETRA: And you know who lacks character? Gyges. Even before his immoral acts of seduction and robbery, he steals the ring. That ring doesn't belong to him. At the very least, it belongs to the king of Lydia. It's the king's land, so what is on his land belongs to him. Gyges is immoral from the start. He's hardly the person to use as a test case of the power of morality.

KYDES: Besides, the story itself is preposterous. Being invisible isn't going to permit you to seduce the queen and steal money. How does an invisible man steal treasure? People aren't going to see it walking down the corridor?!

And is he naked? Are his clothes invisible too? What about the food he puts into his stomach? Can that be seen? How could someone invisible seduce a woman? She's not going to feel him? He's invisible, not bodyless. Once he reveals himself to her, she is going to fall so desperately in love with this shepherd that she'll conspire to murder her husband and hand over control of the country to Gyges?

HERMIAS: Perhaps it is not Gyges who is seductive. Perhaps it is the power of invisibility that seduces the queen, a power she, too, desires to share in. Besides, don't be so literal-minded, Kydes. It's a thought experiment. It's not real.

DEMETRA: The point is to explore whether someone who knew that he couldn't get caught would act immorally if to do so were to his benefit, if he could fulfill his desires. What I don't understand is why Socrates doesn't confront the whole idea. Yes, some people might well act immorally in order to acquire their desires, but not everybody's desires are like Gyges's: seduction, power, wealth. Eavesdropping on conversations? Okay, I can understand that one. But you're not about to steal, murder, or rape. Kydes is right. At the very least, the guilt would be overwhelming. Perhaps we're not going to probe why we would feel guilt, whether it comes from how we were raised or whether it's innate, but you know, Kydes, that you'd feel it.

Some people—

KYDES: Like us?

DEMETRA: Yes, like us. We might well desire other goods—like great poetry and music or philosophical conversation. (They all laugh.) If there is power to be had here through invisibility, could that power be used to acquire greater thoughts or virtue?

HERMIAS: There is still an aspect of Glaucon's challenge that we've yet to address. So far, we've been treating immorality as a power to be used to acquire something. Granted, Deme, your view is that what is wanted is more virtue as opposed to other kinds of goods. Nevertheless, this means that if the goal is to acquire more goods, to profit in some way, even if wanting more virtue, then in that context, immorality is better. But part of the response to the challenge "Why be moral?" is to see morality as a good in itself. One is moral for its own sake, not for anything else.

KYDES: Clearly we can all agree that one person who isn't going to act like Gyges is a person of great virtue. Like Socrates. Surely Plato, too. (The group laughs. Plato simply smiles.) We've learned all our lives that virtue isn't innate. It's learned and practiced, and philosophy is both its expression and the path to it. So, I suspect that Socrates's move in the conversation will be to offer philosophy and, yes, philosophical conversation as a way to undercut Glaucon's thought experiment.

PLATO: Your intuition is correct as far as it goes, Kydes. But Hermias is right: Socrates has yet to entertain the idea of morality for its own sake. Glaucon now addresses this: He introduces a thoroughly moral man, noble in every way, who isn't simply believed to be good but is so. However, his reputation for morality, says Glaucon, must be taken away,

> *"for a reputation for morality would bring him honor and rewards, so that it wouldn't be clear whether he is moral for the sake of morality itself or for the sake of those honors and rewards. We must strip him of everything except morality and make his situation the opposite of an immoral person's. Though he does nothing immoral, he must have the greatest reputation for it. . . . Let him stay like that unchanged until he dies—moral, but all his life believed to be immoral."* (361c1–8)

Now Adeimantus takes a turn to offer up a different angle on the moral/immoral dynamic, but unlike his brother, Adeimantus offers what he actually believes about this situation. Morality might well bring us honors and rewards, but immorality is even better at doing so. What, then, dissuades us from becoming immoral?

Adeimantus then claims that what dissuades us must be our concern about what the gods will think of us and how they might punish us. Still, as we have learned, the gods can be persuaded and appeased by sacrifices, offerings, and prayers. So, *"if we are moral, our only gain is not to be punished by the gods, since we lose the profits of immorality. But if we are immoral, we get the profits of our crimes and transgressions and afterwards persuade the gods by prayer and escape without punishment."* (366a1–4)

Then Adeimantus issued the full challenge to Socrates:

"No one has adequately argued that immorality is the worst thing a soul can have in it and that morality is the greatest good. If you had treated the subject in this way and persuaded us from youth we wouldn't now be guarding against one another's immorality, but each would be his own best guardian, afraid that by doing immoral acts he'd be living with the worst possible thing. . . . So don't merely give us a theoretical argument that morality is stronger than immorality, but tell us what each itself does, because of its own powers, to someone who possesses it, that makes immorality bad and morality good." (367a1–4, b1–4)

This, then, is the challenge put to Socrates by my brothers: If you were, for example, kind and just but had a reputation only for selfish behavior and unfair treatment of others—if, in other words, your virtues were never recognized—could you live well knowing you were moral but never being acknowledged as anything but immoral? In that circumstance, your morality would be for its own sake and for nothing else. Meanwhile, the perfectly immoral person, who gets away with murder and is living a luxurious life full of riches and rewards and high reputation, is thought to be perfectly moral. This person can then get away with his crimes and avoid punishment by expiating their crimes through prayer. Yet, Socrates claims that the unacknowledged moral life is better, happier. How can that be?

ORIGINS OF THE CITY

Socrates admits that the inquiry they now have to undertake is a difficult one, requiring *"keen eyesight"* (368d2). So, he suggests investigating as if our eyesight is weak or we are short-sighted. Large letters are easier to read than small ones. If we were told to read small letters and had to squint our eyes, then we would be grateful if we discovered that *"the same letters existed elsewhere in a larger size and on a larger surface."* We could examine the larger letters first to see whether they really are the same as the smaller ones (368d–e).

My brothers agreed that this would indeed be an improvement for those with weak eyes. But how, they asked, does this relate to an investigation into morality?

Do we not talk, said Socrates, of morality in a single individual and morality in a whole city? And, of course, a city is larger than a single person. So, morality might be easier to see and to understand if we first examine it in a city, since it would exist there on a larger scale. *"If you're willing, let's first find out what sort of thing morality is in a city and afterwards look for it in the individual, observing the ways in which the smaller is similar to the larger"* (368e8–369a2).

DEMETRA: There's no argument here, Plato? Your brothers don't at least query Socrates on this idea that seeing morality is the same as seeing or reading letters?

HERMIAS: Demetra raises a good point, I think. How we see mentally is not the same as how we see physically. To think they are the same is to make a category error. The mind "sees" through concepts and classifications. Our bodies see with physical eyes. Reading isn't about seeing the letters; it's about putting them together in our heads to see what is meant. Shouldn't there at least be some argument raised about this?

PLATO: You would agree, Hermias, would you not, that as a city rises and takes shape, we should be able to see morality rise with it and immorality as well? And would you agree that we would not see either morality or immorality in an individual without the city or community, for moral codes arise within communities? (Hermias nods.) And you two also agree? (Demetra and Kydes likewise nod.) Let us examine, then, as Socrates suggests, how a city comes to be.

KYDES: Here you raise a slightly different point, Plato. A city is called "a city" because it is identified as a unit, an entity. But individuals, although entities themselves, differ within cities and among themselves. You can find morality in a city that is not related to the morality of all individuals within the city. Individuals can have a moral code that is not the same as the city's moral code.

DEMETRA: I don't think that's the point at this stage, Kydes. Granted, not all individuals within the city will be moral according to the city's standards. Nevertheless, it's the city's standards of morality that interests us here. Based on those standards, we can judge whether individuals within that city are moral or immoral, whether how they behave is moral or immoral, at least as far as the city's moral codes extend.

HERMIAS: And you will agree, Kydes, that the standards of morality—that is, what morality is—are easier to see in the city itself than in any individual. Because, as you say, individuals will differ as to what moral standards they adhere to and how they behave morally or immorally. We need the basis or standard by which to identify and judge an individual's moral behavior and ideas.

Besides, clearly Glaucon and Adeimantus themselves haven't "seen" Socrates's arguments to this point. They need a bigger picture for that, and a city might be just the panel for Socrates to paint on.

KYDES: Still, just as individuals within a city differ in their moral outlooks and behaviors, so, too, do cities differ. The morality of Athens, say, establishes its morality as a way of ordering society for the well-being of its citizens and residents. The morality of a different city, however, because of who lives there, the geography of the environment, the goals the residents and citizens share, could be quite different. In addition, a man of high morality, even perfect morality, like Socrates, could transcend the city's morality and reflect universal values in how he lives. Why wouldn't we then examine Socrates the individual and not his city?

HERMIAS: Perhaps we could do that, but would we not end up at the same place—that is, examining morality in the city? In the *Crito* Socrates uses the laws of Athens to explain why he did not flee the city in light of the death penalty against him. Why didn't he? Because he owed it to the city to remain, since he agreed with and adhered to Athens's laws and codes, even and especially in the face of a jury verdict against him.[2]

DEMETRA: A city provides the moral standards to which individuals within the city are to conform. Socrates himself argued that the city provides the structures for developing character. As he says, it is the city that provided the laws by which he and other citizens marry and have children, by which citizens are nurtured and educated. So, in the laws and

---

2. Plato, *Crito*, 50a4–51c4.

institutions of the city we can readily see the system of morality underlying and influencing proper moral behavior.[3]

HERMIAS: Keep in mind, Kydes, that Socrates is not discussing the rise of a particular existing city, like Athens or Sparta or Thebes. That might be because he takes your point about the relativity of morality in the face of extant cities.

DEMETRA: As Hermias said, Glaucon and Adeimantus and Socrates himself are looking for morality in and of itself, not any single instantiation of it. Because cities might well have arisen in the same way and for the same reasons, we might see a pure form of morality in the rise of early cities, before circumstances intruded too deeply. So Socrates is talking about a city "*in theory*" (369a4).

PLATO: Without getting too involved in the *Crito*, can you agree, Kydes, however much you may reject the jury finding of Socrates's guilt, that he accepted the verdict at the very least because it was the outcome from a system of justice, of morality, within the city that he accepted? (Kydes nods.) Then we can see that even in the case of Socrates, a highly moral man, it would be fruitful to examine morality within the city.

KYDES (putting up both hands and laughing): Okay! Okay! I yield.

PLATO: Back, then, to our story. How do cities arise? Well, isn't it through the discovery that no individual is self-sufficient? Each of us has plenty of needs that we cannot fulfill as individuals. So, we associate with others. Those others will, for efficiency, specialize in certain tasks: Some will specialize in building dwellings, others in growing and harvesting food, still others in making clothes or shoes. Because we have so many needs, we will gather with many people. In this way a community arises.

HERMIAS: And yet, Plato, this is not the only way that we can conceive of cities arising. Earlier in the dialogue, when talking about the social contract (358e), Glaucon suggested that people join together so as not to suffer injustice. They make laws and covenants, which they call lawful and just. So, in this case, it is morality itself that leads to the creation of cities.

PLATO: Nevertheless, is this not a form of morality but not necessarily morality itself? The people form a community to thwart injustices that

---

3. Plato, *Crito*, 50d1–51a4.

they are suffering. So, their contract, and their city, arises out of specific circumstances that they have experienced. Is this not the very idea that you earlier warned us about—pegging morality to specific instances or circumstances? We want a story, do we not, that will bypass those and explain how cities arise independent of such circumstances?

HERMIAS: We do, Plato. Forgive the interruption.

PLATO (smiling): Because

> "we are not all born alike, but each of us differs somewhat in nature from the others, one being suited to one task, another to another task, [then] don't we find that one person does a better job if he practices one craft rather than many crafts? (370a8–10) The result, then, is that more plentiful and better quality goods are more easily produced if each person does one thing for which he is naturally suited . . . and is released from doing others." (370c3–5)

DEMETRA: But, Plato, is it really people's natures that determine what they do in the city? Perhaps they don't like raising sheep or weaving blankets; their nature is to write poetry. But they see a need within the city for those goods, and so they become shepherds or weavers. So, it's not their natures that lead them to the work; it's their observation that an aspect of life needs filling.

KYDES: Or they are trained in the family business and simply continue in that business when adults. Or maybe they see a way through weaving and shepherding to make some money, because they produce high-quality products efficiently.

PLATO (Plato smiled.): Strong points. Let us save them for later and at this point complete our city.

We can agree, I think, that we shall need many people in this city.

> "A farmer won't make his own plough, not if it's to be a good one, nor his hoe, nor any of his other farming tools. Neither will a builder—and he, too, needs lots of things. And the same is true of a weaver and a cobbler." (370c8–12)

This is how the city grows. People will need farmers, carpenters, blacksmiths, and all sorts of other craftsmen.

Even so, not everything can be built or created by the city dwellers themselves. Importers are required. So, too, exporters, since people within the city may produce good quality products not just for themselves, but also for those living in other cities that lack the quality craftsmen in certain areas of need. In this way, merchants arise for selling goods and sailors and traders for transporting them. Marketplaces spring up for buying and selling goods, as does a currency for transactions. Among these trades and crafts will be laborers, those physically strong and suited to hard labor, but who lack the mental acuity to join the community. Their trade is their strength, and they will be paid for their hard work (370d–371e).

With the addition of these wage-earners, said Socrates, "*our city has grown to completeness, then, is that not right, Adeimantus?*" (371e4–6). Adeimantus is not entirely sold. "*Perhaps*" is all he says.

Nevertheless, inquires Socrates, at this stage of the city "*where are morality and immorality to be found in it? With which of the things we have examined did they come in*" (371e9–10)?

Adeimantus is perplexed. "*I have no idea, Socrates, unless it has something to do with how these people treat one another.*"[4]

If that is so, said Socrates, then we must examine how people relate to and interact with one another. To do that, let us first

> "*see what kind of lives our citizens will lead when they've been provided for in the way we have been describing. They'll produce bread, wine, clothes, and shoes, won't they? They'll build houses, work naked and barefoot in the summer, and wear adequate clothing and shoes in the winter. For food, they'll knead and cook the flour and meal they've made from wheat and barley. They'll put their cakes and loaves on reeds or clean leaves, and, reclining on beds strewn with yew and myrtle, they'll feast with their children, drink their wine, and, crowned with wreaths, hymn the gods. They'll enjoy sex with one another but bear no more children than their resources allow, lest they fall into either poverty or war.*" (372a6–b7)

At this point, Glaucon interrupted Socrates. "*It seems that you make your people feast without any delicacies*" (372c2). Oh, that's right, said Socrates. I forgot that the people of the city will

---

4. Plato, *Republic* (trans. Waterfield), 372a. It is from Waterfield, as I mentioned in the introduction, that I adopted the term "morality" rather than "justice." The notion of morality, even more than justice, is certainly captured in the idea of how people interact with and treat one another, which is why I prefer Waterfield's phrasing here.

The Ring of Gyges and the Rise of Cities

"obviously need salt, olives, cheese, boiled roots, and vegetables of the sort they cook in the country. We'll give them desserts, too, of course, consisting of figs, chickpeas, and beans, and they'll roast myrtle and acorns before the fire, drinking moderately. And so they'll live in peace and good health, and when they die at a ripe old age, they'll bequeath a similar life to their children." (372c1–d2)

Glaucon interrupted again.

"This is a city fit for pigs, Socrates, for wouldn't you feed pigs the same diet? If these people aren't to suffer hardship, they should recline on proper couches, dine at a table, and have the delicacies and desserts that people have nowadays." (372d3–4, 6–8)

"Oh, I see," replied Socrates.

"It isn't merely how a city comes into being that we're considering, it seems, but the origin of a luxurious city. And that may not be a bad idea, for by examining it, we might very well see how morality and immorality grow up in cities—"

HERMIAS: Just a minute, please, Plato. Isn't there a suggestion here by Socrates that morality can't be found in the "city for pigs," as Glaucon describes it? Socrates asks the question about where morality and immorality came into the simple city. Then Glaucon counters with a need to describe the rise of a luxurious city, and Socrates says that by examining that city, we might well see morality and immorality. Why can't the simple city have morality in it? That's never addressed.

DEMETRA: I think that Hermias is right. First, Socrates needs to show that the simple city doesn't have morality. After that, he can move on to the luxurious city to see whether morality enters that city differently. But since people in the simple city have relationships and families—*"how they treat one another,"* as Adeimantus phrased it—then there must be rules of conduct for how to interact with people within the city, how best to raise children, and why there is a need to limit the size of families. That's all part of a moral system. Is Socrates suggesting that such a system arises naturally? If so, he needs to defend that idea.

Also, notice that Socrates bypasses the point raised by Adeimantus. He talks more of what individuals and individual families will do within the community—build houses, bake bread, drink wine, feast with their children—rather than addressing how people interact with and treat one another, which is where morality arises and can be seen.

KYDES: Also, Socrates says that they will live in peace. So, they have a concept of "peaceful" and, conversely, what isn't peaceful. Isn't that part of morality? Won't there be stipulations on how to conduct behavior to maintain the peace?

Plus, they have virtues in the simple city, since Socrates says that they will drink moderately. Where does the concept of "moderation" come from?

HERMIAS: There has to be within this simple city some notion as well of politics. Disputes will arise. At the very least, romantic disputes can arise among people vying for the same partner.

DEMETRA: And disputes at the marketplace. Disputes among merchants and the artisans who produce, say, clothes or shoes. Disputes with traders from other cities. There must be some understanding, then, of what is a just transaction or what is a fair resolution of a dispute. This implies a political and legal system for resolving such issues and implies a view of justice or morality underlying the system. Why aren't these issues addressed before moving on to the luxurious city? If this city lacks such a system, then in these circumstances it lacks justice. That lack would seem to be far more significant than the absence of couches and rich desserts. Or does Socrates think that this simple city is unrealistic or unimportant?

PLATO: On the contrary, Demetra. Socrates goes on to say, *"The true city, in my opinion, is the one we've described, the healthy city, as it were. But let's study a luxurious city, a city with a fever, if that's what you want"* (372e5–7).

DEMETRA: But that isn't what we want, any of us here. If the healthy city is, as Socrates says, the true city, then that's where we should first see morality. If the first city described is the true city, then it must also be a moral city. Why don't Glaucon and Adeimantus examine that city?

HERMIAS: I agree with Deme. Socrates gave your brothers, Plato, the opening to explore that city—*"Where are morality and immorality to be found in it? With which of the things we have examined did they come in"* (371e9–10)? But then Glaucon described it as a city fit for pigs and pushed on. What Socrates didn't push, and what your brothers didn't think about, is where we find morality in the healthy city. They didn't examine it. And

The Ring of Gyges and the Rise of Cities

since we've also inferred, from what Socrates has already said about the city, that virtues exist within the healthy city and that virtues are part of a moral system, then we need to see the role that philosophy plays among the city's residents, which is how people come to understand, examine, and establish virtuous or moral behavior.

DEMETRA: Because there are children in the city, there must also be some system of education for them. Presumably, the educational system will include moral and character development. Or does it not? That, too, needs to be explored.

PLATO: Tell me, then: Does Socrates's next statement to his brothers surprise you: If you want to discuss the fevered city, *"there is nothing to stop us"* (373a1)?

KYDES: No, Plato, because as we have learned from your other dialogues, Socrates lets the interlocutors determine the directions of the conversations. If that's where they wish to head, then so be it. But from our perspective, the move is premature, at best.

DEMETRA: Of course there is something to stop us. You have told us repeatedly, Plato, about Socrates emphasizing the examination of life: *"The unexamined life is not worth living."*[5] There isn't any of that examination yet visible in the healthy city.

PLATO (smiling): Let's see whether Socrates makes it visible. He says next, *"The things I mentioned earlier and the way of life I described won't satisfy some people, it seems"*—

KYDES (interrupting): By "some people" he means your brothers, Plato.

PLATO (still smiling): Apparently so. Surely, however, they are not alone. So, Socrates says,

> *"Couches, tables, and other furniture will have to be added, and, of course, all sorts of delicacies, perfumed oils, incense, prostitutes, and pastries. We mustn't provide them* [i.e., the citizens of the healthy city] *only with the necessities we mentioned at first, such as houses, clothes, and shoes, but painting and embroidery must be begun, and gold, ivory, and the like acquired. Isn't that so?"* (373a1–8)

---

5. Plato, *Apology*, 38a6.

Both Glaucon and Adeimantus agree.

> "Then we must enlarge our city, for the healthy one is no longer adequate. We must increase it in size and fill it with a multitude of things that go beyond what is necessary for a city—hunters, for example, and artists or imitators, many of whom work in shapes and colors, many in music. And there must be poets and their assistants, actors, choral dancers, contractors, and makers of all kinds of devices, including, among other things, those needed for the adornment of women. And so we'll need more servants, too. Or don't you think that we'll need tutors, wet nurses, nannies, beauticians, barbers, chefs, cooks, and swineherds? We didn't need any of these in our earlier city." (373b2–c4)

HERMIAS: Many of these additions we might well want to include in the simple city, the healthy city. Why should artists and dancers, actors and contractors, barbers and tutors make a city fevered? If they do, then that needs first to be explored, because it says something about the virtue and the morality of the city, if such additions lead out of health and into fever. So, at this point, I would expect your brothers to stop Socrates and raise these issues.

PLATO: They don't intercede, Hermias. One reason might be that we are not yet at the end of the list.

> "We'll need pig farmers as well—a job which didn't exist in our previous community, since there was no need of it, but which will be needed in the present one—and huge numbers of cows and sheep, if they are to be eaten, . . . and with this lifestyle won't we be in far greater need of doctors than we were before." (373c2–4)

KYDES: Certainly, because of all the rich food and gluttony. (Hermias and Demetra laugh. Plato smiles.)

PLATO: "And, of course, although the inhabitants of our former community could live off the produce of the land, the land will be too small now, don't you think?"[6] My brothers did think so. Socrates went on: "Then we'll have to seize some of our neighbors' land if we're to have enough pasture and ploughland. And won't our neighbors want to seize part of ours as well, if they too have . . . overstepped the limit of their necessities?" (373d7–10). That's completely inevitable, said Glaucon and Adeimantus.

---

6. Plato, *Republic* (trans. Waterfield), 373c5–d6.

The Ring of Gyges and the Rise of Cities

"*Then our next step will be war, won't it?*" (373e2). They agreed. So, said Socrates, we have found the origins of war.

DEMETRA: The origins of war, Plato, test the morality that the city presumably already has. The city is seizing neighboring land, and neither of your brothers thought to query that as a moral concern, as saying something about the moral composition of the city and its inhabitants?

The pursuit of additional land for growing crops and feeding animals would be signs of immorality. I say that this action is immoral, because it fails to take into account those from whom the land is seized. The pursuit of luxuries will likewise continue and grow. Money becomes crucial, because the more money you have, the more luxuries you can purchase. Possessions then become a mark of distinction and elevated reputation, perhaps even more than moral character. Displaying one's wealth and luxuries can then supersede signs and acts of kindness to others, concern for one's neighbors, and magnanimity toward all—all virtues—to say nothing of the need to protect one's wealth and possessions. That might require private security and a general wariness of the intentions of one's friends and neighbors, to say nothing of the intentions of strangers.

KYDES: Deme is right. If the city is moving beyond necessities, then growth in these areas is inevitable. On the other hand, this could be a moral development for the city, the rise of martial virtues not present before.

DEMETRA: What martial virtues, Kydes? Courage in battle? That's just a different setting for the exercise of the virtue of courage that can manifest in different ways in the healthy city. Mercy? Justice? We haven't examined where and how those virtues can exist in the healthy city. If they can, and I don't see why they can't, then the addition of martial virtues is unnecessary and is an outgrowth of greed and the desire for acquiring and protecting luxuries.

PLATO: Socrates seems to agree with you, Demetra. He says that war "*comes from those same desires that are most of all responsible for the bad things that happen to cities and the individuals in them*" (373e5–7).

DEMETRA: Then he's suggesting that they examine this development. War shows a rise of immorality, "*bad things*" that happen to people and their cities. Examine, first, those desires that lead to war and to immoral "*bad things.*"

HERMIAS: Even stronger than that, Deme: Socrates seems to be urging Plato's brothers to halt and pull back, to recognize that these desires can destroy the city.

PLATO: This is not a turn that the conversation takes. Instead, Socrates says,

> "The city must be further enlarged, and not just by a small number, either, but by a whole army, which will do battle with the invaders in defense of the city's substantial wealth and all the other things we mentioned." (373e9–374a2)

KYDES: Why don't the citizens themselves defend the city?

DEMETRA: Socrates said that it has to be a whole army.

KYDES: But why? The city enlarges and so does the population. There are many more residents now.

PLATO: Do not forget the mechanism in the origin of the city: the division of labor. The city will not have a single person practicing many crafts or professions.

> "We prevented a cobbler from trying to be a farmer, weaver, or builder at the same time and said that he must remain a cobbler in order to produce fine work. . . . Now, isn't it of the greatest importance that warfare be practiced well? And is fighting a war so easy that a farmer or a cobbler or any other craftsman can be a soldier at the same time? Can someone pick up a shield or any other weapon or tool of war and immediately perform adequately in an infantry battle or any other kind?" (374b5–c8)

KYDES: No one is expecting any citizen to simply pick up a sword and fight. Martial training for citizens can begin at an early age. Then, later in adulthood, training doesn't have to take up much of a craftsman's time. An hour a day? Five hours a week?

HERMIAS: Or is war to become a profession within this city? That in itself might be a hint that something here is off.

DEMETRA: Yes, having professionals fight wars by attacking neighbors and defending the city so that the citizens can be guaranteed the continuation of their life of ease seems to reduce the measure of this city's success to nothing but the possession of luxuries.

Nevertheless, if there is such a profession, and it seems to be so in this city, then I can see that it needs to be treated like any other profession. It needs a skilled class of dedicated warriors, treating war like any other skilled craft. On the other hand, I agree with Hermias. The idea that it is a profession strikes me as "fevered" and thus a natural outgrowth of this unhealthy city.

KYDES: Unhealthy?

DEMETRA: Yes. If the simple city is the healthy city and this one is "fevered," then it is by definition "unhealthy."

PLATO: Demetra anticipates correctly. Socrates says that the work of the "guardians," as he calls those who fight to protect the city, is of such importance that they must be free to pursue it with full devotion. *"Then,"* he says, *"our job, it seems, is to select, if we can, the kind of nature suited to guard the city"* (374e1–2).

3

Philosophical Dogs

PLATO: *"Then,"* Socrates says, *"our job, it seems, is to select, if we can, the kind of nature suited to guard the city"* (374e1–2).

DEMETRA: We talked earlier about this idea that people have natures suitable for one job over others, and I'm glad to hear that they have returned to the subject. But before we discuss that, Plato, I have a concern, and I don't know how to express it.

PLATO: Straightforwardly, Demetra, as always.

DEMETRA: Well, your brothers have taken a wrong turn—not a premature turn, as we said earlier, but a wrong turn.

PLATO: How so?

DEMETRA: I'm sorry to tread over territory already explored, but this is nagging at me. They have moved quickly from the healthy city to the fevered city, because, in their view, people need luxuries to live well. When we studied the *Apology*, you emphasized something Socrates said to the jury:

> *"I went to each of you privately and conferred upon him what I say is the greatest benefit, by trying to persuade him not to care for any of his belongings before caring that he himself should be as good and as wise as possible, not to care for the city's possessions more than for the city itself...."* (36c4–7)

Earlier in that dialogue Socrates said to the jury: *"Wealth does not bring about excellence, but excellence makes wealth and everything else good for men, both individually and collectively"* (30b2–3). That wealth doesn't sound like the luxuries offered in response to Glaucon and Adeimantus. Indeed, as Socrates says, it is only with excellence that wealth can be beneficial for those who hold it and those affected by it. Such wealth begins with excellence found in the soul.

Why, then, do your brothers move toward luxuries without the concomitant of excellence? This is a theme of Socrates's, heard throughout his life, one your brothers had surely heard more than once.

I think that it's imperative to explore the life in the healthy city, because real wealth, the health of one's soul, can develop out of that healthy life. In the healthy city the citizens' needs are met. They have food, shelter, and clothing. They have families and occupations and social interaction. And we established, or at least raised the idea, that they have some kind of morality. In this *"city for pigs,"* the people seem content with the basic necessities of life. They seem content to lie on their rustic beds eating their simple food and singing their ditties. Is all of this the source of excellence? How is that excellence identified and emphasized? Is that where they find the motivation to learn and to grow? And how do the residents keep the city so pure, healthy, and simple?

So, there is the opening for morality and thus for more exploration of this city. Someone needs to have the insight to know what needs to be done to keep the city healthy and excellent. Someone, that is, needs to be able to step back from the city to see what has to be done, maybe even before it has to be done. That's political leadership, and that needs to be examined.

That's also the beginning of philosophy and education. Someone must guide the community in instructing the young about the nature of their community. But someone also must have the perspective to plan for the city, care for the city, protect the city. That's part of philosophy, and that means to know what justice is and when to administer it.

KYDES: Nevertheless, Deme, it seems unrealistic to think that a city that meets only basic needs will be satisfying to all those who live there and will reflect the values that you want to see there.

DEMETRA: How can this city function at all or last for long without recognition of and people's involvement in politics and philosophy that must underlie its order? Those must be present in some form, and both take us beyond satisfying only basic needs.

KYDES: Simply put, people don't want to stay in such a city. People want to move beyond mere necessities to the finer things in life and find excellence there. People want art; people want the Parthenon. People want a thriving agora and a Piraeus for shipping out and receiving abundant treasures. That's what Glaucon is saying. Perhaps only through that refinement, when people have the luxuries that they desire, will they move on to philosophy, asking "Is this enough? What, now, is missing from life?"

DEMETRA: But it's rarely enough. That seems to be part of Socrates's point. How often do our friends and family talk about having fulfilled all their desires for goods and luxuries? They consume, and are consumed by, goods. The pursuit of consumption leaves them with no time for or thoughts of morality. So, in the midst of luxuries it seems difficult to turn to philosophy, to the development of the mind. Look at how few students, young and old, relative to the whole population of Athens, are here in the Academy. That's a clear sign of how little people think about philosophy. War and competition, awards and riches, are what occupy most people's minds. Is that good? And where does this desire for luxuries come from? How is that desire sown within the soul? Is it innate, or is it implanted by society?

HERMIAS: Isn't competition part of our natures as humans? Aren't prizes, whether as increased reputation or additional wealth, worth competing for? Isn't that part of any good life, any excellent life?

DEMETRA: I'm not so sure that it is part of that life. I'm not so sure that competition is essentially part of our natures. If your physical needs can be met, as in the healthy city, and if the step beyond those needs is to fulfill the need for philosophy—that is, for thinking about and examining the nature of life and society—then why do we need war and competition to live happy lives?

HERMIAS: Yet, we don't know whether those living in the healthy city will ever get to the point of wanting philosophy. Maybe we need the presence of war and luxuries to stop and ask, "What are we doing? Is this the best way to live?"

DEMETRA: But Socrates warns against both of those, Hermias. Remember what Plato told us just a while ago: According to Socrates, the residents of the healthy city enjoy sex, *"but bear no more children than their resources allow, lest they fall into either poverty or war"* (372c1). If philosophy and morality are important to the people, and how can they not be, then they must come into a city without the need for luxuries and thus war.

This brings up another point about the healthy city. I don't see why the seizing of land for raising more food is the only reason that the city needs to be protected.

KYDES: Well, what in the healthy city is worth attacking? What might outside enemies want that that city has?

DEMETRA: Are those the right questions? We agree there will be other cities. Can we assume that other cities will have the same morality as our city? We know that the healthy city trades with others. Our city might have much more efficient production or better-quality items because of superior craftsmen. Can we assume that the healthy city does not need to be protected? If it does need to be prepared for attack from outside forces, then who will protect the city?

KYDES: Our healthy city can claim neutrality.

DEMETRA: Neutrality is no guarantee of peace or comity. It cannot assume, even under the most ardent forms of neutrality in the face of conflicts between other *poleis*, that no other city will wish to conquer it. Look, for example, at Mycalessus and the slaughter of its inhabitants by the Thracians.[1] Mycalessus was a small city that had remained neutral between Athens and Sparta during the Peloponnesian War. She did not protect herself, thinking that her neutrality would save her and that no other city would find her worth conquering.

HERMIAS: Let's consider a different angle for the move from the healthy city to the fevered one. Remember, as we have learned here at the Academy, Socrates's interlocutors guide the conversations. Their own level of sophistication or experience leads them to pursue some topics and abandon others. As part of his educational philosophy, Socrates permits them to take the conversation where they think it needs to go. He may later

---

1. Thucydides, *Landmark Thucydides* (trans. Strassler), 443–44.

bring them back to the central topic in ways that, I suppose, he thinks will elevate their own thinking on the subject.

In this dialogue, Socrates has already stated that larger letters are easier to read than smaller ones. Just so, we might more readily find morality by examining a city rather than an individual. Similarly, we might more readily find morality in a fevered city than in a healthy one, because the presence of luxuries and war might make it easier for us to see immorality arising from those developments and thus easier for us to see and understand morality itself. The move to the fevered city seems, then, to benefit Glaucon and Adeimantus, given where they are in their level of understanding to this point.

PLATO (Plato smiled.): These points you all have raised are, of course, philosophical. Will the residents of our two cities—healthy and fevered—be able to raise them? Can philosophy arise and become important in the healthy city? Or does philosophy come only through the presence and pursuit of luxuries and the need for expansion and the possibility of war? Does the fevered city merely make it easier, as Hermias suggested, for us to perceive morality through examples of immorality that luxuries and war might entail? Let us keep these questions in mind as we proceed, but let us return to our earlier focus.

Socrates says that at this point in describing the fevered city,

> "our job is to select, if we can, the kind of nature suited to guard the city. . . . When it comes to guarding, is there any difference between the nature of a pedigree young dog and that of a well-born youth?" (374e7–8, 375a2–3)

(Plato's three students burst out laughing.)

HERMIAS: This is a joke, right?

PLATO: Let us hear him out.

> "Both of them have to be sharp-eyed, quick to catch what they see, and strong, too, in case they have to fight what they capture. And they must be courageous, surely, if indeed they are to fight well. Now, will a horse, a dog, or any other animal be courageous if it is not spirited? Or haven't you noticed just how invincible and unbeatable spirit is, so that its presence makes the whole soul fearless and unconquerable in any situation?" (375a5–b2)

DEMETRA (with undisguised irritation in her voice): Oh, come on, Plato! Socrates is here attributing virtues to dogs: They display courage; they have something that seems akin to *thymos* or spiritedness. But virtues lie within. The behavior of a dog might reflect actions that seem virtuous, but the dogs' actions lack self-awareness. They are simply conditioned responses. They reflect a dog's obedience training, not its character or internal state. It's humans reading virtues into dogs.

HERMIAS: When men act virtuously—

DEMETRA: And women . . .

HERMIAS: . . . and women act virtuously or fail to do so, they know it. They understand what's at stake. Dogs don't have any self-reflection of this sort, and, following Demetra, I'd say that dogs therefore don't have anything resembling virtue.

KYDES: Can a person act courageously without knowing that he is acting courageously? If so, then why can't a dog?

DEMETRA: First, you'd say that the act performed was courageous, but that doesn't make the person courageous. Socrates said that the dog must be courageous. But the dog isn't. One cannot be courageous and not know it. The dog can't judge the act. The dog has no concept of acting courageously.

KYDES: If I act justly, am I not being just?

DEMETRA: Again, focus on the person, not the act itself. Can one perform a brave act or a just act by accident or mistake? We see that the act is just, but we would not necessarily call that person a just person, would we? Does it not require some evidence of inner awareness for us to judge a person to be just? It isn't simply acts over time or performed consistently, since dogs do that all the time.

HERMIAS: Indeed, what kind of protectors of the city can these warriors be, if they are simply raised to be obedient like dogs?

PLATO: Let us find out. Socrates says that in addition to the qualities already mentioned, the guardians of the city must be "*gentle to their own people and harsh to the enemy. Where are we to find a character that is both gentle and high-spirited at the same time, because a gentle nature is the opposite of a spirited one?*" (375c1–8).

KYDES: Right off, I'd say that such character isn't found. It's created; it's made. We raise these citizens, these guardians, to be this kind of warrior. We educate them to recognize their fellow citizens and to treat them gently. Meanwhile, we also teach them to be ruthless toward enemies when need be.

PLATO: As Socrates says, however, don't we see that pedigree dogs have character of this sort naturally? They are gentle to those they know, but the opposite to those they don't know (375d11–e3).

KYDES: No, Plato, we don't see this naturally, and I don't understand why Socrates is going on about this. Dogs learn friendly faces over time. By nature some dogs might growl or bark at those they don't know, or they can be trained to do so. But look how easily dogs can be misled. Placing a square of cloth over your head or wearing a helmet can set the dog barking and growling even when the person is a friendly one, known to the dog.

PLATO: Socrates picks up your point, Kydes: "*When a dog sees someone it doesn't know, it gets angry before anything bad happens to it. But when it knows someone, it welcomes him, even if it has never received anything good from him*" (376a5–8).

KYDES: Well, I argued that a dog can be confused when a friendly face is easily disguised, but I accept the general point that without disguise that is how dogs often react.

HERMIAS: Nevertheless, dogs are bred for certain purposes. Over time some breeds might develop an instinct for certain behaviors. Sheep dogs by instinct, it seems, herd sheep. But they must be trained when to herd and when to stop. Besides, Socrates refers to "*pedigree dogs.*" Those are dogs that are bred with some intention in mind. Granted, the intention, if it isn't just for show, is to breed the dog for some purpose, such as herding sheep, so that might become part of their natures. But no dog owner can rest on permitting dogs only to obey their instincts. Those dogs must be trained further.

PLATO: Socrates here pushes his point. Dogs, as our guardians must be, are philosophical, because they judge anyone they see to be either friend or foe; the dog knows the one and doesn't know the other. How could that reflect anything but a love of learning? And surely love of learning is philosophy (376b1–10).

KYDES: This is drifting into the absurd. Yes, dogs can learn, and perhaps they love learning tricks and commands and even have an instinct for training. But that is in no way a "love of wisdom," which is the definition of "philosophy." At the very least, a dog would have to demonstrate that it could learn on its own in novel situations. That could be wisdom. Yet when does that happen?

HERMIAS: I'm with Kydes on this one. Dogs respond to commands. They don't initiate, and they don't learn on their own who is friend and who is foe. Dogs can be conditioned to obey specific commands. That's training, not education, and it certainly isn't philosophical. If we left our guardians as capable only of obeying commands, then there isn't any judgment or discernment there. Dogs don't judge persons to be friendly or threatening. The judgments made are those of the master, not the dog. Dogs simply react to stimuli.

Without judgment or discernment, our guardians would simply be, at best, rule followers. The guardians will have to judge whether those figures beyond the city's walls are friends or foes. Philosophy pushes behind the rules to see what underlies them and to analyze whether they should be modified, dropped, or obeyed. Sometimes their judgments will lead warriors to violate rules.

When we say that a soldier is well trained, we mean that he has been thoroughly drilled. But that training or drilling is then to be applied to a novel situation, a battlefield experience for which the soldier is prepared through training or drilling, but that is categorically different from what the soldier has heretofore experienced. That is why we place the inexperienced soldiers in the middle of our phalanx, between the veterans in their prime at the front and the elder veterans at the back pushing the youngsters forward.

KYDES: Masters want their dogs to be consistent in their obedience, even blindly obedient. Schoolmasters, good ones anyway, don't want that. A dog cannot interrogate its learning. A dog may "challenge" his master by refusing to obey or by disobeying. But a dog cannot change a behavior because it thought about it.

A guard dog can be commanded to attack, regardless of whether the victim of the attack is a friend or a foe. The dog is responding to the command of its master. Would the soldiers of the fevered city be any different if raised this way?

HERMIAS: Plato, you yourself don't think for a second that dogs are philosophical and that they can be educated. They can be trained, but not educated. Training is putting something into someone, instilling behaviors through repetition of commands or practices. If you thought that that were education, let alone philosophical, then you'd teach very differently here at the Academy. You'd plant opinions that you wanted us to share. You certainly wouldn't use dialectic with your students, as you are doing now. That's the method we use to come to realize what we think and why we think it.

We aren't like these *kraters* (he points) into which wine is poured. We aren't empty vessels into which knowledge and information is simply poured. You might stimulate us with questions and puzzles that we ponder, analyze, manipulate, deliberate about, and even reject. It is what lies inside of us—our curiosity and interests—that we bring to bear, even at an early age, on the questions and puzzles. You want us to think our way to our own conclusions and thereby come to own them. That is hardly something going on inside a dog.

DEMETRA: I think that we've been distracted here. Of course, Socrates knows dogs aren't philosophical, and he must have been waiting for some resistance or outright mockery from Glaucon and Adeimantus. But that doesn't come. So, Socrates continues on this path about natures and philosophy. But why? Why is he introducing, let alone pressing, this idea, which on its face seems ridiculous, as we have been pointing out?

I think he's raising it to probe how philosophy is important to the fevered city. He's proposing that it comes into the city with the need for soldiers as a special "breed." They have to have natures that reflect courage, spiritedness, strength, and also philosophy. But these are no more natural in humans than they are in dogs, and maybe less so, since a dog's breeding may lead it to display what we, not the dog, describe as courage and spirit. We know that we can't breed humans to have certain kinds of natures. There are too many variables. Otherwise, the offspring of our greatest Olympic champions could be bred to surpass their parents. How often has that happened?[2]

---

2. The problem with selective human breeding, known as eugenics, is nicely encapsulated in the apocryphal exchange between the American dancer Isadora Duncan and the Irish playwright George Bernard Shaw. In a letter Duncan is alleged to have written to Shaw: "As you have the greatest brain in the world and I have the most beautiful body, it is our duty to posterity to have a child." Shaw responded, as the anecdote goes, "But it might happen that our child would have my body and your brain. Therefore, I respectfully decline."

As for philosophy? At its center is the heart also of education: Asking questions and pursuing answers or solutions. It is the desire to know and grow. Certainly that seems beyond the capabilities of dogs. The issue seems straightforward to me: If your "students" are pursuing predetermined ends achieved through rote and drill, then you are training them, not educating them. You then measure success by how well they obey, not, as in true education, by how well they assess.

But do we breed persons to be philosophical? We educate them to be philosophical, but we don't breed them. And some persons do show philosophical inclinations without much schooling or education. So, I think at this point that Socrates's talk about natures is to bring his discussion of the soldiers in line with the division of labor he described in the healthy city. Guarding will be our warriors' task or job to the exclusion of other tasks and jobs.

PLATO: Let us see. Socrates summarizes as Demetra did:

> *"Philosophy, spirit, speed, and strength must all, then, be combined in the nature of anyone who is to be a fine and good guardian of our city. But how do we bring him up and educate him? Will inquiry into that topic bring us any closer to the goal of our inquiry, which is to discover the origins of morality and immorality in a city?"* (376c3–8)

My brothers agree. *"Come, then,"* said Socrates, *"and just as if we had the leisure to make up stories, let's describe in theory how to educate our men"* (376d8–9).

HERMIAS: At least Socrates is here acknowledging that these men must be educated and not simply trained.

PLATO: And educated how? We would surmise at this stage, would we not, that such education should involve philosophy?

4

Education of the Guardians

PLATO: Socrates has asked Glaucon and Adeimantus whether examining the guardians' education will bring us closer to understanding the origins of morality in the city.

HERMIAS: Well, certainly it will in one respect: Education in music and poetry leads us to appreciate harmony and order. Taught from infancy on, music and poetry will serve against immorality within one's soul. The ordered and harmonious soul seeks what is most beautiful and good and illuminates all we see.

PLATO: Well said, Hermias. So, we might expect physical training for bodies and arts for the soul, and that is precisely what Socrates says next (377e3–4). To Adeimantus Socrates says, "Do you include stories under music and poetry?"[1]

"I do," answered Adeimantus. Socrates went on:

> "Aren't there two kinds of story, one true and the other false? And mustn't our men be educated in both, but first in false ones. [For] we first tell false stories to children, though they have some truth in them.... You know, don't you, that when they are young and tender, they are most malleable and take on any pattern one wishes to impress on [them]." (377e9–a4, a10–b10)

---

1. In their translation of the *Republic* (Plato, *Complete Works*) Grube/Reeve use the term "music" for arts or cultural education. Music for the Greeks comprised poetry (which includes stories), music, song, dance, calculating, and art.

But we don't tell them just any story told by just anyone. We don't want them to take beliefs into their souls that are opposite the ones that we think they ought to hold. And so,

> "we must supervise the storytellers. We'll select their stories whenever they are fine or beautiful and reject them when they aren't. ... [N]urses and mothers will tell their children the ones we have selected since they will shape their children's souls." (377b3–c3)

DEMETRA: Plato, this doesn't sound like education. It sounds like conditioning—shaping their souls with no input from the children. And what has happened to all that talk about finding the proper nature? This is about creating, not finding, guardians.

KYDES: But this makes sense, doesn't it? The stories that we hear early on are ones that we carry with us when we become older. They show us or reinforce in us how to behave properly. Besides, we all know that little kids don't understand the importance of a sleep schedule. So, we tell them that the gods link beauty and health to good, steady sleep. How many times have we heard you say, Deme, that you need your "beauty sleep"?

DEMETRA: I don't have to be lied to about the benefits of sleep, Kydes.

KYDES: No, not now. But you did when you were six. Otherwise, you'd be up all night trying to talk to the adults.

HERMIAS: And what are the criteria for selecting stories?

PLATO: Socrates tells us: *"When a story gives a bad image of what the gods and heroes are like, the way a painter does whose picture is not at all like the things he's trying to paint"* (377d9–e2, d3), then we must censor, says Socrates, those false stories, such as told by Homer, Hesiod, and other poets. A story that presents

> "the biggest falsehood about the most important things has no good features—I mean Hesiod telling us about how Uranus behaved, how Cronus punished him for it, and how he was in turn punished by his own son.[2]

---

2. Hesiod, *Theogony*, 132–53. From Chaos—literally, a yawning or gaping void and what I shall later describe as the Unmanifest, a state of emptiness yet fullness—are born the five elements: Gaia (the earth goddess), Tartarus (both the god and the underworld itself), Eros (power of love), Erebus (the realm of darkness), and Nyx (the personification of night). Gaia gives birth to Uranus, the "star-studded heaven." Uranus sleeps with his mother (obviously no incest taboo here, though, given what follows, there should

> But even if these stories were true, they should be passed over in silence, I would think, and not told so casually to the foolish and the young. And if, for some reason, they must be told, only a very few people should hear them—people who are pledged to secrecy and have had to sacrifice . . . something so large and scarce that the number of people who hear them is kept as small as possible." (377e6–378a6)

KYDES: Okay, maybe you don't want young, impressionable children hearing these stories. But we heard such stories growing up, and we seem to have turned out all right.

HERMIAS: Well, Kydes, two of us have. (He winks at Demetra.) And who is in that select group, Plato? Who can hear these stories? Also, who chooses the stories? Is it the teachers of the guardians who know the stories and can tell them?

PLATO: Socrates says that no one in the city can tell them.

> "They should not be told in our city, Adeimantus. No young person should hear it said that if he were to commit the worst crimes, he would be doing nothing amazing, or that if he were to inflict every sort of punishment on an unjust father, he would only be doing the same as the first and greatest of the gods.
>
> "Indeed, we must not allow any stories about gods warring, fighting, or plotting against one another if we want the guardians of our city to think that it is shameful to be easily provoked into mutual hatred. After all, those stories are not true either. Still less should battles between gods and giants, or the many other multifarious hostilities of gods and heroes toward their families and

---

have been), and they produce a trio of sons, each with three heads; then they produce the three Cyclopes; and, after, they produce a dozen children known as the Titans. Fearful that one of the Titans would rise up against him and seize power, Uranus decides to engage in perpetual intercourse with Gaia so that the Titans will be locked away in their mother's womb, the interior of earth. Angry and in pain, Gaia asks her titanic-children to get rid of Uranus. Only Cronus has the gall and guile to do so. Gaia gives him a sickle, and Cronus slices away "the genitals of his own father." The Titans are freed, and Cronus becomes their king.

Cronus marries his sister Rhea, but given what he did to his and their father, Cronus fears that his own children might rise up against him. So he swallows his first five children as Rhea delivers them. To save her sixth child, Rhea fools Cronus into swallowing a stone wrapped in baby clothes and then spirits her sixth child, Zeus, to a cave on Crete. Zeus later returns to confront Cronus. With Rhea's help, he induces Cronus to swallow an emetic that causes Cronus to vomit up Zeus's five siblings and the stone. But the now-freed Titans do not recognize Zeus as their leader, and a ten-year war ensues. Zeus ultimately prevails and exiles the Titans to the underworld.

friends, occur in the stories the guardians hear or in the embroidered pictures they see.

"On the contrary, if we are somehow going to persuade our people that no citizen has ever hated another, and that it is impious to do so, then those are the things their male and female elders should tell them from childhood on. And the poets they listen to as they grow older should be compelled to tell them the same sort of thing. Stories about Hera being chained by her son, or about Hephaestus being hurled from heaven by his father when he tried to save his mother from a beating, or about the battle of the gods in Homer, should not be admitted into our city, either as allegories or non-allegories. For the young cannot distinguish what is allegorical from what is not. And the beliefs they absorb at that age are difficult to erase and tend to become unalterable. For these reasons, then, we should probably take the utmost care to ensure that the first stories they hear about virtue are the best ones for them to hear." (378b1–e3)

DEMETRA: But we know, Plato, from our own experiences growing up with these stories that we can evaluate them. We learn growing up what is allegorical and what is not. That is the point of education, especially education in philosophy. We interrogate what we are told. Maybe the first stories ought to be ones about people and gods acting virtuously. That can establish a foundation to build on. For the virtues themselves don't change. How we understand them changes as we grow; how we interpret speeches and behaviors changes as we mature and become more experienced. At some point, however, the young can hear such stories and use them later to examine human behavior and proper living.

HERMIAS: Is this idea of censoring stories a way to test the educational attainment of your brothers, Plato? Can Glaucon and Adeimantus explain why censorship of stories might be a bad idea, as Deme has just done? Can they examine the value beneath and behind poetry, the value that demands that it be an essential part of the city?

DEMETRA: Won't the children of the city at some point want to know why some stories have been excluded from their city? Or do you think the children will never hear them, will never know that there is censorship within their city?

KYDES: At the same time, no one who lives with others, many others as in a city, will fail to hear disagreements and discord among some citizens.

But Socrates is saying that from an early age elders should teach children that no citizen has ever hated another citizen and that it is impious to do so. That's false, Plato, and Socrates just finished telling us that false stories about the gods should be excluded. Well, then, so should false stories about citizens always loving one another. If the guardians hold that false view, then they aren't defending a city. They're defending a fiction.

DEMETRA: Again, Plato, Socrates isn't describing a system of educating the guardians of the city. It's a program of conditioning or training. "Don't let them hear that gods fight among themselves, don't let them hear that citizens quarrel and despise others," because if they do, they might find it permissible not to like all of the city's residents. But if they are educated, and not simply conditioned, then they can see that not all citizens in the city are likeable, but all are worthy of being protected.

And the situation gets worse. Socrates says that even if stories about bad behavior are true (378a1), they should be "passed over." So, now, the truth is to be censored because it doesn't correspond to what the guardians can be allowed to hear? If Socrates is serious about educating the guardians, then he must at some point require them to challenge and investigate the stories they hear and the very censorship that has been imposed on them. If they have been educated in or into philosophy, then surely they will be able to discern the allegorical or symbolic elements within or behind stories. That is part, perhaps the essential part, of philosophical examination. When does that happen? It had better happen soon.

PLATO: It makes sense, does it not, to censor stories about heroes and the gods? After all, children cannot easily judge between what is good and bad, between what is true or false.

DEMETRA: You are right. They cannot judge easily, but that judgment shouldn't be easy. It can be difficult, and that is why education lasts years, especially when it's philosophical. How can it be good for the guardians to learn only one set of facts and fictions showing gods and people as we want them to be? They will then only know how to identify what is good and right and true based on what they have been fed, not what they have judged for themselves. They will see only in black and white: "This is good, because we were taught it is good. All that runs against that must be bad." If something doesn't match the model of what they have come to see as just and good and true, then that something must be and can only be unjust and bad and false. There are no gradations here, no multiple perspectives.

HERMIAS: These guardians have been fed and raised on "true beliefs" that derive from hearing the censored stories of the poets. But those are only beliefs about virtuous actions; they are not themselves true knowledge. To achieve that knowledge requires philosophy or inquiry.

KYDES: Yet can't we say that the just behavior of the guardians, even if only based on true beliefs, is virtuous and moral behavior?

HERMIAS: How different is that behavior from simple blind adherence to the stories told? We can agree that this isn't true goodness or justice or morality, because a person has no knowledge and cannot give an account of why he is behaving as he is and why he should behave that way or behave differently. We're back, then, to the training of pedigree dogs.

DEMETRA: I'm worried, Plato, about your brothers. They don't seem to see that the need for the guardians in the luxurious city is not just about protecting a city that now has abundant land and goods worth seizing. The need is also about protecting the limitations on the education of the guardians themselves. And that education is a farce, since it is not to educate citizens but to train or condition one-dimensional fighters no different from guard dogs.

PLATO: Let us proceed with the dialogue to see whether and how Socrates might address your concerns, Demetra.

Socrates has discussed with Glaucon and Adeimantus the need for forming the characters of the young guardians. To that end, he has suggested that the city ban any stories that paint the gods as quarreling and warring among themselves or that show the gods lying, changing shapes, or acting maliciously. Socrates also wants stories that build and strengthen the guardians' positive outlook on the gods that oversee the city.

To develop their courage, no stories should be permitted that make the guardians afraid of death or that portray the afterworld as frightening. In addition, the city should not portray their famous men as openly mourning dead comrades. Indeed, they should disdain such acts, since those acts belong only to cowardly men and to women (387e9-10). Socrates says, *"as the argument has demonstrated—and we must remain persuaded by it until someone shows us a better one—the guardians mustn't behave like that"* (388e2-4).

DEMETRA: *"Until someone shows us a better one"*? The argument amounts to this: Ban such stories and acts from the city forever, since nowhere does Socrates even hint at reintroducing these stories at a later date, even if they are true (378a1). Instead, they are expunged from the canon of tales of famous men and of the gods. So, the guardians are lied to, and the rulers of the city, whoever they are, hide the truth of human behavior and of the gods' behavior. The base of the guardians' character, then, is lies, and the process of their "education" is indoctrination.

KYDES: So, what is your better argument, Deme?

DEMETRA: We have been talking about it just now, Kydes. Give them the education we received. Tell them the stories of men's lamentations when comrades die in battle. Tell them stories where gods and heroes act poorly. But along the way, ask these young guardians to explain why gods and heroes and brave men might act this way. What does such behavior tell us? Can't we mourn our comrades and still fight in their name, for their honor? Is it really courage to pretend not to care about the death of a fallen comrade, or is Socrates saying that one cannot have true courage and lament publicly, maybe even privately? Even dogs mourn the loss of their masters. Or are those poorly trained dogs, not the pedigree that Socrates seeks?

KYDES: Why do you think that Glaucon and Adeimantus aren't objecting here? They had the same education as Plato and, presumably, one similar to ours.

PLATO: Is it possible that they recognize that sometimes falsehoods can be useful?

HERMIAS: Useful how, Plato? For cultivating the morality that we think the guardians will need?

DEMETRA: Or is Socrates showing us the opposite of morality, since this is prescribed behavior within a fevered, unhealthy, city? Since Socrates is engaged with Plato's brothers in dialectic,[3] then perhaps showing them the opposite of morality can highlight morality itself.

---

3. As I wrote in the introduction, dialectic is a method of investigation and interrogation—often in question-and-answer form—often aimed at identifying faulty or limited assumptions and at reaching clarity about understandings or definitions of important concepts or ideas. See footnote 10. I shall have more to say about dialectic later in this text.

HERMIAS: Then the falsehoods are useful for keeping citizens' and guardians' behavior in line with the prescribed strictures. But, as Deme said, this isn't education, since the work of developing morality and acting morally here is based on imposition from without. It is external conditioning. There is not yet, anyway, anything like internal work, processes by which someone comes to interrogate these strictures and form their behaviors according to what they have come to know themselves through examination.

KYDES: And who knows what is false and what isn't? The city's rulers do, but the people, including the guardians, do not, because they never know anything but the stories permitted within the city. Everything is censored and controlled.

DEMETRA: Socrates's concern seems to be that if the people, especially the guardians, hear stories about the gods doing bad things or about famous men lamenting deaths, then the people and the guardians themselves will in turn do bad things and lament. But that doesn't follow if the guardians are educated and not conditioned; that is, if they can examine, as we have done all our lives here at the Academy, what is presented and not simply drink it down like watered wine.

KYDES: And is this morality? Is telling people certain stories and prohibiting other kinds of stories the basis of morality, instilling good behavior by permitting people to hear only certain stories and by forcing them to behave only in certain ways? As Deme and Hermias said, this is imposing character from the outside. It isn't developed from within, from within the soul. Having behaviors and perspectives imposed persuades no one. People may obey, but do they know and understand?

PLATO: Kydes brings us back to our inquiry: What is morality in and of itself? Why should we be moral? He alludes to "good behavior." Though we don't yet know what "good" means, we do think, as Socrates says, that *"surely nothing good is ever harmful, is it"* (394b3)?

Anyway, at this point, Socrates changes direction somewhat. He says, *"This concludes our discussion of the content of stories. We should now, I think, investigate their style"* (392c5–6).

Adeimantus then says, "I don't understand what you mean."

KYDES: Quite right, Plato. I don't know what Socrates is pointing toward. Style? What does he mean, and why is that important, as important as content?

PLATO: Well, as Socrates goes on to say, everything said by poets is either narration or imitation, is that not so?

KYDES: I'm not catching the significance of this, Plato.

PLATO: When speaking in narration, the poet is not trying to make the listener think that the speaker is anyone but himself. On the other hand, when speaking as someone else, to make himself sound or appear as another, is to imitate that other person. When you have a combination of narration and imitation, then you have epic poetry. Right?

KYDES: So far.

PLATO: Socrates then says,

> "What I want you to consider, then, Adeimantus, is whether our guardians should be imitators or not. Or does the answer follow from what we have said already—namely, that whereas each individual can practice one pursuit well, he cannot practice many well? ... Then doesn't the same principle also apply to imitation—namely, that a single individual cannot imitate many things as well as he can imitate one." (394d11–e5)

KYDES: I don't see why not. We have many fine actors who can mimic almost perfectly our leaders and generals. Those who are talented in this way can imitate many voices and characters, not just one. But I'm curious to see where this is leading, Plato.

PLATO: Socrates next says to Adeimantus,

> "So, if we are to preserve our first argument, that our guardians must be kept away from all other crafts so as to be the most exact craftsmen of the city's freedom, and practice nothing at all except what contributes to this, then they must neither do nor imitate anything else. But if they imitate anything, they must imitate right from childhood what is appropriate for them—that is to say, people who are courageous, temperate, pious, free, and everything of that sort. On the other hand, they must not be clever at doing or imitating illiberal or shameful actions, so that they won't acquire a taste for the real thing from imitating it. Or haven't you

noticed that imitations, if they are practiced much past youth, get established in the habits and nature of body, tones of voice, and mind?" (395b8–d2)

HERMIAS: Let me see whether I understand what Socrates is pointing out. His fear is that if the guardians imitate someone else, then they might be in danger of behaving over time like that someone else. Repeated behaviors, repeated imitations, could lead those guardians to become this other person, who might display, for example, humorous though weak character.

If that is so, then these guardians themselves display weak, even fragile, character. All of this, it seems to us, stems from their lack of education. No one is in danger, when repeating parts of the *Iliad*, of thinking that she is Homer or in danger of becoming Homer.

DEMETRA: We are back now to philosophical dogs, Plato. The guardians, if they imitate at all, can imitate those behaviors that have been deemed in the city to be good—courage, temperance, piety, and the like—the virtues, in short. Just so, they can't be permitted to imitate "illiberal" or "shameful" acts, lest they become illiberal and shameful. This is because, like guard dogs, they learn commands and behaviors external to them. They become what they practice. But they aren't practicing any kind of inquiry, any pursuit of knowledge. They certainly aren't engaged in dialectic, a back-and-forth involving questions, responses, and especially opposites. Again, Plato, it is their lack of education that lies at the root of the guardians' problems. Let the guardians "imitate" philosophers by practicing dialectic.

PLATO: If you agree, Demetra, that persons often become what they practice, then you might agree that in this city we do not want our guardians imitating, say, metal workers or other craftsmen, rowers in the triremes, slaves, cowards, or, going farther afield, madmen, lest they become tainted.

> "Suppose, then, that a man who through clever training can become anything and imitate everything were to arrive in person in our city and wanted to give a performance of his poems. It seems that we would bow down before him as someone holy, amazing, and pleasing.
>
> "But we would tell him that there is no man like him in our city, and that it is not lawful for there to be one. Then we would

anoint his head with perfumes, crown him with a woolen wreath, and send him away to another city.

"But, for our own benefit, we would employ a more austere and less pleasant poet and storyteller ourselves—one who would imitate the speech of a good person and make his stories fit the patterns we laid down at the beginning, when we undertook to educate our soldiers." (397e9–398b3)

DEMETRA: This man at our gates is one who has received "clever training." In that sense, he is not unlike the guardians themselves. The guardians, as we have been saying, are no more educated than this poet. Because they haven't been educated, certainly not in and through dialectic, they cannot be trusted to hear this cleverly trained poet, for they lack discernment to see that he is a poet only and not those things and persons he imitates.

HERMIAS: And I assume, Plato, that much the same will be said about music permitted in the city. Just admit those modes that are harmonious. Nothing atonal; nothing experimental. Only tones and rhythms that stir courageous guardians into battle?

PLATO: So Socrates says (398c–399e3).

HERMIAS: Now we have our well-trained "philosophical" dogs, which, as we've covered, is no philosophy at all.

PLATO: Well, even more than that, Hermias. Socrates then observes, "And without being aware of it, we have purified the city we recently said was luxurious" (399e4–5).

HERMIAS: Purified it? How? By denying the guardians an education through dialectic? By denying them any chance to inquire into the practices we put them through; any chance to challenge poets and teachers; any opportunity to question the manner and lyrics of musicians and even craftsmen? And, by the way, the city has hardly been purified of its seeming addiction to luxuries and war.

DEMETRA: This is a city ruled by dictates from . . . well, someone or somebody. We have yet to discuss who is behind all of this censorship, who is making these judgments. I'd wager that these rulers haven't been raised as the guardians are raised. Otherwise, these ruling "philosophical dogs" couldn't discern what is good and decent from what is shameful and harmful. They could only repeat what they themselves had heard and been taught, been conditioned into. They couldn't purify a luxurious city, because they wouldn't know anything different.

It's the opposite of purification. It's preservation. How do you preserve luxuries? Well, not all can have luxuries. Otherwise, they aren't luxuries anymore. The term's very meaning involves what goes beyond life's necessities; that is, what we saw in the healthy city. Luxuries involve what is costly, even excessive and extravagant. Not everyone can have those, which is why the guardians don't just protect the city, but protect those within the city who live in luxury. To do that job requires the guardians themselves to be sheltered from the selfish and wasteful practices of many in the city whom they are raised to protect.

PLATO: You are right, Demetra, that we have yet to discuss who is ruling this city. Right now, we must focus, as you three are doing, on the qualities that our guardians need to have. But your inference is correct. There is a plan behind what the guardians learn and how they are raised. As Socrates says, *"This sort of fine and good character has developed in accordance with an intelligent plan"* (400e2–3).

You are correct also, all three of you, that the city requires, well, let us follow Socrates and call it "supervision." If we are to have the purified city as he proposes, then he asks,

> *"Is it only poets we have to supervise, then, compelling them either to embody the image of a good character in their poems or else not to practice their craft among us? Or mustn't we also supervise all the other craftsmen, and forbid them to represent a character that is vicious, unrestrained, slavish, and graceless in their images of living beings, in their buildings, or in any of the other products of their craft? And mustn't the one who finds this impossible be prevented from practicing in our city, so that our guardians will not be brought up on images of evil as in a meadow of bad grass, where they crop and graze every day from all that surrounds them until, little by little, they unwittingly accumulate a large amount of evil in their souls? Instead, mustn't we look for craftsmen who are naturally capable of pursuing what is fine and graceful in their work, so that our young people will live in a healthy place and be benefited on all sides as the influence exerted by those fine works affects their eyes and ears like a healthy breeze from a good place, leading them unwittingly from earliest childhood into being similar to, friendly toward, and concordant with the beauty of reason?"* (401b–d2)

HERMIAS: "*Beauty of reason*"? We have already tried to argue that censorship, the main practice in this city, eliminates the need and the opportunity for reason.

DEMETRA: Eliminates even the need to think. The music and poems you hear in the city are good; those that are foreign are bad.

HERMIAS: That's right. To know that your city's practices and music and poetry are good, you need to know their opposites and figure out why one is good and another harmful. Censorship eliminates that. There is no room for pursuit of knowledge here, for there is no dialectic, no inquiry, no education, and thus no philosophy.

KYDES: Socrates says as much. Everything bad is accumulated "*unwittingly*" in the soul. So, too, is everything good. There is no room for examining practices and their effects. Nothing is taken into the heart, into the head, into the soul and there thought about, criticized, and accepted. We, then, own nothing in our souls. Everything is planted by forces outside of us. I don't understand, Plato, why your brothers don't see this, don't see the lack of true education in this city.

PLATO: What about this, Kydes? Socrates says,

> "*Anyone who has been properly educated in music and poetry will sense acutely in their soul when something has been omitted from a thing and when it hasn't been finely crafted or finely made by nature.*" (401e1–3)

KYDES: With that I agree, Plato. But that is not what is happening to the guardians. They aren't "*properly educated*." That's what we've been saying. They cannot assess music and poetry acutely or otherwise. All they can do is sense that something they are hearing is not like that which they have heard before. Since they have never heard that before, what they are hearing must be inferior to what they have been brought up on. Thus, the different is inferior and bad. There is no assessment, no judging the qualities of what is performed. There is only the reaction that this music or poem is not like what we have in the city. There is no trying to understand what is different, how, and why. There is only the recognition that this is different and therefore bad, even evil.

Is there anywhere in this luxurious city where one can even hear discordant music or poetry? Is there a seedy place like the Piraeus, a place where the stimuli are various, unfettered, and even unpredictable?

PLATO: Socrates is not without an appreciation for what you three have pointed out. But, he wants to postpone what you are describing as the guardians' education. Right now, at their early development, he wants them to hear uplifting stories and music.

> "Neither we nor the guardians we claim to be educating will be musically trained until we know the different forms of moderation, courage, generosity, high-mindedness, and all their kindred, and their opposites, too, which are carried around everywhere; and see them in the things in which they are, both themselves and their images; and do not disregard them, either in small things or in large, but accept that the knowledge of both belongs to the same craft and discipline. . . . Therefore, if someone's soul has a fine and beautiful character and his body matches it in beauty and is thus in harmony with it, so that both share in the same pattern, wouldn't that be the most beautiful sight for anyone who has eyes to see?" (402b9–d3)

DEMETRA: At least Socrates is admitting that thus far the guardians aren't educated and that the opposites of moderation, courage, generosity, and high-mindedness are present—though, frankly, I don't know how that can fit in with what he said earlier. But as I said earlier, he'd better hurry up. Because there is now a lot of indoctrination and training and little else.

Also, the very forms of what is to be known and interrogated—that is the virtues and morality—are here assumed to be available and evident in the city, which is the point of our inquiry; namely, where do morality and immorality come into being in the city? At this stage, without arguing that point, I can say that so far I see only immorality in the unquestioned values and behaviors inculcated through the censorship imposed by the rulers.

So, to answer Socrates's question, no, having a fine and beautiful character is not the most beautiful sight to see, since that character has been done for you, even to you. It is not set in the soul, it is not etched in the soul, since it is not one you own, as Kydes said. It is not a character that is yours, because it is not anchored through knowledge led by inquiry and examination. Can the guardians know goodness, know beauty? I don't see how they can without philosophy.

KYDES: On the other hand, why isn't being surrounded by beauty and goodness enough? If your circumstances reflect only what is judged to be good and beautiful, then why isn't having those circumstances sufficient for creating good and strong character?

DEMETRA: If the goal is to have guardians who are obedient, who respond to commands and react to what is set before them, then having such circumstances is probably enough. But Socrates is talking throughout about educating the guardians, and thus far we aren't seeing anything that we agree is education.

Besides, circumstances can change. Will the guardians be able to adapt and change if the rulers were to decree what might even be the opposite of what the guardians have learned? The emphasis seems to be, then, on what surrounds them and not on what is itself good and beautiful and why it is good and beautiful. If one can be led into goodness without knowing why it is good, then they can be led out of goodness. The rulers of the city are the ones setting the circumstances.

5

The Noble Lie

PLATO: So, let us now discuss these rulers of this city. Who, Socrates asks, is to rule and who is to be ruled? The rulers are those, he says, who are knowledgeable and capable and who care for the city.

KYDES: That doesn't help us much, Plato. Knowledgeable about what? Capable how? Of guarding the city? Isn't that all that they, beyond others, are knowledgeable about in the city?

PLATO: Yes, but consider this: In guarding the city the rulers want only what is advantageous to the city and would be unwilling to do anything to undermine it. Then we must seek out those guardians who have the abiding quality of always doing what they believe is best for the city, for the city is their sole focus. So, for rulers let us choose, says Socrates, those who are most enthusiastic throughout their lives for doing what benefits the city.

> "I think, then, that we will have to observe them at every stage of their lives to make sure that they are good guardians of this conviction. (412e4–7) . . . [W]e must discover which of them are best at safeguarding within themselves the conviction that they must always do what they believe to be best for the city. We must watch them right from childhood, and set them tasks in which a person would be most likely to forget such a conviction or be deceived out of it. And we must select the ones who remember and are difficult to deceive, and reject the others. Do you agree?" (413c5–d2)

KYDES: Yes, I agree we want rulers who are committed to doing what is right and good for the city. We don't want those who are easily swayed to veer away from that commitment and do, instead, what is best for them or best only for one segment of the city.

DEMETRA: Why only the guardians? Why are they the ones who know best what is best for the city and will commit to it? Why not certain farmers or merchants? Traders or craftsmen? They, too, are residents of the city and must care for its welfare.

HERMIAS: And how are convictions and commitments best set in one's character? Is that not through thorough examination and argument? Isn't it best done through dialectic? As we've been saying, we don't yet see that among or within the guardians.

PLATO: Let us see what Socrates says about this.

> "We must subject our young people to fears and then plunge them once again into pleasures, so as to test them much more thoroughly than people test gold in a fire. And if any of them seems to be immune to sorcery, preserves his composure throughout, is a good guardian of himself and of the musical training he has received, and proves himself to be rhythmical and harmonious in all these trials—he is the sort of person who would be most useful, both to himself and to the city. And anyone who is tested as a child, youth, and adult, and always emerges as being without impurities, should be established as a ruler of the city as well as a guardian." (413e3–414a1)

DEMETRA: Okay. I see the value of testing children, youths, and adults to see how they perform over time to determine what individuals are best suited to rule the city. Those who perform best will be rulers of the city. I understand that. But Socrates is saying that only those who perform well can be rulers and guardians. Thus, if someone is the child of a farmer or a blacksmith and tests well throughout, then that child will be raised, if he continues to perform well as a youth, to be a guardian. He can even be a ruler. But does anyone have a choice about what he, or even she, will become?

HERMIAS: And, Plato, who is offering these tests? Who is making these judgments? Is it Socrates himself? Is he the sole judge of what tests to administer and how to evaluate the results? Or is it all philosophers? But were they themselves ever guardians? Is it the generals and admirals who judge, or are the founders those who judge? Yet don't they live outside or even "above" the city and drop in to manipulate and impose this educational scheme on the city dwellers?

PLATO: It is a city in speech that we are discussing. It is a hypothetical. Socrates provides, as he himself says, tests and procedures "*only as a general pattern and not the exact details*" (414a6).

At this point, Socrates suggests that those guardians tested as children, youths, and adults who show the requisite character will be eligible to be rulers. These he calls "complete guardians." Those who don't pass muster at this point will be guardians and guardians only, now known as "auxiliaries."

With such a division, how can we make certain that there is unity and solidarity among all of the guardians?

DEMETRA: Is that even a question that needs to be raised? Socrates has just spent time telling us that these guardians-in-training will be put through physical training and character-building—what he might call education in music and poetry, but which we aren't willing to call education at all—and will be tested on their convictions and commitments. Isn't that enough to unify them? Give them that "fellow-feeling"?

PLATO: You can imagine that those who remain "auxiliaries," who are not fit to be "complete guardians," might be envious of those selected to be rulers. Some children of merchants and traders might think more of their own merits than they do some of the guardians they see and interact with. How, asks Socrates, can we overcome dissension and discord in the city? He suggests that the founders of the city tell the residents a "useful falsehood," something emanating from the gods that could unite all of those in the city and persuade them of the need for and the wisdom of placing people in specific classes.

THE NOBLE LIE

This is a story, Socrates says, from Phoenicia[1] that has been used in many places, though it will require a lot of persuasion to get the people of the city to believe it. Socrates proceeds:

---

1. Phoenicia was a seafaring state on the eastern coast of the Mediterranean, largely occupying today's Lebanon, but including some territory of today's Israel and Syria.

> "*I will first be trying to persuade the rulers and the soldiers, and then the rest of the city, that the upbringing and the education we gave them were like dreams; that they only imagined they were undergoing all the things that were happening to them, while in fact they themselves were at that time down inside the earth being formed and nurtured, and that their weapons and the rest of their equipment were also manufactured there. When they were entirely completed, the earth, their mother, sent them up, so that now, just as if the land in which they live were their mother and nurse, they must deliberate on its behalf, defend it if anyone attacks it, and regard the other citizens as their earthborn brothers.*"
> (414c12–e5)

KYDES: "*Formed and nurtured*"? You mean that they were born not of humans but of the earth, who is their mother? They are asleep and dreaming through their childhood into young adulthood, and when they awaken, they are "*entirely complete*," with all of the requisite beliefs firmly and permanently planted in their character, within their souls. (Plato nods.) Well, that seems convenient. Certainly bypasses all that messy educating that we thought was necessary.

DEMETRA: We have to stop here, Plato. Holding aside the ridiculous nature of this story, one that I'm sure even Glaucon and Adeimantus chastised Socrates for trying to pass off, there is a significant problem from the outset. Earlier you told us that Socrates had said that a falsehood to be useful must be "*as much like the truth as we can* [make it]" (382d2–3). This lie isn't anywhere near the truth. But even worse, Socrates says that what everyone hates and will accept least of all is a lie about the most important things, and that would be a lie that is false to one's soul (382a11–b5). So, everyone would especially hate and refuse to accept this lie about the soul itself, the very most important thing.

PLATO: This is another reason why Socrates says that it will be difficult for those in the city to accept.

HERMIAS: So, why tell it at all?

PLATO: Let me finish the story, what Socrates calls "the Noble Lie," and perhaps the answer will become clear.

> "'*Although all of you in the city are brothers,*' we will say to them in telling our story, 'when the god was forming you, he mixed gold into those of you who are capable of ruling, which is why they

are the most honorable; silver into the auxiliaries; and iron and bronze into the farmers and other craftsmen. For the most part, you will produce children like yourselves; but, because you are all related, a silver child will occasionally be born to a golden parent, a golden child to a silver parent, and so on. Therefore, the first and most important command from the god to the rulers is that there is nothing they must guard better or watch more carefully than the mixture of metals in the souls of their offspring. If an offspring of theirs is born with a mixture of iron or bronze, they must not pity him in any way, but assign him an honor appropriate to his nature and drive him out to join the craftsmen or the farmers. On the other hand, if an offspring of the latter is found to have a mixture of gold or silver, they will honor him and take him up to join the guardians or the auxiliaries. For there is an oracle that the city will be ruined if it ever has an iron or a bronze guardian.' So, have you a device that will make them believe this story?" (415a1–c7)

KYDES: A device to make them believe this story? No, not as it's told. When Socrates says, "*we will say to them*," who are "we" here? Who is telling this story so that they might be believed? Are they already rulers of the city? Rulers of some other city who are forming this new city? Philosophers like Socrates? Whoever it is, the story rests not on its contents but on the reputations of those telling the story. Because, ultimately, these founders of the city are going to judge the natures of infants born in the city.

HERMIAS: And how do they judge the natures of these infants? They are making their judgments when these infants are really newborns. They aren't and can't reveal their characters or natures, their talents and skills, at that age. Or are all children raised the same until a certain age? Raised how and by whom? Do the rulers dictate to all parents how their children are raised?

Socrates says that some putatively gold child might really be silver, and a bronze child might be gold. And at what age do the rulers decide to which class a child belongs? Such decisions can only come after years of education and development, when the child proves himself to be with or without the requisite abilities to guard or rule. But the bronze child? Does he have the benefit of any of the training of the gold and silver children who have undergone schooling in music, poetry, and physical fitness?

DEMETRA: Stop, Hermias! You're getting caught up in the tale as if it is operative, as if it is useful. You're already thinking of how this falsehood might play out in the city. The whole notion is wrong from the outset. And what happened to the idea, presented earlier, of testing children, youths, and adults over time to determine what they are best at? That seems such a better method than accepting some fanciful and, quite frankly, absurd idea of the myths of the metals. I'd be surprised if your brothers ever allowed that idea to go forward.

Let's recapitulate for a moment. After Socrates described the healthy city, he asked his interlocutors where morality and immorality entered in. Glaucon avoids this challenge when he moves the conversation to discussing the need in the city for luxuries. This luxurious city Socrates describes as the fevered city, in contrast to the healthy city, which Glaucon has labeled *a city for pigs*.

So, now we find ourselves with Socrates discussing the unhealthy city, the fevered city. But the question remains, where in this city do morality and immorality enter in? We have seen how guardians and auxiliaries are raised to be good soldiers protecting this city. Now we see that the entire foundation of the city, the division of persons into classes within the city, rests on a lie. Calling that lie "noble" doesn't help, because we have to ask: Can anything moral, can any just system, rest on a lie?

Also, if it is the gods who implant the metals in our souls, then the gods from the outset made us unequal. But if the gods can only do good, as Socrates wants the city's stories to reflect, then inequality must be good. That would not be surprising in a city, based on this "Noble Lie," where immorality poses as morality.

KYDES: And it is the human rulers, in recognizing and judging the metals within individual souls, who perpetuate inequality. Again, hardly a moral system, even if the gods created this inequality for *"good reasons."*

DEMETRA: Think of our own lives. How would we fare in this city? Hermias would be seen as bronze or iron, at least to start. He was Eubulus's slave from Atarneus.[2]

KYDES: But he proved himself to be gold or silver, which is how he ended up here at the Academy.

DEMETRA: Well, which is it? Is he gold or silver?

KYDES: He's clearly gold.

---

2. Atarneus was an ancient Greek city in Asia Minor.

DEMETRA: Would it be so clear to the founders of this city? And what about you, Kydes? You were known from youth on as an athlete. Would you then be assigned to the silver class because of your physical gifts and athletic prowess? Would you thereby be deprived of being a gold soul, of being a ruler?

KYDES: Would I not prove myself as Hermias had done?

HERMIAS: Maybe, but maybe not. It depends on what the founders thought. And what about Demetra? As a woman, would she even be eligible for consideration? Or would she be relegated to the home, learning only those skills useful for managing a house, raising children, and pleasing her husband?

DEMETRA: Have we not seen this before in this Socratic dialogue? The Noble Lie undermines thinking. It prevents free thought and inquiry, since only those already designated gold and silver will have even the training that we have argued is not really education. And because this is training—really, conditioning to respond in certain circumstances in prescribed ways—and not education, the guardians might accept this Noble Lie, this myth of metals, but not necessarily believe it. They accept it as a way of keeping the bronze souls in check.

Yes, there is order within the city, because there are delineated classes. But it is the rulers or founders making the judgments about the natures of people and thereby assigning them to their "proper" class. What are the criteria for their judgments? Are those criteria ever subject to questioning or criticism? If not, then their judgments degrade human character and purpose. There may be exceptions, but most judgments will be fixed unless the outcome is obviously wrong. Yet, again, those judgments rest with the founders, and later the rulers, who judge without delineated criteria that we, the people, can assess and question.

HERMIAS: Now you're getting caught up in the lie, Deme. Our brief conversation here demonstrates its seductiveness.

Still, I see the importance of undermining this lie as best we can. We cannot lose sight that the Noble Lie stops people from thinking about how we should live our lives. Should we let the state sort us into classes based on some early views of our talents and inclinations, or do we permit people to develop at their own pace, free to change their minds and think about who they are and what they want to do? As Deme said, can we challenge the rules and roles that society has laid out, or do we blindly accept them as edicts from the gods or from our rulers? Is there to be any questioning of this social order, or do we acquiesce here to rulers like Sophocles's Creon in *Antigone*—"Anyone who disobeys in any way will die by public stoning"?[3]

DEMETRA: Shouldn't every child in a moral city be taught the skills necessary to direct her own life and thereby express her harmony and integrity in pursuit of fulfilling her purpose, her *telos*? How can anyone assume that a child will exhibit her defining talents and skills or interests at an early age? To restrict that child to only certain kinds of work is to miss her latent talents and skills and to cut that child off from her own self-direction. Haemon says, again to quote from *Antigone*, "The gods endow mankind with reason, the highest quality that we possess."[4] Why would the city deprive any child of developing that highest quality?

KYDES: We agree, with reference to Hermias, that persons can rise up out of a poor, even a vicious, environment to make something fine and decent of themselves. Will the judges miss that? Will they overlook someone whose soul is gold, not bronze? Will that person show noble traits too late in adolescence to be selected for education as a silver or gold soul?

HERMIAS: In my environment I was surrounded by injustice and viciousness. I saw it and had to avoid it every day. In such an environment you want to survive, so you latch onto whatever helps you do so. But I always knew that others lived better lives. I saw them, too, in my master's house and in his environment. That was something that I latched onto, aimed for, longed for. To survive I did some things that I was not proud of, but I never felt that those things attached to my soul. Indeed, the injustices that I saw, experienced, and committed have actually strengthened my soul by serving to impress on me how not to behave and by showing me the arduous daily struggles of so many in our cities.

DEMETRA: Hermias's own life shows the central deficiency in this Lie. People can learn in and rise above even the most challenging and deplorable conditions. The rulers deprive people of that opportunity by assigning them to classes when quite young.

---

3. Sophocles, *Antigone*, 37–38.
4. Sophocles, *Antigone*, 667–69.

KYDES: Plus, people change. They change their interests, their pursuits, their perspectives. This scheme locks them into a class from which only the most obviously misapplied can escape.

DEMETRA: What this story covers up, what it hides, is the necessity, and the hard work, of providing every child with a rigorous education, as rigorous as he or she can handle. If, during that education, some children demonstrate that they cannot handle advanced math or demanding argumentation, then at that point, and I urge only at that point, should they be assigned different kinds of tasks and lessons, but, nevertheless, still educational tasks and lessons. Never should they be consigned, however, to a life devoid of free thought and choice.

But the founders or the judges want instead to relegate children at an early age according to some criteria that remain mysterious. This Socrates wants to pass off as moral, as just? Socrates is using his dialectical method throughout his entire story to educate Glaucon and Adeimantus. I fear that to this point, especially with the Noble Lie, they aren't getting the message. Here morality rests solely with the judgments of founders and rulers, which others within the city might easily see as arbitrary and capricious, which is not justice at all. Look at the lengths, Plato, to which Socrates must go to make this fevered city appear moral.

KYDES: But would the citizens see these judgments as arbitrary and capricious? Could they? Isn't the whole point of this tale to cloud the minds of the citizens with thoughts that these judgments are made by the wisest, if not by the gods? Isn't that a part of the scheme of censorship that we discussed earlier?

HERMIAS: It doesn't help to suggest that the gods themselves will make the judgments, an addition to the story that only children could believe. If rulers or priests claimed themselves to know the judgments of these gods, then, again, the divine intercession remains always unseen to adults and children alike.

DEMETRA: Morality cannot be dictated to the citizens. It must arise out of their own interactions, relationships, and controversies. Morality cannot exist independent of politics. We alluded to this when we talked about morality in the healthy city.

KYDES: Because of the very preposterousness of this story, of this Lie, I can only think that force might be required to install and maintain the social order. Rather than quelling civil unrest, this Lie might well exacerbate it.

PLATO: Here is what Socrates says next related to your point, Kydes:

> "When we have armed our earthborn people . . . they must go and look for the best place in the city for a military encampment, a site from which they can most easily control anyone in the city who is unwilling to obey the laws, or repel any outside enemy who, like a wolf, attacks the fold." (415d6–e2)

KYDES: Well, there it is, Plato. Socrates recognizes that not everyone is going to be happy and go along with this scheme. Here he anticipates that there might well be uprisings and resistance. Hard to see how this is a city of unity and harmony, at least at the outset.

HERMIAS: At least until the Noble Lie has taken root within the city. But that can only be because it has been accepted without obvious disquiet or rebellion.

PLATO: Although the city and the guardians might plan for possible rebellion, is there really a danger of it? Are the gold and silver children really better off than those of bronze or iron? Will their lives be ones that the bronze and iron children want or that their parents want? Here is how Socrates describes gold and silver lives:

> "First, none of them should possess any private property that is not wholly necessary. Second, none should have living quarters or storerooms that are not open for all to enter at will. Such provisions as are required by temperate and courageous men, who are warrior-athletes, they should receive from the other citizens as a salary for their guardianship, the amount being fixed so that there is neither a shortfall nor a surplus at the end of the year. They should have common messes to go to, and should live together like soldiers in a camp. We will tell them that they have gold and silver of a divine sort in their souls as a permanent gift from the gods, and have no need of human gold in addition. And we will add that it is impious for them to defile this divine possession by possessing an admixture of mortal gold, because many impious deeds have been done for the sake of the currency of the masses, whereas their sort is pure.
>
> "No, they alone among the city's population are forbidden by divine law to handle or even touch gold and silver. They must not be under the same roof as these metals, wear them as jewelry, or

> *drink from gold or silver goblets. And by behaving in that way, they would save both themselves and the city. But if they acquire private land, houses, and money themselves, they will be household managers and farmers instead of guardians—hostile masters of the other citizens, instead of their allies. They will spend their whole lives hating and being hated, plotting and being plotted against, much more afraid of internal than of external enemies— already rushing, in fact, to the brink of their own destruction and that of the rest of the city as well. For all these reasons, let's declare that that is how the guardians must be provided with housing and the rest, and establish it as a law. Or don't you agree?"* (416d5–417b7)

KYDES: I'm not sure that I do agree. Socrates is saying that if this city is to have luxuries, which we have been at pains to accept, then those who guard the city must themselves be kept from those luxuries. Men, Socrates says, who are temperate and courageous don't need property or gold and silver. They don't need luxuries, and to have them or to want them is impious. This is to imply, if not outright state, that luxuries conflict with and corrupt virtues and thus undercut morality.

HERMIAS: It is as if we are thrust back into the healthy city, for here Socrates is describing a life "fit for pigs," as Glaucon said. In the healthy city there was no need or desire for luxuries. But unlike people living in the healthy city who have limited possessions and goods, the founders of the fevered city have eliminated from the guardians all property and goods, while others in the city have them.

DEMETRA: Purifying the fevered city, as Socrates said was being done, means returning it, at least in part, to the healthy city. But now the guardians who defend the unhealthy city from internal rebellion and outside attack are denied the very riches that give character to the city. And, as Kydes pointed out, if these riches corrupt the virtuous, then what does this say about the nature of the city itself? Do the rulers want to preserve luxuries at the expense of virtue? Why would the virtuous guardians protect the riches of the corrupt and impious?

PLATO: Adeimantus takes your point. He challenges Socrates:

> *"How will you defend yourself, Socrates, if someone objects that you are not making these men very happy and, furthermore, that it is their own fault that they are not? I mean, the city really belongs to them, yet they derive no good from the city. Others own land,*

> build fine, big houses, acquire furnishings to go along with them, make their own private sacrifices to the gods, entertain guests, and also, of course, possess what you were talking about just now: gold and silver and all the things that those who are going to be blessedly happy are thought to require. Instead, one might say that your guardians are simply settled in the city as mercenaries and that all they do is watch over it." (419a1–420a1)[5]

KYDES: I'd say, "That's right, Adeimantus. I agree with you . . . and perhaps for the first time." But at least the guardians, like all those in the healthy city, can enjoy their families and friends. That could be a sufficient compensation for them to valiantly protect the city and to make them happy.

PLATO: We shall return later to the idea of happiness, but now I want to examine Kydes's sensible notion that the guardians, at least, can enjoy their families. For Socrates the notion is not that straightforward. He tells his interlocutors that just like other sorts of possessions, families will be held in common.

KYDES: He's saying that wives and children will be held in common?

PLATO: Yes, but understand something first. Wives are no more possessions of husbands than husbands are of wives. Socrates says,

> "Do you think that the wives of our guardian watchdogs should guard what the males guard, hunt with them, and do everything else in common with them? Or should we keep women at home, as incapable of doing the same kind of guarding as men, since they must bear and rear the puppies, while the males work and have the entire care of the flock?" (451d4–8)[6]

DEMETRA: Will your brothers agree with this, Plato? I mean, so few men over the years have argued against how women throughout Hellas have been treated. Until recently, women were relegated to the household, rarely ventured out even to the marketplace. Oh, they wielded influence, but always behind the scenes, like Aspasia with Pericles. What a waste, leaving undeveloped the talents and capacities of half the population.

---

5. This odd numbering appears as is in the text.

6. Notice that the Stephanus numbers have jumped here into the 450s. This is because this section and much of this chapter come from Book V of the *Republic*, which comes later in the dialogue than at the point where we are now in my treatment.

PLATO (and Plato smiled): Consider, Deme: Who is to be a suitable parent for the child of a guardian? Is it not someone raised and educated as a guardian? If that is so, then must we not raise and educate women to be guardians as well?

DEMETRA: You don't have to convince me, Plato. But (pointing to Kydes and Hermias) what about these two?

KYDES: This arrangement isn't strange to us, Deme. We've grown up with you as an equal. But it is odd to think, Plato, that your brothers would go along.

PLATO: Why is that odd? What is the weakness of the argument? If you accept the Noble Lie, as they do, that some infants have gold and silver in their souls, then are not females with gold and silver the equals of the male gold and silver infants?

KYDES: Yes, holding aside the whole problem of gold and silver infants, they are equals.

PLATO: And this my brothers accept, though Glaucon then stipulates that *"females are weaker and males stronger"* (451e1–2).

DEMETRA: That's clearly wrong, because it's a gross generalization. Some females will be stronger than some males, even if those males have gold souls.

KYDES: You'll admit that men are faster than women.

DEMETRA: Again, I'll admit that most men are faster than most women. But if an enemy is chasing us, we women only have to be faster than the slowest man the enemy is pursuing.

KYDES: Would women be expected to fight?

DEMETRA: I can answer that for Socrates: Of course! If they are guardians, then they would be expected to fight and defend the city. What, you don't think women capable of that?

KYDES: Can they wield the sword and shield? Can they function wearing heavy armor?

DEMETRA: Yes, they can. They can carry lighter shields and swords and wear armor proportional to their bodies. A lighter sword can inflict as much damage as a heavier sword. Besides, if you examine the results from the Olympic Games, you will find that women are better shots with the bow than are men. That skill would be useful in warfare, would it not?[7]

And women have as much dexterity as men and are often more flexible, which is why they are so effective in *pankration*.[8] They may lack the same brute force as men, but that simply requires them to be quicker, more flexible, able to use an opponent's temper and aggression against them, and highly skilled in using their legs to compensate for male arm strength.

KYDES: But do women have the temperament to fight and kill?

DEMETRA: Do all men? This emphasizes the importance of training and educating both men and women so that they can develop their fighting prowess and so that they can reveal whether they have the proper temperament. Again, this highlights how wrongheaded the idea is that such prowess and temperament can be identified in children, male or female.

PLATO: Perhaps a better criterion for sorting out persons is this: One person is better suited for something if

> "one learns it easily, the other with difficulty; that the one, after a little instruction, can discover a lot for himself in the subject being studied, whereas the other, even if he gets a lot of instruction and attention, does not even retain what he was taught; that the bodily capacities of the one adequately serve his mind, while those of the other obstruct his? Are there any other factors than these, by which you distinguish a person who is naturally well suited for each pursuit from one who is not?" (455b5–c3)

HERMIAS: That is certainly a better criterion than the myth of the metals, as Deme was saying about testing for aptitude and temperament as a better method.

PLATO: "Then," says Socrates,

---

7. See Graeber and Wengrow, *Dawn of Everything*, 278. The authors do not specify the weapons involved, but make the general claim that "various military forces . . . discovered that women also tend to be much better shots."

8. *Pankration* was an event in the Greek Olympic games that combined wrestling, kicking, boxing, and submission holds. Pankration, meaning "all force" (*pan* or "all" and *kratos* or "strength" or "power"), was the forerunner of today's mixed martial arts.

> "there is no pursuit relevant to the management of the city that belongs to a woman because she is a woman, or to a man because he is a man; but the various natural capacities are distributed in a similar way between both creatures, and women can share by nature in every pursuit, and men in every one, though for the purposes of all of them women are weaker than men." (455d6–c1)

KYDES: Just so, and to determine those capabilities we need to train, educate, and test persons to ascertain what they, men and women, can do well. But we have argued ourselves that it is false to say that women are weaker than men simply on the basis of their sexual and bodily differences. Most women are physically weaker than most men. Yet doesn't character often compensate for physique? Aren't some able to perform at the highest level not because of physical gifts, but because of perseverance, effort, initiative, imagination, and other such traits? Women with those traits might well be superior in performance to many men.

HERMIAS: In addition to now agreeing with Deme, Kydes is getting at a significant point, I think. It is not on the basis of their bodies but on the basis of their souls that females can be guardians. Take, for example, what Socrates said in the *Meno*: He learned the doctrine of recollection from "*men and women wise about divine matters*" (81a5). As with divine matters, guarding the city is a matter of the nature of one's soul, whether man or woman.

PLATO: So, you would agree that women selected to be guardians should receive the same training and education as the men.

KYDES: We would, and we do.

PLATO: So, you also agree with Socrates: "*We declare that our male and female guardians must share all their pursuits, and that our argument is somehow self-consistent when it states that this is both viable and beneficial*" (457b9–c2)?

KYDES: Yes.

PLATO: And do you agree with this:

> "All these women are to belong in common to all these men, that none are to live privately with any man, and that the children, too, are to be possessed in common, so that no parent will know his own offspring or any child his parent." (457c10–d3)

KYDES: I agree only if, as you alluded to earlier, all these men are to belong in common to all these women.

DEMETRA: What is the point of this "possession in common" arrangement, Plato? And does Socrates think that the city will be calm, let alone happy, when parents are deprived of knowing their own children?

PLATO: The point is to unify the city. Common possession of property, partners, and children produces unity, which stabilizes the city. Can you imagine, Demetra, that not knowing your children will permit you to avoid feeling possessive about them? Then might you fight for all children in the city because you do not know which is yours?

DEMETRA: Why would these selected guardians, educated in the virtues, not fight for all children in the city, their own and those of others?

HERMIAS: Well, I can see that a guardian might race first to be certain that his or her own child is safe before trying to secure the children of others. This might eliminate that.

DEMETRA: I think I'd rely on the education in virtues to eliminate that.

KYDES: But you admit that it could be a danger.

DEMETRA: I do, but I do not think that parents will tolerate this arrangement. Besides, who is raising these children? Is there an "artisans'" specialty where bronze women, and possibly bronze men, are responsible for that? There must be, since male and female guardians are specially selected for only defending the city.

Yet how can the rulers of the city turn over nurturing and educating gold and silver children to bronze types? Also, where will these children be raised? Certainly not with bronze families. That would taint them, no? So, they too live in barracks and eat in dining halls, having tasted nothing of family life?

PLATO: You are right, Demetra, that guardian men and guardian women must focus on their tasks as warriors, and they will

> "have shared dwellings and meals, and none of them has any private property of that sort, they will live together; and through mixing together in the gymnasia and in the rest of their daily life, they will . . . I take it, have sex with one another . . . ." (458c8–d3)

DEMETRA: But what of their children? Does Socrates say where they will live and be nurtured? Plus, this communal arrangement won't eliminate jealousy among the warriors, which could lead to serious trouble among them and thereby undermine the harmony of the city.

PLATO: Just so, Demetra. Thus, Socrates suggests that sexual intercourse must be regulated by creating *"sacred marriages"* (458e4).

KYDES: Wait, now, Plato. I thought that all guardian men and women were given to one another, all having all in common, and no one living privately with anyone else.

PLATO: That is so, Kydes, but being in a sacred marriage regulates eroticism. It does not then permit a male and a female guardian to live together separately and privately and to raise a family. The conditions of communal living continue.

KYDES: How do these marriages come about? Do the males and females select their partners?

PLATO: I think that you would be surprised if they did. No, the rulers select who is to marry whom.

> *"The best men should mate with the best women in as many cases as possible, while the opposite should hold of the worst men and women; and that the offspring of the former should be reared, but not that of the latter, if our flock is going to be an eminent one."* (458d6–9)

HERMIAS: Stop right there, Plato. Let me make sure that I understand this: Children from parents that the rulers judge to be the worst guardians are to be destroyed, as done in Sparta—cast down like stones off of cliffs or left on some mountainside to be the food for predatory beasts. Is that right? Or are those children adopted by bronze families, which, on the whole, sounds like an outcome better for these children, better even than the fate of the best gold and silver children?

PLATO: Socrates does not specify here, at least not yet. May I continue? (Hermias, with a look of disgust on his face, nods.)

> *"And all this must occur without anyone knowing except the rulers—if, again, our herd of guardians is to remain as free from faction as possible. . . . So then, we will have to establish by law certain festivals and sacrifices at which we will bring together brides and*

bridegrooms, and our poets must compose suitable hymns for the marriages that take place. We will leave the number of marriages for the rulers to decide. That will enable them to keep the number of males as constant as possible, taking into account war, disease, and everything of that sort; so that the city will, as far as possible, become neither too big nor too small." (459d7–460a5)

HERMIAS: The expectation is that the guardians, devoted to the city, will permit this to happen, to have marriages arranged for them? To have the rulers judge who among the guardians are the best and who the worst? And all of this is done in secret. Is that it?

PLATO: Socrates acknowledges the willful use of deception in these marriage arrangements:

> *"It will be necessary for the rulers to use many drugs."* (459c) *"Among those drugs will be 'a great deal of falsehood and deception.'* (459c–d) *. . . I imagine that some sophisticated lotteries will have to be created, then, so that at each marriage the inferior people will blame chance rather than the rulers when they aren't chosen."* (460a7–10)

HERMIAS: We have seen plenty of lying and deception since the introduction of the Noble Lie.

KYDES: You know why it is done in secret? To hide what is actually going on. If the rulers were truthful about this, if they were themselves virtuous and able to defend with good arguments what they were doing, then they would not need to lie and plot in secret. Since the rulers do need to lie and plot, then Socrates must be intimating that the guardians would resist such programs and perhaps rise up against the rulers and the city.

DEMETRA: What good arguments, Kydes? Are there any for forbidding guardians from having families and raising their own children? All we've heard is that the guardians must love virtue and duty above gold and possessions, and so they must be deprived of goods and property; that they cannot have their own families and children, lest they love them more than the city itself and all the inhabitants in it.

These seem to me to be admissions that the rulers do not know how to educate for virtue and for a commitment to the common good. If they did, then they would be confident that the guardians would through their own inquiry come to see the value in limiting their possessions, to see the value in all lives within the city, and to see the value of defending this city because it had just laws and virtuous citizens. Instead, the city needs all of this deceit because it is founded on a lie, which the rulers must perpetuate along with all of its required offshoots.

Does it not seem as if your brothers, Plato, in going along with this deceit and secrecy, are acknowledging that the rulers can act immorally in the name of establishing their version of "morality"? Acting immorally seems to benefit the rulers, the stronger, as they foist morality on the weaker. Loving the city seems only to be a product of deceit.

KYDES: Now we're back to where we were earlier: How do the rulers judge who is best and worst? By what criteria? What measures are used to determine that a child, an infant, is deficient? Is it simply a matter of who their parents are, which the rulers know but no one else does? And isn't this simply the idea of breeding humans the way we breed dogs and horses? We've already covered how fraught this area of human interaction is. We were dissatisfied with how your brothers responded the first time the issue was raised. Socrates must be baiting them again. How are your brothers not asking questions like these and raising issues like Deme's?

HERMIAS: Leaving aside the issue of breeding, since Kydes has pointed out that we've already touched on it, I am disturbed that your brothers also aren't objecting to the level of emphasis Socrates has placed on the discernment of the rulers. From the fiction of identifying the metals in a person's soul to arranging marriages for the guardians, the rulers claim sole power of determining the quality of the lives of everyone in the city. How is this acceptable? How is it any form of morality? So far, I've not heard anything persuasive as an answer to the question, "Why be moral?" Quite the opposite.

6

The Good City

PLATO: You three have raised strong objections and interesting questions. But let us return to the second half of Kydes's statement: What about happiness? The mission, as Socrates points out, is not to make any single group happy, but to make the whole city happy. *"We take ourselves to be fashioning the happy city, not picking out a few happy people"* (420c1–3).

If the whole city is to be happy, then the guardians, like everybody else, must be compelled or persuaded (421c1) to be the best possible craftsmen at their own work. Their education and upbringing will make them reasonable men and women, and *"they will easily see things for themselves. . . . Good education and upbringing produce good natures, and useful natures"* (423e3, 424a5). They, like the other groups in the city, will fulfill their natures and thereby generate a happy city.

KYDES: Plato, this is just what we've been arguing—and repeating, I might add: the guardians don't have that education, at least not yet. I agree that educated men can find out for themselves and see things for themselves. But Socrates hasn't introduced that system. So far, it's all training. I'm willing to wait to hear when they learn to follow dialectic and think for themselves, but that has not been offered and certainly can't be assumed.

HERMIAS: Nor have I heard how doing your own work necessarily makes you happy, especially when your work is the result of being assigned as a child to a class of workers, where you have no choice over what you can do. Socrates notes this, and your brothers miss it. Socrates says that all the people, including the guardians, must be persuaded to do their own work well. If they can't be persuaded, well, then they must be compelled. This presupposes that doing your best work makes you happy, even if you don't and wouldn't choose that kind of work yourself, and that everyone doing so makes the city happy as well.

PLATO: Since we are talking of happiness, can we say that a happy city is a well-structured city? Can we say that a well-structured city is a good city?

HERMIAS: You presume this, Plato; neither you nor Socrates has argued that yet. This city is structured, is ordered. But is it necessarily good? And are the citizens truly happy because they know their place and do their jobs well?

PLATO: If we found courage, wisdom, moderation, and justice in the city, then would we not say that the city is good?

HERMIAS: I agree we would, Plato.

PLATO: So, Socrates says, *"I think we can clearly see wisdom in the city, because the city has good judgment"* (428b3–4).

KYDES: Whose judgment are we talking about here, Plato? The rulers? Surely not the guardians, since we don't yet see where they are educated to exercise judgment at all, let alone good judgment. So far, all we see is their responses to commands or commandments. How can we assess, then, whether the judgment mentioned here is wise or good?

HERMIAS: It is knowledge and inquiry that lead to or permit good judgment. Do the guardians know anything beyond what the edicts are that they must follow? Do they question anything?

PLATO: Let us explore that. Carpenters have knowledge, yes, which they glean from their experience with and skill in carpentry? And farmers know how to grow and harvest crops and investigate when to plant, when to rotate crops, and the like? Are these the sorts of knowledge and inquiry that we would say make our city wise?

KYDES: Well, they can add to the city's wisdom, though I'm not sure that their knowledge is what we mean by "wise."

PLATO: What, then, do we mean when we say that a city is wise? Is it not, as Socrates says, that

> "there is some knowledge possessed by some of the citizens in the city we just founded that doesn't judge about any particular matter but about the city as a whole and the maintenance of good relations, both internally and with other cities?" (428c11–d2)

KYDES: I agree that that would be wisdom, and the citizens in the city who have that wisdom are the rulers.

PLATO: You mean the guardians whom we have been describing.

KYDES: No, Plato, I do not. We have already pointed out, perhaps *ad nauseum*, that the guardians, whether auxiliaries or complete guardians, lack the education in philosophy or dialectic to form and exercise good judgment.

PLATO: So, you say that the rulers have the good judgment about the city to warrant being called "wise," but you do not accept that the guardians themselves are wise.

KYDES: That is so, though I don't really know anything about these founders of the city, or rulers as you call them, and so I can't say for certain that they are wise. Using lies and myths to compel behavior doesn't strike me necessarily as "wisdom," since wisdom is a virtue, a moral good, and lies and deceptions aren't that.

DEMETRA: The rulers might have had insight into seeing that the people of this city needed to hear the myth of the metals and the Noble Lie to be able to take orders from the rulers. But to perpetuate that rule, the founders would then also have to see that the citizens, whether guardians or auxiliaries, could not be educated. For then they might come to think for themselves, examine for themselves, and thereby overturn the system of classes built solely on a lie. That would be, to my mind, wisdom and good judgment.

PLATO: If the complete guardians became rulers, would they be wise?

HERMIAS: They would not, unless we could see, as we've been saying and as Demetra just repeated, when their training turned into education, when they learned to challenge and question and develop knowledge about more than responses to commands. At this point in the story, they could perpetuate the Lie quite possibly by believing themselves that the myth of the metals was true. That is not wise. At best, that is prudent.

PLATO: Prudent? Is not prudence part of wisdom? If so, then, as Socrates goes on to say, perhaps *"we have found one of the four virtues, though I don't know how we found it"* (429a5).

HERMIAS: He doesn't find it, Plato. Socrates implants it.

DEMETRA: Socrates assumes it.

PLATO: For the moment, let us continue. What about courage?

KYDES: If there is one virtue in this city that seems to stand out, it is courage. I imagine that the guardians will be courageous in their defense of the city. I can grant them that.

DEMETRA: I can't, Kydes, and I've expressed to you earlier why. Courage and all of the virtues are internal. They grow from within. They rise out of and express our souls. I am not convinced by Socrates's argument that the guardians, reared as dogs to respond to commands, exhibit courage. You just said yourself that wisdom, if it exists, has been implanted.

KYDES: But do you know, Deme, that the virtues cannot be instilled from the outside, not by imposition by others but by our responses in various circumstances? Can't one learn to be courageous by undertaking courageous acts? Those circumstances are external, and our actions, undertaken over time and repeatedly, could leave an imprint of courageous behavior on our souls.[1]

DEMETRA: As I said earlier, Kydes, such a person acts virtuously, but is he virtuous? Perhaps he responds to such circumstances courageously, but lacks the judgment, the good judgment, to know how to act in novel situations. In a new situation, his previous courageous action might

---

1. This is how Aristotle, Plato's most famous student, describes the way in which persons develop virtuous character: Moral virtues are "the result of habit.... [W]e learn by doing them.... [W]e become just by doing just acts, temperate by doing temperate acts, brave by doing brave acts" (Aristotle, *Nichomachean Ethics*, 1103a33–b25). Formed and performed only through habit, moral virtues would then seem to require no judgment or thought. That is not the case with Aristotle, since persons, he further tells us, must decide on the right action depending on the circumstances.

Social psychologist Philip Zimbardo claims that a statistical analysis of twenty-five thousand social-psychological experiments conducted over one hundred years and involving eight million subjects reveals the robust finding that circumstance or situation strongly influences behavior and character (Zimbardo, *Lucifer Effect*, 323).

instead be foolhardy and uncalled for. But I take your point. If there is virtue in this city, then courage seems to be the most likely one at this point.

PLATO: Socrates seems to be following this part of your conversation in his metaphor of wool dyeing. He says,

> "When dyers want to dye wool purple, they first select from wools of many different colors the ones that are naturally white. Then they give them an elaborate preparatory treatment, so that they will accept the color as well as possible. And only at that point do they dip them in the purple dye. When something is dyed in this way, it holds the dye fast, and no amount of washing, whether with or without detergent, can remove the color." (429d4–e5)

Similarly, Socrates continues, we selected and raised our guardians so that

> "they would absorb the laws in the best possible way, just like wool does a dye; that as a result, their beliefs about what things should inspire terror, and about everything else, would hold fast because they had the proper nature and rearing; so fast that the dye could not be washed out even by those detergents that are so terribly effective at scouring." (430a1–6)

KYDES: This is what we've been saying, Plato. The guardians absorb the laws; they don't examine and challenge them. They simply take them on.

DEMETRA: And they hold fast to the beliefs they have absorbed, because they have been put through the "*elaborate preparatory treatment*," which we've identified as conditioning, not education. Can the guardians exercise good judgment in discerning what actions a novel situation requires? Beliefs lodged deeply within one's character are difficult to dispel or alter. Notice that something is being done to the wool. One cannot be dipped in education as if it is imposed on or installed in someone. Education in philosophy must be active and must provide the mechanisms, as Kydes said, for doing that—examination and challenge.

PLATO: Glaucon takes up your position . . . in part. He responds to Socrates by saying that he accepts this account of courage, provided *"that you don't consider the correct belief about these same things, which you find in animals and slaves, and which are not the result of education, to be inculcated by law to be courage"* (430b6–9).

KYDES: Then we must disagree with Socrates here, because, as we've been saying, the guardians' absorption of these *"correct beliefs"* has not been through education. I don't know how animals and slaves absorb such beliefs, as Glaucon posits, but whatever that method, it is the one also used by these guardians.

PLATO: So, are you three united on rejecting what Socrates says as the way to instill the virtue of courage? (The three nod their agreement.) Then we shall join Socrates as he demurs and says, *"we shall discuss political courage more fully some other time"* (430c4–5). For now, we must consider the other two virtues: moderation and justice—the four virtues, in addition to others, pointing to or highlighting morality overall.

Moderation is a kind of order, a form of self-restraint in the face of certain pleasures and desires.

HERMIAS: Yes, and a kind of prudence, which we discussed earlier in the context of wisdom. So, prudence linked to moderation then linked to wisdom (wise moderation) might give us a foundation in morality overall, depending on what justice looks like.

PLATO: Hold that in mind, Hermias, as we proceed. Anyway, in self-restraint who is the self doing the restraining? Is it not one's own self? There is, then, a kind of self-mastery here, and is not such a term, as Socrates now says,

> *"trying to indicate that within the same person's soul, there is a better thing and a worse one? Whenever the naturally better one masters the worse, this is called being master of oneself. At any rate, it is praised. But whenever, as a result of bad upbringing or associating with bad people, the smaller and better one is mastered by the inferior majority, this is blamed as a disgraceful thing and is called being weaker than oneself, or being intemperate or immoderate."* (431a2–b1)

Of course, in a city such as the one we have created, there will be all sorts of diverse desires and pleasures, and only a few people will have

> *"desires that are simple, measured, and directed by calculation in accordance with understanding and correct belief, . . . the few people who are born with the best natures and receive the best education."* (431c4–7)

DEMETRA: And those select few, no surprise here, are the guardians. Right?

PLATO: Correct. In this city the desires of the inferior many are controlled by the wisdom and desires of the superior few (431c9–d1). The few, having both wisdom and moderation—

KYDES (interrupting):—And the virtue of courage as well, since the complete guardians were raised first as auxiliaries.

PLATO: True, Kydes. So, the few will control their desires by both the virtue of wisdom and the virtue of moderation.

HERMIAS: We are going in circles here, Plato, merely retracing the complaints that we all have expressed earlier. We have not established, in fact we have argued against, the idea that the Noble Lie in any way identifies the best or superior people. Indeed, selecting children, when they are very young, for different classes offers no systematic way to discern who is born with the best natures. Moreover, we have already stipulated that no real system of education has been offered to anybody in the city, let alone the guardians. So, this is just more presumptions to assure that one class of people will rule over the other classes, who are rendered, because judged to be, inferior.

PLATO: Would you agree, however, that if we could properly identify those who were wise and moderate, who had desires that were simple, measured, and directed by reasoned calculation, then they should be the ones to lead this city? That that would be a kind of justice for the city?

KYDES: I think we can agree with that.

PLATO: Then holding your dissent in mind, let us move on to trying to find justice in the city in accordance with what I just suggested. Socrates says,

> "What we laid down and often repeated, if you remember, is that each person must practice one of the pursuits in the city, the one for which he is naturally best suited.... Moreover, we have heard many people say, and have often said ourselves, that justice is doing one's own work and not meddling with what is not one's own. This, then, Glaucon, provided it is taken in a certain way, would seem to be justice—this doing one's own work." (433a7–b5)

HERMIAS: Justice, then, rests on everyone in the city accepting the myth of the metals. That is the basis of the agreement that the people will obey the laws and edicts of the complete guardians, who belong in the ruling class because they have gold souls, while everyone else—the silver and bronze people—are either auxiliaries or "craftsmen." In that way, sticking to your own work and not meddling in others' work can be a kind of justice, thereby providing people with what is their due.

KYDES: And as we have said, there is as yet no good reason for accepting that myth, which is a lie. Therefore, without the Noble Lie, doing a job that you did not choose, and perhaps do not like, cannot be considered a form of justice. Likewise, meddling with the work of others, perhaps as a way of finding a different craft that you prefer, could be construed as just and moral.

PLATO: As Socrates says,

> *"If a carpenter attempts to do the work of a shoemaker, or a shoemaker that of a carpenter, or they exchange their tools or honors with one another, or if the same person tries to do both jobs, and all other such exchanges are made, do you think that does any great harm to the city?"* (434a4–6)

KYDES: Under the circumstances that I laid out, or under any circumstances really, the answer is "no."

PLATO: Socrates agrees with you, as does Glaucon. But, Socrates says, if a craftsman or some sort of money-maker tries to enter the class of auxiliaries or an auxiliary tries to become a ruler or guardian, then that meddling might destroy the city.

HERMIAS: If a money-maker uses his money as a substitute for learning the skills and knowledge necessary for being an auxiliary, then that is unjust. Likewise, if an auxiliary uses his reputation as a soldier or uses some other kind of influence to worm his way into the guardianship, then that, too, is unjust and immoral. But if they show the talents or aptitude for those jobs, then they should pursue that desire. That ability to pursue what inspires you is as it should be. Isn't that the sort of city we want to live in, where people are not prematurely consigned to a class where they do not belong? And if they are so consigned, then in the sort of city we want to live in, they can work to get out of that class, whether that means moving up or down.

DEMETRA: I want to push this point even further. Remember in the *Lysis*, Socrates asks Lysis: *"Do you think a man happy if he's a slave and is not permitted to do whatever he likes?"* Lysis responds, *"No, by Zeus, I do not think so."*[2] That is what is happening in this city. We are willing to sacrifice a worker's happiness for a sense of justice that arises out of a Noble Lie where rulers pretend—because so far Socrates has offered nothing about their methods that we can evaluate—that they can determine with precision what work people are best suited for. We are willing to consign them, then, to work that they may well loathe, thereby trapping them *"in a perpetual condition of servitude."*[3]

The limits of *"permitting him to do whatever he likes"* are established by the system of justice, the system of morality, operating in the city. In the healthy city, as I see it, that system is not imposed from above, as through the Noble Lie, but is, instead, deliberated about by the people themselves. An imposed system is the product and desire of tyrants, those who wish to dictate, not govern. Justice requires dialectic, not edicts.

PLATO: What if we returned, at this point, to Socrates's original mission, which is to find what morality is within each individual person? Recall that Socrates supposed that it would be easier to see morality in some larger thing—a city, in our case—than in an individual. *"So,"* he says,

> *"let's apply what has come to light for us* [in the city] *to an individual, and if it is confirmed, all will be well. But if something different is found in the case of the individual, we will go back to the city and test it there. And perhaps by examining them side-by-side and rubbing them together like fire-sticks, we can make justice blaze forth and, once it has come to light, confirm it in our own case."* (434e3–435a2)

DEMETRA: I want to point out, Plato, that when talking about the healthy city, Socrates asked your brothers where morality and immorality entered the city. Well, we now see that it enters the unhealthy city in the assignment of the people to classes and jobs and in the notion of "justice" of each doing his own work and minding his own business. Those assignments are lies based on the myth of the metals.

But since the healthy city also has specialized jobs and tasks for those living in it, then justice and morality can enter in the same way—through

---

2. Plato, *Lysis*, 207d9–11.

3. Plato, *Lysis*, 208e7.

the nature of duties and tasks and the interactions and relationships among the people doing them.

The difference is that while Socrates presupposes an educational system for the guardians, we have seen that it is really a system of training and indoctrination. That leaves an opening in the healthy city for educating all of its children, all of its people, without first assigning them arbitrarily to classes. Then, when they take on crafts and jobs, including judging and ruling, they do so with judgment and discernment, having been educated beforehand. If, for example, people in the healthy city are to discuss whether sharing duties is moral or whether it is, say, unjust, then that supposes that philosophy needs to be in the city. The presence of philosophy also supposes the presence of education to develop and foster philosophical thinking. That makes the city moral and healthy, though more needs to be said to fill out our picture of that city.

I am curious now to see how a moral individual reflects the alleged morality of the fevered city, how the classes of the city echo the soul of each person.

PLATO: We have arrived at the point, have we not, where we can see the virtues distributed within the city? The artisans, the bronze children, have the virtue of moderation of their tastes and desires.

KYDES: Oh, please, Plato! Artisans and their bronze children can hardly be said to have the virtue of moderation. If their tastes and desires are moderated, it is only because the auxiliaries and guardians enforce rules and behaviors. At best, the moral system here rests on the fear of punishment. But do go on.

PLATO (smiling): Thank you, Kydes. The auxiliaries, those of silver, display the virtue of courage. Meanwhile, the complete guardians, in whom the gods placed gold, have the three virtues of wisdom, moderation, and courage. Justice, then, our fourth virtue, is found in each class holding to its own business. This is the city's moral system overall, which is the proper ordering of virtues. If the system is moral, then the system is good. The rulers are those who preserve morality, preserve the structures of the three classes, and thus preserve goodness in the city.

HERMIAS: Holding aside our fundamental objection to the Noble Lie that initiated the rise of certain characters, and thus the rise of classes, within the city, then, yes, I agree that this is the outline for what Socrates is proposing. But without addressing our objections, then the whole outline is a farce.

DEMETRA: Yet, at this stage, Plato, let us not deter you as Kydes did for a moment, since, I dare say, we three are eager to hear how each individual reflects these virtues.

PLATO: So, we shall proceed.

If the just or moral city has three parts in balance, as we have seen with the three classes, then, given the isomorphism we accepted earlier on—that is, that the city, for easier viewing, is an individual writ large—we should expect each individual soul to have three parts.

7

The Tripartite Soul

PLATO: Socrates observes that each of us has a soul with three parts. One part within is appetitive, another part is spirited or willful, and a third part is rational. Does that seem to comport with your experiences?

KYDES: Are you asking, Plato, whether each person has within desires, emotions, and reason? If so, then, yes, I agree. (The other two nod.)

PLATO: Good. And, as Socrates asks,

> "do we learn with one, feel anger with another, and with yet a third have an appetite for the pleasures of food, sex, and those closely akin to them? Or do we do each of them with the whole of our soul, once we feel the impulse?" (436a8–b1)

KYDES: That's a tricky one, Plato. We separate in our minds, for example, emotions from reasoning. But I'm thinking now that we do them with the whole of our soul.

PLATO: Let's see whether Socrates clarifies.

> "Wouldn't you say that the soul of someone who has an appetite wants the thing for which it has an appetite, and draws toward itself what it wishes to have; and, in addition, that insofar as his soul wishes something to be given to it, it nods assent to itself as if in answer to a question, and strives toward its attainment?" (437c1–5)

HERMIAS: I agree, and, for me, this example points toward acting with the whole of our soul. We want something; we have a desire for it. We then draw near to it, which is the rational way to attain what we want. If there is an obstacle in our way, we determine how much we want this thing. If we have a strong emotional draw to it, we figure out or reason ways to overcome the obstacle. Our parts are all present and working together.

PLATO: Let us say that we are talking about an appetite for something to drink. Would we claim that persons have an appetite for drink rather than for good drink? For food or for good food?

HERMIAS: It depends on the circumstances. If I am dying of thirst, I'll drink muddy water from a puddle. But if I am thirsty after exercising, then I'll look for clean water to quench that thirst.

PLATO: Socrates seems to agree.

> "A particular sort of thirst is for a particular sort of drink. Thirst itself, however, is not for much or little, good or bad, or, in a word, for drink of a particular sort; rather, thirst itself is, by nature, just for drink itself. Right? Glaucon says, 'Absolutely.'" Socrates follows up: "Hence the soul of the thirsty person, insofar as it is simply thirsty, does not want anything else except to drink, and this is what it longs for and is impelled to do. To which Glaucon responds, 'Clearly.'" (439a4–b2)

KYDES: I don't have the confidence of Glaucon. What is "thirst itself"? I've not had that experience. There isn't "thirst." I am thirsty. Why? As Hermias said, I just exercised, or I just woke up, or I've been trapped in the desert for two days. Those are different thirsts, not "thirst" in and of itself. My companion and I stumble onto a well in the desert. We long to drink. But he says, "I think this well is poisoned." Do we drink anyway? No. We exercise judgment. We use our reason. I am shipwrecked in the sea. Do I gulp down seawater though I am dying from thirst?

PLATO: But you will admit that Socrates has a point.

> "It would not be unreasonable for us to claim, then, that there are two elements, different from one another; and to call the element in the soul with which it calculates, the rationally calculating element; and the one with which it feels passion, hungers, thirsts, and is stirred by other appetites, the irrational and appetitive

element, friend to certain ways of being filled and certain pleasures." (439d3–8)

There is your thirst that pulls you toward drinking from the well and your reason or rational part that holds you back.

KYDES: I agree with that.

DEMETRA: Nevertheless, Plato, although we can grant Socrates this view that there are two elements in or two parts of the soul, why suggest that they are working separately, even independently? It seems to be the whole soul working here. Indeed, once Socrates introduces the idea of "good drink" versus "drink," then it is unavoidable that reasoned judgment—rationality—enters in here. Otherwise, how could we assess what "good" means?

PLATO: Holding that point aside for the moment, right now we seem to agree that we have identified or distinguished two elements in the soul. Now, is there a third element, a spirited or, as you have called it, an emotional element? Glaucon raises the point that this element might itself be part of the appetitive element and not independent. Socrates then offers this example:

> *"I once heard a story and I believe it. Leontius, the son of Aglaeon, was going up from the Piraeus along the outside of the North Wall when he saw some corpses with the public executioner nearby. He had an appetitive desire to look at them, but at the same time he was disgusted and turned himself away. For a while he struggled and put his hand over his eyes, but finally, mastered by his appetite, he opened his eyes wide and rushed toward the corpses, saying: 'Look for yourselves, you evil wretches; take your fill of the beautiful sight!'"* (439e6–440a3)

Socrates comments that this story suggests that anger sometimes wars against the appetites, and Glaucon agrees.

HERMIAS: I'm not sure why Glaucon agrees. I can see that Leontius's initial desire is to want to look at the corpses, but his emotional response, his visceral reaction, is disgust that turns him away. But how does the desire to look overcome the disgust? Does it have its own force of will, stronger than the visceral reaction of disgust? There is also a competing desire—the desire to look away.

And where is reason in all of this? When Leontius's desire "masters" his emotions, how is that done? Do appetites have their own reasoning part and that part overcomes the disgust? Or is the war between emotions and desires mediated by reason? If so, then the whole soul is engaged.

DEMETRA: This story reminds me of the allegory from the *Phaedrus* that you told us about, which also discusses the tripartite soul. Two horses represent two parts of the soul. These can be stand-ins for appetites and passions and for will and emotions. The charioteer represents the third or rational part. He drives and directs the horses.

One horse is white with a noble, upright frame, well jointed, with a high neck, and is a lover of honor and modesty and self-control. The other horse is black, crooked, and really a jumble of limbs going every which way. Socrates describes this horse as *"a companion to wild boasts and indecency . . . is shaggy . . . deaf . . . and barely yields to the whip."*[1] The white horse is our will and emotions, most often easily controlled by the charioteer or our reason. The unruly black horse is our appetites.

As the chariot approaches a beautiful boy, the charioteer is suffused with desire. The white horse, our emotional element, is obedient as the charioteer drives forward but is also filled with shame at the lust of the charioteer. The black horse of desire simply wants to leap forward and jump the boy.

The three are not in harmony, and the elements of the soul are not working together. The rational part, the charioteer, is lured by the beauty of the boy and the nature of Beauty itself (254b7). Yet the two horses buck because they are at cross-purposes with the charioteer—one filled with lust and the other filled with shame. This allegory reinforces the idea of the tripartite soul, but doesn't the situation determine which parts work together and which work at cross-purposes? Regardless, doesn't the whole soul need to be accounted for in any circumstance?

PLATO: So, you would not agree with Socrates here that no one would say that they have ever seen the spirited part of the soul partner with the appetitive part.

HERMIAS: I would not agree with Socrates, and I don't know why your brothers would. Consider this example. A merchant wants his business not just to do well but to grow so as to provide him with abundant gold and silver. He has a taste for the luxuries that the city is founded to

---

1. Plato, *Phaedrus*, 253c7–e5.

provide, so much so that he dreams day and night of swimming in gold and silver coins. He imagines holding them, running his hands through piles of them. His heart races at the thought. He feels the glory of walking into his room full of gold and silver and luxuries of all sorts. He bursts with pride at his success. But his rational part recognizes that his business selling cloth can never fulfill this appetite. Nevertheless, that recognition does not diminish his desire or the emotions associated with that desire.

PLATO: Would you agree with Socrates and Glaucon on this proposition: *"Just as there were three classes in the city that held it together—the moneymaking, the auxiliary, and the deliberative—is there also this third element in the soul, the spirited kind"* (440e10–441a4)?

HERMIAS: That seems to be so. Haven't we already acceded to this image?

PLATO: Further, would you three agree that it is best if the rational part rules, *"since it is wise and exercises foresight"* (441e2–3)? (The three nod their heads.) And that would be true for the individual as well as the city?

KYDES: Speaking for all of us, we can agree to that.

PLATO: And is it best if the spirited part supports the rational part when the appetitive part gets out of hand and pursues pleasures of the body out of all proportion? So that whether in the city or the individual soul

> *"these two elements, having been trained and having truly learned their own jobs and been educated, will be put in charge of the appetitive element—the largest one in each person's soul and, by nature, the most insatiable for money. They will watch over it to see that it does not get so filled with the so-called pleasures of the body that it becomes big and strong, and no longer does its own job but attempts to enslave and rule over the classes it is not fitted to rule, thereby overturning the whole life of anyone in whom it occurs."* (442a4–b2)

HERMIAS: Yes, if you bear in mind the distinction that we have maintained throughout and which your brothers have overlooked—namely, that having been trained is not the same as having been educated. Training alone, as we saw with dogs, is insufficient for developing the rational part of the soul to rule over the whole soul, let alone the city.

PLATO: And isn't it so that every part within each person does its own work, whether it is ruling or being ruled? Similarly, every class within the city does its own work. This principle that it is right for someone who is, by nature, a shoemaker to practice shoemaking and nothing else, for a carpenter to practice carpentry, and the same for all the others is a sort of image of morality. This morality pertains not simply to what one does externally, but with what is inside him, with what he is truly himself and is his own (443c2–d1).

DEMETRA: Little of that follows for me, Plato. First, we have already taken issue with the idea that anyone, but especially the founders of this city, will be able to identify the nature of every person within the city when those persons are young, especially when they are toddlers or infants. Socrates admits as much when he rests his "principle" on the myth of the metals, which is a lie.

Second, the very image of the tripartite soul shows the ridiculousness of this lie. Any sense of morality, and system of justice that reasonable people will accept, requires that the people themselves deliberate about it. They can deliberate and they must deliberate provided they are educated. And educated they all should be, because as Socrates lays out, every soul—not just the souls of guardians and auxiliaries—contains the three parts. Therefore, every soul, not just souls of gold, has a rational part that needs to be developed.

The Noble Lie is not noble at all. Even if every person were assigned to the proper class, every person in every class has a tripartite soul. Perhaps you don't want carpenters meddling in the business of cobblers, but you want them to use their rational part to meddle in the business of morality as it pertains to carpenters and cobblers. Just as the rational part of each soul rules over the morality within that soul, so too should the rational part of each soul participate within the city in ruling and being ruled.

As this fevered city stands now, for the artisans in this city, whose class is to make money at their crafts and leave all else to the guardians and auxiliaries, what is the point of having a rational part of their souls? Or a spirited part? Any city that excludes those parts of their souls, leaves them undeveloped, or lets them atrophy does harm to those souls. A system that does harm to souls cannot be a just and moral system.

PLATO: So, Demetra, would you agree with this assessment by Socrates?

> "[Morality] *is not concerned with someone's doing his own job on the outside. On the contrary, it is concerned with what is inside;*

with himself, really, and the things that are his own. It means that he does not allow the elements in him each to do the job of some other, or the three sorts of elements in his soul to meddle with one another. Instead, he regulates well what is really his own, rules himself, puts himself in order, becomes his own friend, and harmonizes the three elements together, just as if they were literally the three defining notes of an octave—lowest, highest, and middle—as well as any others that may be in between. He binds together all of these and, from having been many, becomes entirely one, temperate and harmonious. Then and only then should he turn to action, whether it is to do something concerning the acquisition of wealth or concerning the care of his body, or even something political, or concerning private contracts. In all these areas, he considers and calls just and fine the action that preserves this inner harmony and helps achieve it, and wisdom the knowledge that oversees such action; and he considers and calls immoral any action that destroys this harmony, and ignorance the belief that oversees it." (443c8–e7)

DEMETRA: I agree in part—

KYDES: No surprise there—

DEMETRA: That's right! I don't really know what Socrates means by not permitting the three elements within one's soul "*to meddle with one another.*" Meddle? They are different parts, and they interact. How do they meddle?

Anyway, I certainly agree with the rest of it: he regulates and rules himself; he puts himself in order, becomes his own friend, and harmonizes the three elements together; he binds these together to become one, temperate and harmonious. In politics or business, in any action really, anything that preserves this inner harmony and helps achieve it is moral, and any action that disrupts or destroys inner harmony is immoral. Every person does this, which means every person is deserving of the education that helps him achieve this harmony and this rule. Every person.

HERMIAS: If Deme is right, and she certainly seems to be, then the tripartite soul itself undercuts, if it doesn't outright destroy, the Noble Lie. In doing harm to each soul by relegating persons to classes where elements of their souls are underdeveloped and even overlooked, the city itself is immoral.

KYDES: Besides, if we take literally what Socrates says in the Noble Lie, then no one in the city can be moral, because no one in the city has a complete soul. Socrates said, *"The god who made you mixed some gold into those who are adequately equipped to rule. . . . He put silver in those who are auxiliaries and iron and bronze in the farmers and other craftsmen"* (415a3–5).

HERMIAS: That's right. He doesn't say mixed "more gold" in those who will rule and "more silver" in those who will defend the city.[2] That would be more congruent with the idea of each soul having three parts and having different qualities or certain virtues. But even here Glaucon and Adeimantus should be objecting, because with all three parts, no child will display which mixture he or she has so early in life.

PLATO: Immorality within each soul is a kind of civil war among the parts, what Socrates calls

> *"a meddling and doing of another's work, a rebellion by some part against the whole soul in order to rule it inappropriately. The rebellious part is by nature suited to be a slave, while the other part is not a slave but belongs to the ruling class."* (444b1–5)

Does this help clarify anything?

DEMETRA: Yes, it does. It shows just how flawed this whole scheme is. If the appetitive part of the soul is *"by nature suited to be a slave"* to the ruling and spirited parts, to cause no trouble or disruption, then what does this say about the class of artisans in the city? That class is by nature suited to be a slave class, beholden fully to taking orders from the ruling class, orders that are in turn enforced by the auxiliaries. Would the city not then be in constant rebellion, since it denies the exercise, even the existence, of the three parts that compose each individual's soul?

PLATO: What about what Socrates says later: *"If we claim to have found the moral man, the moral city, and what morality is in them, then I don't suppose that we'll seem to be telling a complete falsehood"* (444a3–5)?

HERMIAS: As we have been saying, Plato, not a complete falsehood. The description of the tripartite soul seems relevant and accurate. But it undercuts the Noble Lie and therefore undermines the very foundation of

---

2. I have not found any translations that take this position of mixing in "more gold" or "more silver." All the translations are clear that the god mixed in gold in some, silver in others, and bronze and iron in the rest.

the city. So, a moral man within this city? No. That is a falsehood, because the city founded on this Lie cannot be moral. You might find a moral man within the city, but that would be in spite of the city's organization, not because of that organization. That your brothers don't recognize this is both a surprise and a disappointment.

KYDES: At this point, I'm not even sure that the idea of three parts is accurate. Are there really three parts, as if they are distinct? We can all acknowledge that we have appetites, reason, and emotions. But are they divided neatly or at all in three discrete parts? Don't they all blend and intermingle all the time? When there is conflict between what I want, my desires, and what I think is good for me—cabbage rather than figs—I experience some internal conflict. But is that conflict really between two warring parts or just a conflict of motivation of one person and thus of one soul?

PLATO: One soul with differing motivations in different situations, is that it, Kydes? Not three separate parts, like three tiny persons, warring like neighbors about the proper action.

KYDES: Quite so, Plato.

PHILOSOPHER KINGS AND QUEENS

PLATO: Perhaps we can agree with Socrates on his next move. He addresses why cities have failed to be moral or virtuous or, perhaps, why they have fallen away from morality and virtue. The problem, from his perspective within this story, begins and ends with the nature of rulers and ruling. All of you have argued throughout our conversation that much rests on the discernment of the founders and rulers of the city. You have also objected to the idea that whatever the basis of this discernment, it cannot be adequate for determining at birth or early in childhood the rank or class of each person. At this point in the dialogue, Socrates emphasizes what has concerned you three—the absence of adequate preparation in philosophy. For Socrates, such preparation readies the nascent philosopher to know what is permanent and unchanging in the world. That knowledge permits the philosopher to establish a city stabilized through unity and beyond decay. So, you might not be surprised to hear this next from Socrates:

> "Until philosophers rule as kings in their cities . . . , that is, until political power and philosophy entirely coincide, while the numerous natures that now pursue either one exclusively are forcibly prevented from doing so, cities will have no rest from evils, my dear Glaucon, nor, I think, will the human race. And until that happens, the same constitution we have now described in our discussion will never be born to the extent that it can, or see the light of the sun." (473c10–e1)

DEMETRA: And leading women, too, no? Philosopher kings and philosopher queens. Otherwise, what is the point of all this chatter about complete women guardians being equal to men?

PLATO (smiling): Quite so, Demetra. Quite so. The people Socrates means are those *"fitted by nature both to engage in philosophy and to rule the city, while the rest* [of the population] *are naturally fitted to leave philosophy alone and follow their leader"* (474b6–c2).

HERMIAS: Wait now, Plato. Socrates's mission in this dialogue is to tell us what morality is and to explain why being moral is better than being immoral. At this point, Socrates has stated that morality for the city is to do one's own job and not to meddle in the jobs of others, just as morality within one's soul is to have each part do its own work and not usurp the work of the other parts.

Holding aside any objections to this assumption, for it is hardly an argument, I need to point out that Socrates violates morality in the city. He now suggests that the rulers will do two jobs. They will philosophize, and they will rule. This, by his own definition, is immoral. He makes the rulers immoral and thereby forces them to live an immoral or lesser life.

PLATO (Again, Plato smiled.): We shall revisit this very good objection, Hermias, as we proceed. For now, let me repeat that Socrates's mission, as you called it, is not at this juncture to make any single person happy or any class happy. It is to make the city happy overall. Might that require sacrifices from some on behalf of the city to assure unity and happiness?

DEMETRA: Not so fast, Plato. As Hermias points out, the morality of the city now seems to rest on the immorality of the rulers, just as the founding of the city rests on an injustice, on a lie. Can we really stabilize and perpetuate morality on the basis of lies and immorality?

HERMIAS: Unless philosophizing is not itself an occupation. For a philosopher, a true philosopher, it might be like eating or breathing. At some point, philosophizing for them becomes second nature.

KYDES: Or perhaps ruling is what becomes second nature to them. They rule as an aspect of their love of wisdom, not as something separate from it. What looks like two jobs really isn't two at all.

DEMETRA: Also, bear in mind that we have yet to see how and where philosophy enters this city. It certainly isn't in and through education, which we have argued the guardians have yet to experience.

PLATO: Maybe understanding better who these philosophers are can help us see how the city can be moral and how philosophizing fits in. Philosophers are those who are initially ruled by a desire, a passionate desire, for wisdom—not for knowledge about one part or another part, but for knowledge about all parts. That is, the philosopher moves beyond loving particulars to loving that which something is (475b7–8).

KYDES: Okay, that makes some sense. Here the philosopher's initial move is to follow an appetite and use both his passion and his reason to attain it. He's using all three parts of the soul.

PLATO: That is correct, and a philosopher is not one who simply loves to learn about many things. A philosopher is one who is a lover of knowing the truth (475e3). Not seeing the truth merely of this or of that, but of seeing the truth itself. He or she is interested in the knowledge of what is, to know what it is as it is.

Some learning might bring us, and exercise in us, the power of belief or the power of opinion. But these powers leave us in the realm of the binary, where something, for example, described as beautiful must carry with it the opposite—that is, ugliness—if we are to understand it. This must be so when we look at the appearance of anything. Anything we see and wish to make sense of always appears with its opposite, though we may not recognize that: Beauty needs ugliness, good needs bad, justice needs injustice, and so forth.

The things we see and make judgments about appear in relation to some standard that we create based on multiple experiences interacting with that thing. In the background lurks always that which the thing is not; that is, its opposite. In such a case, we are interested in particulars that we deem beautiful—beautiful colors or shapes or sounds. Whatever flaws this beautiful thing has relates to its opposite. And flaws there must be, because the object is not perfectly beautiful. It cannot be perfectly beautiful, because such perfection can only exist beyond this world.

So, we hold a belief or opinion about this particular object or person, and in judging it, we discount its opposite. We do not hold the two "qualities"—beautiful and ugly—simultaneously, nor do we transcend the binary to see that which can be both of these qualities and neither of them simultaneously.

> *"Those who look at many beautiful things but do not see the beautiful itself, and are incapable of following another who would lead them to it; or many just things but not the just itself, and similarly with all the rest—these people, we will say, have beliefs about all these things, but have no knowledge of what their beliefs are about."* Whereas, *"those who in each case look at the things themselves that are always the same in every respect, won't we say that they have knowledge, not mere belief?"* (479d11–e9)

KYDES: Are you saying, in the context of our discussion, that we can come to know beauty or morality or justice in itself, know its purity, know it totally?

PLATO: I am, Kydes, and those who are passionate and in love with knowing things in themselves are "lovers of wisdom" or philosophers. By the way, recall that one of Socrates's tasks as laid out by my brothers is to explain not only what morality is, but also how it can be good in and of itself, even as the moral person is thought to be immoral.

DEMETRA: And somehow, Plato, knowing things in themselves will permit the rulers, these philosopher kings and queens, to be able to rule this city and to perfectly assign children to their proper classes. Is that what you are saying?

PLATO: Here is what I am saying, Demetra, which follows from what Socrates has been saying: *"What is completely is completely knowable"* (477a3). In coming to know what is complete, what is perfect, unchanging, and permanent, to know it as it is in and of itself and to know it in its totality (477b10), what happens to such a philosopher? Well, let us hear what Socrates says about that.

8

The Good

PLATO: Socrates has been suggesting that the best rulers are those who can create laws and practices that establish and perpetuate a moral and happy city. That can happen only when philosophers are rulers or rulers are philosophers. He also suggests that those who know what is unchanging, what is permanent, what is always the same in all respects are philosophers, while those who "*wander among the many things that vary in every sort of way*" (484b4–5) are not. This latter group has no clear model in their souls, and so they cannot look at what is most true. We should not expect, therefore, that non-philosophers can establish, guard, and preserve laws and conventions that are most just, most fine, and good.

If we continue to follow Socrates here, we should then agree that the learning that philosophers love is knowledge of "*the being that always is, not what wanders around between coming-to-be and decaying*" (485b1–2).

KYDES: If you want the city to last, then avoiding decay is paramount.

DEMETRA: If the laws of the city are to be good, must they not also be true? If they are true, then can they exist on a foundation of lies such as the Noble Lie?

PLATO: Socrates says that our philosophers must be truthful and "*must never willingly tolerate falsehood in any form. On the contrary, they must hate it and have a natural affection for the truth*" (485c4–5).

DEMETRA: So, a philosopher king or queen could not tolerate the Noble Lie and thus could not rule as a "lover of wisdom" over the fevered city that we have been describing. Isn't Socrates pointing out—painfully, as I see it—to your brothers that the fevered city is a sham? If philosophers are rulers and rulers are philosophers, then they could never rule in this city.

PLATO (Plato smiled.): Let us see whether Socrates agrees. Adeimantus raises an issue that might well point to what you are saying, Demetra. Socrates lists some of the inherent qualities of philosophers—namely, they are good at remembering; quick to learn; high-minded; graceful; and a friend and relative of truth, justice, courage, and temperance. It is to these people, because of their education, age, and maturity, that we entrust the ruling of the city (487a1–10).

HERMIAS: Before you continue on to Adeimantus's issue, Plato, I need to stop you. I don't see, or haven't heard, in any description of the guardians' education so far, which we have suggested is mostly training and not education *per se*, anything about participating in dialectic. Nothing about interrogating pronouncements by the founders or rulers. Maybe the education the guardians receive reinforces the virtues that you listed, but I don't see how the guardians, even if they have such inherent qualities, can become philosophers through censored stories and limited rhythms and songs. Don't they need to hear what is deleted or banned to understand the fullness of, basis for, and truth behind what the city has accepted? Don't they need to wrestle with dilemmas and problems, contradictions and possible oppositions? That is the nature of dialectic. Or is that the whole point of the Noble Lie? They can't rule until they see the falsity, the utter groundlessness, of such a tale? This point reinforces what Deme has been saying.

PLATO: I am glad you raised that, Hermias, but as you will see, there was no need to stop me. Adeimantus picks up something quite similar. He says,

> "No one, Socrates, would be able to contradict these claims of yours. But all the same, here is pretty much the experience people have on any occasion on which they hear the sorts of things you are now saying: they think that because they are inexperienced in asking and answering questions, they are led astray a little bit by the argument at every question, and that when these little bits are added together at the end of the discussion, a big false step appears that is the opposite of what they said at the outset." (487b1–7)

DEMETRA: As I was saying, this is just what has happened to your brothers, Plato! Both Adeimantus and Glaucon have failed at each turn to ask the questions that we've been troubled by since the outset. Now Adeimantus, at least, senses that something has gone wrong with the argument to this point. The big step has happened; the city, this fevered city, cannot support philosophers as rulers if it is built on and perpetuated by falsehoods. Yet, I would think that your brothers would be far more experienced in dialectic, in asking and answering questions, since they have been students of Socrates for some time.

PLATO: Would you then anticipate that my brothers would reorient this discussion toward the issues that you all have raised?

KYDES: We would.

PLATO: Sadly or otherwise, that is not where they venture next. Adeimantus's concern is that philosophers who are in love with and in pursuit of that which never changes, that which always is, will be the least qualified to lead the city, which needs practical guidance, not theorists and dreamers. The city needs people who understand how to rule a city, not who know the abstract nature of ruling itself.

Of course, as Socrates has intimated and as he shall develop in more detail going forward, the real dreamers are those trapped in a reality of appearances and opinions, who mistake resemblance for identity. Nevertheless, how is it that the philosopher can rule this city? Socrates offers a parable:

> "Imagine, then, that the following sort of thing happens either on one ship or on many. The ship-owner is taller and stronger than everyone else on board. But he is hard of hearing, he is a bit short-sighted, and his knowledge of seafaring is correspondingly deficient. The sailors are quarreling with one another about captaincy. Each of them thinks that he should captain the ship, even though he has not yet learned the craft and cannot name his teacher or a time when he was learning it. Indeed, they go further and claim that it cannot be taught at all, and are even ready to cut to pieces anyone who says it can. They are always crowding around the ship-owner himself, pleading with him, and doing everything possible to get him to turn the rudder over to them. And sometimes, if they fail to persuade him and others succeed, they execute those others or throw them overboard. Then, having disabled their noble ship-owner with drugs or drink or in some other way, they rule the

ship, use up its cargo drinking and feasting, and make the sort of voyage you would expect of such people. In addition, they praise anyone who is clever at persuading or forcing the ship-owner to let them rule, calling him a 'sailor,' a 'skilled captain,' and 'an expert about ships' while dismissing anyone else as a good-for-nothing. They do not understand that a true captain must pay attention to the seasons of the year, the sky, the stars, the winds, and all that pertains to his craft if he is really going to be expert at ruling a ship. As for how he is going to become captain of the ship, whether people want him to or not, they do not think it possible to acquire the craft or practice of doing this at the same time as the craft of captaincy. When that is what is happening onboard ships, don't you think that a true captain would be sure to be called a 'stargazer,' a 'useless babbler,' and a 'good-for-nothing' by those who sail in ships so governed?" (488a8–489a2)

KYDES: We don't have to go very deeply into this parable, Plato, to see the parts of the city in play here. The captain could be the founder of the city—the original selection to guide the ship—and the crew are the ambitious and often clueless politicians eager to seize control of the city. Or the crew might even be sophists, those philosophers who use arguments not in the service of truth but in the service of their own interests, especially money. The philosopher is the "good-for-nothing" off in the corner gazing at the stars. Lost on the crew is the stargazer's ability to navigate the ship—that is, govern and protect the city—safely and well.[1]

HERMIAS: I recall a maxim; I can't remember when or where I heard it. Perhaps it was in Atarneus: "Where there is no vision, the people perish."[2] People want rulers who have a sense of where the city or community is headed, as well as a path for getting there.

KYDES: That's the concern expressed by Adeimantus, one that I share. Philosophers might well have the vision of where the community needs to go, but do they know how to get to it? Can they align people to achieve that goal? Do they have those skills?

---

1. Useless stargazers? The Mayflower was headed to the colony of Virginia, but the crew didn't know the science of astronomy—how to read the stars—and ended up in Massachusetts. That might have been a fine destination, but it was not their intended one. For almost half of the voyagers died, making Massachusetts their abrupt and unanticipated final destination.

2. Proverbs 29:18. The earliest collection, called "The Proverbs of Solomon," was written around 700 BCE. Since Hermias did not die until around 341 BCE, he might well have heard this proverb.

HERMIAS: Philosophers will have a clear idea of what the vision is and why it is significant and achievable. And I think that they can communicate that to people and have them agree.

KYDES: Yes, but can they get the people, the city, to the goal? Can they show them how it's attainable? How can their "stargazing," how can their pursuit of knowledge of the eternal unchanging, help in that endeavor?

DEMETRA: I don't mean to divert the conversation, but I want to examine more closely this parable. Notice, first, that Socrates uses the same word to describe the ship-owner—"noble ship-owner"—as he does the founding myth of the city—the "Noble Lie." I don't think that's an accident. The ship-owner is noble in just the same way: The ship-owner is "taller and stronger" than the others; the Noble Lie is a massive falsehood, large and powerful enough to found and organize a city.

But the Lie itself, like the ship-owner himself, is shaky—hard of hearing, shortsighted, and deficient in knowledge of seafaring; in the case of the Lie, it is metaphorically deaf and shortsighted when it comes to criticisms and objections. The Lie is also deficient in knowledge, since there is nothing about it that constitutes knowledge at all, as Socrates uses the term. It is fake all the way down. I think that Socrates displays the same skeptical attitude toward the acceptance of the Noble Lie as he does toward the nature of this ship-owner.

Let's assume for the moment that Hermias is right. The stargazer, or our philosopher, could expertly guide the ship. Notice that no one on board thinks so. He's useless, isolated, and ignored. Like the stargazer, the philosopher in the city will barely be noticed, so different are his manner, interests, and knowledge from everyone else in the city. How could he possibly rule? Like the stargazer, the philosopher has no interest in seizing the rudder and murdering those who stand in his way. The people in the city will ignore him. Here, then, is the moral man in an immoral city—ignored and dismissed. At least we've now found him and can see his place.

PLATO: Socrates agrees: *"The best among the philosophers are useless to the majority,"* and they will not recognize that he speaks the truth (489b3–4).

KYDES: This is breaking apart for me, Plato. Who cares whether the majority finds the philosopher useful or useless? In the city with its three classes, isn't the majority relegated to doing their crafts? What do they have to say about who rules? That would be meddling in the business of the guardians. It is only the guardians who have the wherewithal to understand who can rule and why, and probably only the complete guardians in this case. They are the ones who must be persuaded, which the philosopher himself, not interested in seizing the rudder, doesn't want to do.

Since they are all supposed to be brothers and sisters, would they turn against the philosopher? If so, then it must be because the philosopher is so far removed from their own understanding and experiences that he or she appears to be nearly foreign. Perhaps, as they are citizens of the city, the philosophers can't be driven from the city, but they can be ignored. So even the complete guardians may well not recognize the philosophers' wisdom.

PLATO: Recall how we began our discussion. Remember that the challenge is to see, as Deme reminds us, the most moral person as someone thought to be immoral, someone who is viewed as without virtue and, perhaps we can add this here, someone who is useless to a city that presents itself as virtuous. Nevertheless, our philosopher is not and cannot be dissuaded from the pursuit of truth, for he or she is

> "[a] real lover of learning . . . , neither losing nor lessening the erotic love until he grasps the being of each nature itself . . . and that, once getting near what really is and having intercourse with it and having begotten understanding and truth, he knows, truly lives, is nourished, and—at that point, but not before—is relieved from the pains of labor." (489e3–490b6)

HERMIAS: This passage points out to us, doesn't it, Plato, the value of morality in and of itself? The philosopher is shunned, misunderstood, and viewed as if without virtue. Clearly, he lives for and according to morality even in the face of being thought immoral. He is not seeing or using morality as any means to an end, like luxuries or enhanced reputation. There is no extrinsic reward for him in being moral.

KYDES: And if a philosopher is relieved of the pains of giving birth, then clearly women can be philosophers. They know about those pains first hand.

DEMETRA: We saw that, didn't we, with Diotima in the *Symposium*, a female philosopher of the first order who taught Socrates a thing or two?

The Good

PLATO: Male philosophers, also, know such pains. Once they grasp the nature or being of each thing itself, he no longer suffers the pains of striving. He has seen and knows and is thus released.

Back to your earlier concern, Kydes: Socrates points out that the majority cannot be philosophic (494a3).

KYDES: Yes, of course, Plato. Why would we expect artisans sticking to their crafts to be philosophic? They lack the education and temperament.

PLATO: Some of them might be attracted to philosophy, which retains a "*grand reputation*" compared to lesser crafts (495d6). But many artisans have "*defective natures . . . souls cramped and spoiled by their menial tasks as their bodies are warped by their crafts and occupations*" (495d6-e1). They cannot associate with philosophy in a way that is worthy of her.

HERMIAS: This is true of the majority, as Socrates says, whether we are discussing a city in speech, like the fevered city, or an actual city, like Athens.

Nevertheless, when presenting the Noble Lie, Socrates did say that some exceptional children might be born of bronze or iron and can thus elevate their positions. Those exceptional children could be educated to become philosophers, though certainly not the majority. Likewise, some gold and silver children might prove to lack the nature reflective of the guardian class.

PLATO: Socrates repeats something like your point, Hermias. He says, "*A very few might perhaps come to philosophy from other crafts that they rightly despise because they have good natures*" (496b4-5).

DEMETRA: As if to suggest that the nature of an artisan is not a good nature, which Socrates can't believe for one second. After all, they too have tripartite souls.

I take his point, and yours, Kydes and Hermias, about the majority, but I want to reiterate our objection here: Although the majority won't be drawn to or be fully capable of knowing the nature of objects in themselves, we cannot predict from childhood, let alone infancy, who will be so capable and appropriately drawn. Since every person has three parts to her soul, since all people therefore have gold in their souls, then every person is deserving of a chance to learn philosophy and express their philosophical leanings to the fullest extent possible. Every person, not just some fanciful class of gold and silver souls. When we accept the dictates of the founders and their myth of the metals, then we are trapped in their falsehoods and in their fevered city, just as the citizens within the city are trapped in their roles.

And look at what happens to those who are trapped in this way: Socrates says that their "*souls [are] cramped and spoiled by their menial tasks as their bodies are warped by their crafts and occupations*" (495d6–e1). This is what their consignment to the artisan class has done to them. They have been forced to abandon the development of all aspects of their souls.

What would happen if we reverted to the healthy city, Adeimantus's city for pigs, and introduced to every citizen an education in philosophy fit for the guardians of the fevered city? Given the strictures of how Socrates describes the character and qualities of philosophers, I doubt that the majority in the healthy city would become philosophic. But they should be able to try.

PLATO: What do you think, Demetra, of this comment by Socrates: When asked by Adeimantus which of the current constitutions in effect is suitable for philosophy, Socrates responds,

> "None of them. . . . There is not one city today with a constitution worthy of the philosophic nature. . . . But if [philosophers] find the best constitution . . . it would be clear that it is really divine and that other natures and ways of life are merely human." (497b1–c2)

DEMETRA: First, I think that Socrates has limited his response to actual constitutions framing actual cities, not theoretical possibilities. So, in that context, no constitution is suitable, though it must be said that Athens raised Socrates, but he did not and would not rule the city.

Second, the healthy city is a theoretical possibility and not an actual city, and, as such, it might well be suitable for philosophers if we added to the city philosophical education for the citizenry. That is what was missing from the healthy city and, I think, what Socrates pushed your brothers to identify when they diverted the discussion early on to the luxurious city.

Third, unless you educate the majority, then you can't have philosophers rule, because, lacking education, the majority will not recognize the insights of philosophy and will ignore what philosophers say. In that situation, without education, the majority will be susceptible to demagoguery and to stupid myths like the Noble Lie. Educated, however, the

The Good

people can come to see that when philosophers rule, it is really their reasons that rule, not the persons offering the arguments and judgments.

PLATO: Well, what about that other theoretical city, the one that Socrates and my brothers have been constructing? Could the fevered city be suitable for philosophers?

HERMIAS: Continuing to hold aside our objections to the Noble Lie as the cornerstone of the city and our objections to the failure of the interlocutors to see the immorality of denying the majority of the citizens an education by assigning them to the artisan class, I think it might be suitable.

KYDES: How can you think so, Hermias?

HERMIAS: Because the rulers are at least dedicated to a philosophic education for some segment of the population, even if that segment is not the majority and might have been selected inappropriately.

PLATO: *"It is not impossible,"* Socrates says, for

> *"the muse of philosophy"* to gain mastery of a city; difficult, yes, but not impossible. (499d4–5) *"No city, constitution, or individual man will ever become perfect until either some chance event compels those few philosophers who are not vicious (the ones who are now called useless) to take charge of a city and compels the city to obey them, or until a god inspires the present rulers and kings or their offspring with a true erotic love for true philosophy."* (499b1–6)

KYDES: The city will be moral and just when philosophers are kings or kings are philosophers.

PLATO: Just so, Kydes.

DEMETRA: Or when philosophers are queens or queens, philosophers.
    (And Plato smiled.)

HERMIAS: What kind of *"chance event"* does Socrates have in mind? And how might philosophers as rulers *"compel"* the city to obey? Must it really be through compulsion? Why doesn't Socrates say *"persuasion"*? Is he acknowledging that the majority, being without adequate reason, cannot be persuaded?

PLATO: Not exactly, Hermias. Socrates says this: The masses can come to hold a different view of philosophy if *"you soothe them and try to remove their slanderous prejudice against the love of learning"* (499¹e1–3), because they have never seen a philosopher full of virtue in word and deed, one who pursues the truth and who keeps his distance from sophistries (498e3, 499a4–6). Instead, the masses are suspicious of philosophy and learning, because all they have seen is *"outsiders . . . who have burst in like a band of revelers, abusing one another, indulging their love of quarreling, and always arguing about human being . . ."* (500b1–4).

KYDES: Sophists, you mean . . . like the legendary Thrasymachus.

PLATO: Let's not devolve to the personal here, Kydes.

DEMETRA: Here is an opening, then, for the majority to come to an appreciation for philosophy. *"The masses,"* Socrates calls them. So, he recognizes that the masses can appreciate philosophers, admire their pursuits, and perhaps learn from what they have to teach. Therefore, the artisans ought not to be isolated, kept to their own work alone, and forced to avoid philosophers for fear that they would thereby be meddling in others' business, rendering themselves immoral by that path.

PLATO: Ah. So, Socrates asks, *"Do you think there is any way to prevent people from associating with what they admire?"* (All three exclaim simultaneously, "There is no way.") And is there any way to prevent those in association with someone they admire from imitating that person (500c4–6)?

KYDES: Look at us with you, Plato.

DEMETRA: Though we are hardly the masses, Kydes.

And isn't it so, Plato, that in your view we grow in reasoning and thought when we are exposed to those who think better than we do? If true, then the masses themselves will grow in thinking or better thinking by associating with true philosophers. Again, the masses ought not to be excluded from learning, which is what the founders and the rulers of the fevered city are trying to do with those they deem bronze or iron.

PLATO: Must this not also be true for the philosopher himself? By pursuing things as they are, *"by consorting with what is ordered and divine,"* will he or she not *"become as divine and ordered as a human being can"* (501c6–8)?

KYDES: That must be so, Plato.

PLATO: As Socrates says,

> "And if he should come to be compelled to make a practice—in private and in public—of stamping what he sees there into the people's characters, instead of shaping only his own, do you think he will be a poor craftsman of temperance, justice, and the whole of popular morality?
>
> And when the masses realize that what we are saying about him is true, will they be harsh with philosophers or mistrust us when we say that there is no way a city can ever find happiness unless its plan is drawn by painters who use the divine model?" (500d3–e2)

HERMIAS: They won't be harsh with them, Plato, because they understand what the true philosophers are trying to do, which can only mean, as Demetra has been saying, that the majority can follow and comprehend the plan and their role in it. That must entail more than simply doing their artisanal work and nothing else. They are, at the least, both artisans and citizens.

PLATO: Indeed, Hermias. Socrates then adds something germane: The majority would seek a divine model by taking "*the city and the characters of human beings as their sketching slate, but first they'd wipe the slate clean*" (501a2–3).

HERMIAS: Wipe it clean? How?

DEMETRA: Wipe it clean by eliminating the Noble Lie! Socrates is giving Glaucon and Adeimantus a chance to reverse course here. You don't need that Lie to find or develop philosophers. Each person is wiped clean of the Lie. Take this fevered city, wash it clean of the Lie, and then provide an education for each person. Each person, regardless of birth or station, can improve in character, even if not every person can be a philosopher.

Still, Plato, I'm disturbed that Socrates describes the philosophical practice as "*stamping the things ordered and divine into the characters of the people.*" That hardly seems to be a philosophical approach, certainly not one that Socrates or you have ever used. You educate by drawing insights from us and letting us wrestle with problems, dilemmas, and knotty issues. You don't pour or stamp content into us.

PLATO: Socrates moves to a different metaphor, which might be more acceptable to you. He says that the people would "*mix and blend the various ways of life in the city until they produce a human image based on what Homer too called 'the divine form and image' when it occurred among human beings*" (501b4–7).

HERMIAS: Mixing and blending the various ways of life in the city would destroy the Noble Lie where people are consigned to a certain class of citizen and to near-immutable occupations by some worthless judgment about the basic metal in their souls. The human image produced, divine in form and image, is the model for all persons living in that city, not just for those flattered to be called gold or silver. Deme is right about that.

DEMETRA: Notice, too, who is doing the wiping and mixing and blending; notice who is producing the image. It is the majority. Unless Plato was careless in his use of grammar, and when has that ever happened, then the only plural construction in these excerpts, the only "they," is the majority. Otherwise, Socrates speaks only of "the philosopher," in the singular.

KYDES: What is the significance of this for you, Deme?

DEMETRA: Don't you see, Kydes? If it is the majority blending the various ways of life, then it can't be a single class or two classes. This can only mean that everyone has the potential within to have a soul of gold, to be a soul of gold.

PLATO: Then can we agree with Socrates when later he says, "*every soul pursues the good*" (505e1)? (All nod their heads.) Nevertheless, is it not so, perhaps even with this divine image as a template for the city, that the majority mostly believes that pleasures or appetites are the good?

KYDES: That seems to be so. Many people believe that; certainly most of the people in a city of luxuries will do so, though others think that knowledge is the good.

DEMETRA: You said, "the good," Plato, which seems to contrast with, say, good food or a good poem.

PLATO: This is an important distinction. People don't want to acquire things that are merely believed to be good; everyone wants the things that really are good (505d7–9). But to know what is really good, one must know what the good is. Can we say or grasp what "the good" is? Perhaps it is best to take Socrates's route here and first discuss an offspring of the good, that which is most like it (506e3–4).

THE ANALOGY OF THE SUN

DEMETRA: I want to remind you, Plato, of something you told us about the time you tutored Dionysius of Syracuse. You said that he claimed to have already a sufficient knowledge of many important subjects, one of which must be the good.[3]

PLATO: That is so, Demetra, for I have said that among important subjects, the most important, the *megiston mathema*, is "*the form of the good*" (505a1).[4]

DEMETRA: You went on to say that you have never written on these matters and never would, for this knowledge is not something that can be put into writing.[5]

PLATO: Correct, again, Demetra. This subject cannot be frozen into words. Most often a reader, even if as intent as you three, will fixate on the words, on the text itself, using all her resources to tease out meaning. The written word lends itself to that exercise, which is understandable, since the words do not move or change. But when I point up to the moon, I do not want you focused on my arm and hand and finger. That is what reading too often does, and the reader then misses the experience of seeing the moon.

The knowledge can only be born in the soul after long-continuous interchange between teacher and pupil, in joint pursuit of the subject. Only then is it born in the soul suddenly, like light flashing forth when a fire is kindled.

KYDES: Why, Plato? Why can't a skilled teacher like you use the written word to serve as that flashing light?

PLATO: A very good question, Kydes. As a skilled teacher, a philosopher knows that the power of dialectic comes not simply from what he says, but also from how he says it. The tone, the cadence, an inflection, a

---

3. See Plato, "Seventh Letter," 341a7–b2, in Plato, *Plato Complete Works*, 1659.
4. *Megiston mathema* means "the greatest thing to be learned."
5. Plato, "Seventh Letter," 341c5–d1, in Plato, *Plato Complete Works*, 1659.

gesture, a look all have an effect on how his interlocutors are reacting to the discussion. None of that can be duplicated in or through the written word. That is why writing, in my experience, cannot serve as the spark needed to ignite the soul.

KYDES: But your dialogues can be an echo of the dialectic as used by Socrates.

PLATO: Nevertheless, they remain an echo. In my written dialogues, even if I am merely repeating verbatim what Socrates has said, I cannot capture precisely how he has said it or the effect of how he has said it.

KYDES: Is this why you want to begin by talking about an offspring of the good?

PLATO (smiling): Yes, that is one reason, but bear in mind that at this point, it is Socrates who is speaking of the offspring.

So, as you know, if we are talking about Truth itself or Beauty itself or the Good itself, we are referring to "the being" of each, which is the Form of each.

KYDES: We have talked of the Forms before, for example, when we discussed the *Phaedrus*.

PLATO: That's right. So, this is not new for you. And we said, as Socrates says now, we can differentiate many beautiful things and good things, as we were saying about good food or good drink. These things are visible. On the other hand, the Forms—Beauty itself or Truth itself—are intelligible but not visible (507b2–10).

To see the visible we need our eyes and properties—colors, say—in the things we are looking at. We also need light. The source of light is, most readily, the sun. Of course, sight or the eye is not the sun. But only with the sun can we see the visible; the power of sight, it can be said, comes from the sun. We might even say it is the cause of sight (508b4–7).

HERMIAS: I can agree with most of that, Plato. But the sun doesn't cause sight. It is essential for it, because we can't see without light.

PLATO: Let us stay with that, Hermias. The sun makes seeing things possible, just as the Good makes knowing things possible. The sun is to visible things as the Good is to intelligible things. "*What the good itself is in the intelligible realm, in relation to understanding and intelligible* *things, the sun is in the visible realm, in relation to sight and visible things"* (508b12–c1). Would you accept that from Socrates?

HERMIAS: I would, because I have no reason to dispute it at this point.

PLATO: To state this another way, Socrates says:

> "When our eyes no longer turn to things whose colors are illuminated by the light of day, but by the lights of night, they are dimmed and seem nearly blind, as if clear sight were no longer in them. Yet whenever they are turned to things illuminated by the sun, they see clearly, and sight is manifest in those very same eyes.
>
> "Well, think about the soul in the same way. When it focuses on something that is illuminated both by truth and what is, it understands, knows, and manifestly possesses understanding. But when it focuses on what is mixed with obscurity, on what comes to be and passes away, it believes and is dimmed, changes its beliefs this way and that, and seems bereft of understanding." (508c4–d9)

KYDES: So, just as things appear dim and shadowy at night when the sun is down, so things of the soul like beauty are grasped dimly if we focus only on particular objects that decay or shatter and not on the subject of Beauty itself.

HERMIAS: What is true of sight, of seeing things, is also, I suppose, true of the soul.

PLATO: Demetra, do you also accept this? (She nods, but does not comment.) Good. Now then,

> "what gives truth to the things known and the power to know to the knower is the Form of the Good. And as the cause of knowledge and truth, you must think of it as an object of knowledge. Both knowledge and truth are beautiful things. But if you are to think correctly, you must think of the Good as other and more beautiful than they. In the visible realm, light and sight are rightly thought to be sun-like, but it is wrong to think that they are the sun. So, here it is right to think of knowledge and truth as 'good-like,' but wrong to think that either of them is the Good—for the Good is yet more prized." (508e1–509a5)

DEMETRA: So, the Good is superior to knowledge and truth, for they depend on the Good? The Good causes both knowledge and truth, but is itself beyond them? Still, that cause can be known.

PLATO: Yes. The objects of knowledge owe their being to the Good, but "*the Good is not being.*" It is "*superior to being,*" beyond being "*in rank and power*" (509b6–9).

DEMETRA: Because the Good cannot come into being. It already always is. That is because although the Good can be an object of knowledge, it is also the ground of all knowing, of knowing anything. It had to be before anything is.

The Good is that out of which all being arises. It must already "be" for being to arise. It cannot come into being, which would be something that is now, but that was different or was not before. It cannot itself arise if all being arises from it.

HERMIAS: All objects owe their being to the Good. That is, all objects come from the Good. But how can they come from that which is "not being"?

PLATO: To answer that, Hermias, is to attempt to trap the Good. The Good isn't "not being." The Good is both being and not being. Or the Good is neither being nor not being. From this being/non-being all things emerge. The Good is the one source. It is one.

DEMETRA: Well, one what? It isn't being; Socrates clearly states that it is "not being," but is superior to being. So, it isn't the one source; it's the "none" source.

KYDES: Seriously? You all are killing me with all of this "being/non-being" talk.

HERMIAS: Let's break this down for both our sakes, Kydes. The Good is not being.

KYDES: Right, just as Socrates said.

HERMIAS: But then how can anything that is, how can any "being," come from "not being"? How can something come from nothing? Because the Good is "no-thing." It is, but not as any object. As Plato said, the Good must, therefore, be both being and not being.

KYDES: At the same time? Well, that's a paradox: The Good is both being and not being. It doesn't make sense.

DEMETRA: I don't think it's supposed to make sense. If it did, then we'd think that somehow we'd captured its meaning and knew the Good. Besides, Socrates said clearly that the Good is not being. So, if it makes "sense" to say that the Good is both being and not being, then we have to add, following Socrates, that the Good is neither being nor not being. (Kydes throws up his hands.) We can't define it as if we can understand it.

HERMIAS: Maybe this analogy might help us think about it. Let's imagine that the Good is like the night sky, but the sky beyond the stars, beyond anything we can see. That sky beyond the stars looks empty. It is nothing but black, a vast ocean of blackness, of darkness. Yet out of that nothingness all the stars arise. That means that the emptiness we see isn't really empty. Nothing is there—"no-thing" is there—but the potential for everything, every form of being, is there. The Good could be like that.

DEMETRA: But calling it the sky or an ocean of blackness is already to put boundaries on it. Trying to describe it is to contain it, "to trap it," as Plato said. That's what language does. It defines and bounds ideas. Even ideas have shape or form.

HERMIAS: But where do ideas come from? Don't they often pop into our heads, just appear? They aren't there, then suddenly we're aware of them.

DEMETRA: So, the Good could be like an unbounded field of awareness in which things take shape and form? Out of the unbounded field arise all forms. But now we're back to the same problem. The "field of awareness" is like our "empty sky." It has shape or form. It's now "in being" and therefore can't capture the Good, which is superior to and beyond being.

KYDES: Well, how about calling it the "unbounded unmanifest"?

HERMIAS: How does that help?

KYDES: It's vague, with just enough opacity to be compelling—a limitless expanse that is itself but only as what holds all that will be.

HERMIAS: However vague you can be, Kydes, you're still describing "a thing" that has being. That's what language does. It shapes ideas and gives form as words, images, and symbols. The Good is itself beyond language and is ineffable. Look at how we tried to describe it a minute ago: The Good is, the Good is not, the Good both is and is not, and the Good neither is nor is not.

DEMETRA: So, the Good is beyond thought, since thought is done in images and symbols.

KYDES: Then we can't think our way to knowing the Good, if it's beyond thought, since thought is in being.

HERMIAS: But Socrates said, "*What is completely is completely knowable*" (477a3). So, we can know the Good, but we can't think our way to the Good or even think about the Good? Anything we say will be a distortion and inaccurate.

KYDES: Hermias, remember telling us about that time you were riding in the wagon. The sun was shining on your face, the horses' hooves clomped in rhythm, and the wagon swayed gently as you rode. Relaxed in the back, your eyes opening and closing peacefully, you found yourself in almost a dream world. In an instant—

HERMIAS: I disappeared. Everything I saw and heard was intimately connected. Everywhere I looked I saw unity. I was everything, and everything was "me." But there was no "I" to see this, to experience this. I had disappeared. Left was this oneness, this unity among everything. Yet things weren't there any more than I was there. There was just this, this oneness.

KYDES: You knew this, even though you didn't think it or think about it. You simply experienced it. Or, rather, there was simply this experience, this awareness with no "you" to acknowledge it, to know it.

HERMIAS: Yes, that's right. I knew it, but there was no "me" there to process anything. It was direct knowing, beyond thought and language. I just knew.

KYDES: Like intuition, a different kind of knowing.

HERMIAS: I guess something like that.

DEMETRA: But how can the Good be known by any method if it is beyond or superior to being? To be known it must "be" something, which means that it is. So, it has always been, yet is also beyond that, since it is not being. Is any of this . . .

Suddenly, all three became still. Plato observed them. They were staring off, looking at nothing. Plato recognized the state they were in or were edging their way into. He leaned forward and, in a voice just above a whisper, he said slowly: *"By consorting with what is divine and ordered ... you will become as divine and ordered as a human being can"* (501c6–8).

Hearing this, the bodily positions of the three altered. Each sat back. Plato could see them falling silently into themselves. Those around Plato, Meno for example, referred to such moments of *aporia*—an impasse in the dialogue that resulted in silence—as if being stung by a stingray, rendering the mind and tongue numb.[6]

Plato knew from experience that *aporia*, this impasse or perplexity, was not the silence of deep thought or a fall into analysis. It was, as Meno said, the numbing of the mind, a silence beyond thought.

What happens in *aporia* when all motion ceases and thought stops? You are at a dead end. The end seems like death, because it is. You have stopped. But your heart still beats, your blood still flows, you continue to breathe. So how can you be at the dead end?

Because the self you thought you were is not who you really are. The world continues, the clouds move, and you breathe. At the dead end, all of this is happening. But at the dead end all of this is happening, but you are not part of it. You are all of it. That is you. You are neither what looks at the world nor what you look at. There is now only what is by itself, for itself.

Aporia is the silence of stupefaction, of trance, of the vastness of space before the moment of realization. This is a silence so profound, so engorged, so poignant, that these three, being speechless, frozen, and numb, were at the gateway to the transcendent, the state of true knowledge and eternal freedom. Theirs was the stillness before the spark from the fire jumps into recognition, into awareness. Their silence and stillness were a moment of pure witnessing, when one's self has disappeared but before their being aware of it, aware of anything but the emptiness of silence and stillness itself.

The infinite, the absolute, the unchanging and eternal, is only known when the intellect surrenders to the transcendent; that is, when the intellect surrenders to silence. Then can come direct contact with the Good, the unnameable, which was like nothing, no-thing. Yet it was everything at the same time.

---

6. See Plato, *Meno*, 80a6. The term *aporia* means a "puzzle" or, literally, "without passage" or "a barrier on one's journey." Although seemingly a barrier, I am using *aporia* also as an opportunity.

Plato knew that one cannot fight the silence. You must embrace it. That is difficult to do, because it is so sudden, original, and extreme. It is death. Yet dialectic can bring on this surrender in the right circumstances with the right people even against their will. Dialectic, properly used, can prepare a student for realization. Its cross-examination, as the three had been doing all night, can provide an intellectual impetus as preparation for what is beyond the intellect. Otherwise, without some mechanism like dialectic, they could not accept or grasp the direct realization of the Good or eternal Being lying behind the phenomena of existence, including thought itself. Dialectic can generate a state of receptivity and openness, a state of vulnerability. Such was the state of Kydes, Hermias, and Demetra. Plato thought to himself, "Lao Tzu said it well: *'The Master leads by emptying people's minds and filling their cores,'* their souls."[7]

---

7 Lao Tzu, *Tao Te Ching* (trans. Mitchell), verse 3. Mitchell uses no page numbers in his translation of the *Tao*.

9

The Forms and the *Tao*

Plato waited patiently. He was in no hurry. This scene with his three protégés frozen in their transcendent states reminded him of the incident described by Alcibiades that Plato had included in the *Symposium*:

> "One day, at dawn, [Socrates] *was thinking about some problem or other; he just stood outside, trying to figure it out. He simply stood there, glued to the same spot. At midday, many soldiers had seen him, and, quite mystified, they told everyone that Socrates had been standing there all day, thinking about something. He was still there when evening came, and after dinner some Ionians out of curiosity brought out their mats and slept in the open air mainly to watch him and see whether he would stand all night. And so he did; he stood on the very same spot until dawn. With the return of light he offered up a prayer to the sun and went his way.*"[1]

Transfixed, unmoving, Socrates stood from dawn to dawn. Was he lost in thought? Given the experiences of most Athenians, even the best educated Athenians, this was the conventional, and logical, perspective. But no one who is lost in thought, Plato knew, is immobilized like that. No one, not even the deepest thinker. Yes, everyone has had the experience of losing a sense of time or even a sense of one's self when hearing certain music or following a line of thinking. But to be transfixed from dawn to dawn? That is to conflate intellect with transcendence.

You can get lost in the transcendent, so lost that you can remain motionless only to be amazed, when "coming to," that many hours had

---

1. Plato, *Symposium*, 220c6–d5.

passed when time for the entranced seemed to have been but the blink of an eye. That occurs when thought, even the deepest thought, is transcended, when the thinker himself is not simply lost but is altogether absent.[2]

At the beginning of the *Symposium*, Socrates has a similar episode, though of much shorter duration. While on his way with Aristodemus to dinner at Agathon's home, the setting for the symposium, Socrates does lapse into deep thought. That lapse soon turns into something like a trance state—another conventional perspective—as Socrates stands motionless on the porch of one of Agathon's neighbors. Sometime later, Socrates enters Agathon's house to share in the meal and conversation. Agathon says,

> "Socrates, come lie down next to me. . . . [I]f I touch you, I may catch a bit of the wisdom that came to you under my neighbor's porch. It's clear you've seen the light. If you hadn't, you'd still be standing there."[3]

Seen the light, not through one's eyes or through one's thinking, but through the soul. Yes, seen the light, the light of the Forms radiating from the Good, now stepped down and grasped as illuminated thought or wisdom.

As with Socrates, Plato's three students would soon come to their senses. He knew from their own stories, told to him, that they had each, to varying degrees, experienced the disappearance of self, the overwhelming sense of Oneness among all things, the incalculable sense of unboundedness and joy associated with experiences of the transcendent. Over time, they might come to embody the knowledge of what they had experienced, were experiencing, and would experience again and again

---

2. Here is a contemporary example of a similar, if not exact, phenomenon. Vernon Kitabu Turner—author, poet, artist, Zen master, and martial-arts expert—tells of one of his own transcendental experiences:

"I was sitting in Dunkin' Donuts holding a cup of coffee, and when I looked up, there was a policeman standing in front of me. So, I said, 'Yes, Officer? May I help you?' 'Is everything okay?' he asked. 'Well, yes,' I said. 'What's wrong with drinking a cup of coffee?' 'Nothing is wrong with drinking a cup of coffee,' he told me. 'It's just that you've been looking at that cup for the past eight hours.' I thought to myself, 'Oh, my God. Eight hours have gone by. I'm in a public place. People are working here. They've been watching me, but I haven't been aware of them at all.' And then I said to myself, 'Vernon, you'd better be careful, because you're not in Asia, where they understand these things. You're in the U.S. of A. where they definitely don't.'" Turner, "Mind Like Water," 120.

3. Plato, *Symposium*, 175d1–3.

through the proper use of dialectic. But for now, early tastes of the Good could not be prolonged. Bringing them back gently, his voice soft but clear, Plato said:

PLATO: You have raised two questions that we ought to pursue. First, how do we describe, can we describe, the Good, that which is not Being, which is superior to or beyond or prior to Being, but from which all being arises? Language seems to fail us here. Language leads to the second question: How, then, can we know the Good? We'll return to Socrates and the second question later, but first . . .
(The trio of students came back slowly to full attention as Plato begins to rummage behind his couch. He turns back to the group with several parchments in his arms.)

PLATO: I want to share with you some of what is written here, and before I do, I need to issue a brief preface. Demetra quoted me correctly from my "Seventh Letter." I want to amend that statement somewhat. Some persons have written on the Good, though in a manner different from what I imagined when I wrote my Letter. So now I say this: The very best writing on the most important subjects can serve as reminders of what the writers know for those who likewise know, however limited their knowledge of the subjects might be. Such writing can deepen understanding, but it cannot substitute for experience. As I mentioned earlier, what is written on the soul comes through experiences such as you have been wrestling with, which can be stimulated by dialectic. What is written on the soul, what is lasting and indelible, can then be recollected through written prose and especially through verse, where rhythm and emphasis can play an important role. Yet, written words cannot plant experience in the soul, and too often reading words can distract as much as instruct.

(He unscrolled one of the parchments.) I have mentioned my former student Ladmon to you. He returned recently from the Far East, from the lands of Seres and Sinae.[4] He brought with him several parchments, translated by Ladmon, that he thought might be of interest to me. I think, in light of our conversation, they might also be of interest to you.

The parchments are the text of a philosophical and religious system known in those lands by the term "Taoism." This text, known as the *Tao Te Ching*, is the centerpiece of that system. The author of the text is

---

4. The ancient Greeks referred to China as two lands rather than one. The root *sēr* is the Greek word for silkworm, which might come from the Chinese name for silk. *Sērikḗ* means "land of silk."

known as Lao Tzu. That name is actually a title that translates as "Old Master." There is some doubt, according to Ladmon, whether Lao Tzu is the single author or whether he is the author at all. For our purposes, that is irrelevant. The title, *Tao Te Ching*, has several meanings, but the one that Ladmon thinks provides the most flavor related to the text is "The Classic Way of Integrity," where "integrity" stands for the totality of a person's morality.[5]

I think that you will find, as I have, that this text has some pertinence to what we are now discussing. The translation of the text is Ladmon's own. How well he understands the language of the original I cannot say, but he has been there many years. Perhaps it is a literal translation; perhaps he has embellished it. I am not sure, but, given what is here, that might not matter. Consider this description of the Tao or the Way, which we might link to our discussion of the Good. Indeed, as far as I can, I am going to substitute the word "Good" where the word "Way" appears. Here is the opening passage:

> *The Good that can be told*
> *Is not the eternal Good.*
> *The name that can be named*
> *Is not the eternal Name.*[6]
>
> *Heaven and earth*
> *begin in the unnamed:*
> *Naming is the mother*
> *of all particular things.*[7]

KYDES: This is what we were trying to say! Once you say "the Good," you've labeled it and bounded it. You can't name it. Beyond language is the Good, beyond all boundaries. Once you provide a name, then you have something, a thing that is, that is in being. (Kydes threw his hands into the air.) I've stopped making sense.

DEMETRA: No, you haven't. Well, yes, you have. But that's because little sense, but some sense, can be made of this.

---

5. I borrow the spirit of this translation from Mair's translation of the *Tao Te Ching*, xix. See also his afterword, 130–36.

6. Lao Tzu, *Tao Te Ching* (trans. Mitchell), verse 1.

7. See also Lao Tzu, *Tao Te Ching* (trans. Le Guin), 3.

HERMIAS: Plato, is the first rising of "particular things," this first naming, is that what you call the "Forms"? They would be the primordial or primeval manifestations, the perfect models, of everything.

PLATO: Let us hold that in mind for now as a working hypothesis. (Plato continued reading from the parchment:)

> *Mystery and manifestations*
> *Arise from the same source.*
> *This source is called darkness.*
>
> *Darkness within darkness.*
> *The gateway to all understanding.*[8]

KYDES: That is what we were trying to say using the night sky, the dark sky beyond the stars. All manifestations arise from the darkness, the unbounded unmanifest.

HERMIAS (exasperated): Do you have to keep using that phrase, "unbounded unmanifest"?

KYDES: I know it's ungainly, but doesn't it point to what we're trying to describe? I'll stop when you come up with something better.

PLATO: How about this phrase from Lao Tzu:

> *The Good is like the eternal void:*
> *Filled with infinite possibilities.*[9]

HERMIAS: "Eternal void filled with infinite possibilities." That seems to capture what we've been trying to say. Kydes?

KYDES (with some petulance): Okay, but I don't see why it's any better than "unbounded unmanifest."

HERMIAS: Maybe because "eternal void" is not ugly?

KYDES: Oh, we're going for mellifluence now? Excuse me. I thought we were going for meaning.

DEMETRA: Steady on, boys. We're all working together here. How about we use whichever one suits us at the time? So, the Good, like the Tao, is itself not a Form?

---

8. Lao Tzu, *Tao Te Ching* (trans. Mitchell), verse 3.
9. Lao Tzu, *Tao Te Ching* (trans. Mitchell), verse 4.

HERMIAS: It is beyond form . . .

KYDES: . . . and formlessness.

HERMIAS: Right. It's, ah . . . beyond and prior to all manifestations.

PLATO: Lao Tzu writes:

> *Form that includes all forms,*
> *The form of the formless,*
> *Image without an image,*
> *Subtle, beyond all conception.*[10]

DEMETRA: He is focused here on the Forms, but not on the Good. You can't describe the Good, which is unqualified, beyond all thoughts, feelings, concepts, and qualities at all. You can't call the Good perfect or even formless. Such terms at best could only describe the Forms, which are primal manifestations from the Good, the unborn.

PLATO: Lao Tzu again:

> *The world is formed from the void . . .*[11]
> *The Good is beyond is and is not . . .*[12]
> *When you look for it, there is nothing to see.*
> *When you listen for it, there is nothing to hear.*
> *When you use it, it is inexhaustible.*[13]

DEMETRA: So, here is where I am with all of this: The Good is not itself a thing. It is that in which all things arise and appear. Our language tries to pinpoint the Good, to make it a thing that we can point to. Even to refer to it as "The Good" is to create a limit and maybe an image.

Perhaps the closest we can come in language to describing the Good—that which is itself beyond description—is to think of it as emptiness that through some excitation manifestations arise out of it. This emptiness is the realm of pure potentiality out of which all things are and can be generated but is nothing (no-thing) itself.[14]

---

10. Lao Tzu, *Tao Te Ching* (trans. Mitchell), verse 14.
11. Lao Tzu, *Tao Te Ching* (trans. Mitchell), verse 28.
12. Lao Tzu, *Tao Te Ching* (trans. Mitchell), verse 21.
13. Lao Tzu, *Tao Te Ching* (trans. Mitchell), verse 35.

14. Modern physicists refer to dark energy as the quantum vacuum of virtual particles. That is, it is the unmanifest "realm" about to be born as matter. Perhaps Plato comes closest to this idea when Socrates discusses "the *khôra*" or characterless, unqualified "space" in Plato, *Timaeus*, 49a5–52d1.

PLATO: Lao Tzu says it like this:

> *The Good . . . is empty yet infinitely capable.*[15]
> *The Good is . . . empty yet inexhaustible,*
> *It gives birth to infinite worlds.*[16]

KYDES: Paradoxes piled on top of conundrums on top of riddles.

DEMETRA: How else could it be, if we're wrestling with the ineffable?

KYDES: Can we even say there is a Form of the Good? Isn't it outside of being and thus beyond form?

DEMETRA: As Lao Tzu said, it is, and it isn't. It is empty but full, being but not being, nothing but everything.

HERMIAS: The Good is beyond being. The Good is beyond. The beyond is not far away. It is right here. How could it be otherwise? Since It is beyond time, it must be now. It can only be now.

KYDES: So, "now" is not in time?

PLATO: Parmenides tells Socrates, "*There is no time in which something can, simultaneously, be neither in motion nor at rest.*" Socrates agrees. Yet, Parmenides continues, "*something cannot change from rest while rest continues, or from motion while motion continues. Rather, there is this queer creature, the instant,* [which] *lurks between motion and rest.*"[17] The instant, "this queer creature," is outside of time. It is not time. Anything that is past, a memory, cannot be recalled except in the present; any future event can only be thought of or anticipated "now." "Now" is not in time, but is also the only time we actually have. Change occurs only in the now, which is not itself in time. Therefore, Parmenides is correct: Something can only be in motion and at rest "at no time."

HERMIAS: So, the Good is like the "now"? That means that it is not in time, nor out of time; it is beyond time. When it is both being and not-being at the same time, then that can only be the same instant, the now. Placed in time, the Good can be one or many, because it is neither and yet both.

KYDES: Good grief!

15. Lao Tzu, *Tao Te Ching* (trans. Mitchell), verse 5.
16. Lao Tzu, *Tao Te Ching* (trans. Mitchell), verse 6.
17. Plato, *Parmenides*, 156c5–e3.

DEMETRA: Maybe this will help you think about the Good, Kydes. The Good is absent from nothing (no-thing). Empty a room of all its furniture. What remains?

KYDES: Walls. Doors. Windows.

DEMETRA: What is the room full of? Emptiness. Full of emptiness. So, too, the Good. To know it, empty yourself, become nothing. Empty yourself of all thoughts and feelings. In that moment, the Good is, and you are full. Only by being empty can you know this fullness. Open yourself. Empty yourself. The Good remains as always. It cannot be found, because it always is.

KYDES: So, if it always is and is never absent, then it is right here. Why do anything? Why empty yourself?

DEMETRA: To recognize what is already here. To remember what you can never get away from.

KYDES: You're wrong, Deme.

DEMETRA: About which part?

KYDES: About this helping me think about the Good. Again, can we say that there is a Form of the Good?

HERMIAS: The Forms come from or out of the Good. Those are in being; those exist. Perhaps we should focus on those.

KYDES: Is this what Lao Tzu meant when he said "use the Good"?

HERMIAS: Use it to understand manifestations, the first manifestations, what we've been calling the Forms. That might be a good place to start.

PLATO: About manifestations in the world, Lao Tzu says this:

The Forms and the Tao

In the beginning was the [Good].
All things issue from it;
All things return to it.
To find the origin,
Trace back to the manifestations.[18]

KYDES: The Forms are nameable. They come into being out of the Good. Because they are nameable and exist, they have boundaries and limitations, including the Forms' opposite. We can talk about them, but then we have to talk as well about their opposites, no?

HERMIAS: You're saying, then, that the moment manifestation takes place, the moment something takes form, then that something carries with it its opposite: night and day, light and heavy, beautiful and ugly, life and death. One cannot make sense without that other, that opposite.

KYDES: It seems so.

HERMIAS: I'm not so sure. The subtlest level of creation, the finest level of experience, is the level of the first or primordial manifestation, the Forms. Why is that so? Because that subtlest level is closest to Being and thus is in this initial impulse perfect and pure. The Forms exist. They are universals or essences that are real. But do they have opposites?

DEMETRA: Why should they have opposites? The first manifestations out of the Good are "archetypes" (*arkhetypon*)[19] or the Forms. These are the original models or patterns from which all subsequent forms arise. The Forms are universals, perfect and unchanging, beyond all particularities. Yet they are also beyond any concept or thought. Any form—animal, vegetable, or mineral—is nothing but the organization of patterns into form or condensed into consolidated shapes. As such, why should these archetypes have opposites?

KYDES: Because everything we see and think has an opposite—tall/short, heavy/light, living/dead, moral/immoral, beautiful/ugly. We understand the terms in relation to their opposites.

DEMETRA: I see your point, Kydes, but that's how we operate "down here," away from the unchanging and eternal, away from the archetypes,

---

18. Lao Tzu, *Tao Te Ching* (trans. Mitchell), verse 52.

19. *Arkhetypon* is Greek for "pattern" or "model" or "first form," from *arkhē* meaning "beginning, origin, first place" (noun from verb *arkhein* or "to be the first"); *typos* meaning "model, type, or mark."

and amid objects that decline and decay. We live in a world of separate objects with distinct properties. So, for example, is there an opposite of "chariot"? It is a discrete object, and we search out the qualities that make it so. In that search, we might well look to anything that "opposes" a chariot; that is, anything that isn't a chariot. That is its opposite.

At some point, however, in examining a chariot, we might ask about the properties all chariots share. What are the qualities that connect them? Then, I think, we are moving toward the qualities about an object that might be unchanging and eternal; qualities, that is, that might reflect the Form underlying the object. Pursuing that kind of inquiry might bring us to the essence of the object, the truth of the object. Would an essence have an opposite?

HERMIAS: Recall what Socrates said in the *Phaedrus*: The soul can see (*noēsis*)

> "what is outside heaven. The place beyond heaven . . . is without color and without shape and without solidity, a being that really is what it is, the subject of all true knowledge, visible only to [intuition], the soul's steersman."[20]

He is describing the first manifestation, when "*a being really is what it is, but without color or shape [form] or solidity.*" It is the essence of the being, prior to content; the first Form outside of formlessness, the first pattern below heaven or the Good. This is way beyond discrete objects.

The soul is here "*seeing what is real and watching what is true.*"[21] On this "*high ridge of heaven,*" where being comes into existence in the primordial place that is not beyond heaven, heaven itself moves in a circle. The soul's gaze moves from what is "*outside*" or "*beyond*" heaven to seeing what is "*true*" and "*real,*" the first manifestations of "*what is.*" These are the Forms.

> "The circular motion brings the soul around to a 'view of justice as it is; it has a view of Self-control; it has a view of knowledge—not the knowledge that is close to change, that becomes different as it knows the different things which we consider real down here. No, it is the knowledge of what really is what it is. And when the soul has seen all the things that are as they are and feasted on them, it sinks back inside heaven and goes home.'"[22]

---

20. Plato, *Phaedrus*, 247c2–d1.
21. Plato, *Phaedrus*, 247d4.
22. Plato, *Phaedrus*, 247d5–4.

The soul goes back down to our world and to everyday reality.

Socrates says, "*Only a philosopher's mind grows wings*"[23] to ascend to these heights, because only a philosopher uses or follows dialectic. At these heights,

> "He is the only one who is as perfect as perfect can be. He stands outside human concerns and draws close to the divine; ordinary people think he is disturbed, like the stargazer aboard the ship, and rebuke him for this, unaware that he is possessed by god. . . . [When] *he sees the beauty down here, he is reminded of true beauty.*"[24]

Why should we expect to see the opposite of true Beauty there?

KYDES: So, the beauty we see down here is relative to its opposite? This image is beautiful relative to other images that are less beautiful and even ugly? But in the realm of the Forms, inside heaven, there is only Beauty without an opposite.

HERMIAS: What these philosophers saw, says Socrates, was revealed sacred objects—what we are calling the Forms—

> "that were perfect and simple and unshakeable and blissful. That was the ultimate vision, and we saw it in pure light because we were pure ourselves, not buried in this thing we are carrying around now, which we call a body, locked in it like an oyster in a shell."[25]

These philosophers were perfect and free, but those of us down here, locked like oysters in our shells, don't see the Form of Beauty when we gaze at images and objects. We see beauty through our senses, including our thoughts.

DEMETRA: When we see something we think is beautiful, we aren't seeing the Form of Beauty, the thing-in-itself. We are seeing beauty instantiated and thus qualified in some way. This is beauty that changes, that fades, that comes into being and dies. As such this cannot be the Form of Beauty itself, for every instantiation, having taken form, must itself be imperfect and impermanent.

---

23. Plato, *Phaedrus*, 249c6–7.
24. Plato, *Phaedrus*, 249c8–d5.
25. Plato, *Phaedrus*, 250c3–6.

This reminds me of what Socrates says in the *Symposium* about what he learned from Diotima on love and beauty: In the beginning, a person will find that someone else is beautiful. She might fall in love with that other person. Soon, however, she can come to realize that the beauty of one body "*is brother to the beauty of any other and that if* [she] *is to pursue beauty of form* [she'd] *be very foolish not to think that the beauty of all bodies is one and the same.*"[26]

Soon, she'll come to see that beneath the beauty of people's bodies is the beauty of their souls and the beauty of ideas. That, then, leads her to gaze at the beauty of what beautiful souls can create—that is, customs and laws and institutions, which are patterns. What has led to these patterns? Then she will look to see the beauty of the knowledge that lies beneath and informs these patterns, these laws and institutions. And that beauty, so abstract and vast, will lead her to "*the great sea of beauty*" (210d5).

At this stage, having given birth to many gloriously beautiful ideas and theories through loving wisdom, she will "*all of a sudden catch sight of something wonderfully beautiful in its nature*," something that always is and neither comes to be nor passes away, neither waxes nor wanes. "*It is not beautiful this way and ugly that way; it is not beautiful at one time and ugly at another, nor beautiful in relation to one thing and ugly in relation to another*" (210e6–211a9). She will see beyond, as Kydes pointed out, the beauty down here that is relative. It is not beautiful for some people, but ugly to others; it is not beautiful simply as one idea or one kind of knowledge.

Instead, "*it is not anywhere in another thing, as in an animal, or in earth, or in heaven, or in anything else. [It] is itself by itself with itself; it is always one in form; and all the other beautiful things share in that*" (211b1–5). This beauty is never shrunk or lost and never suffers any change. This is the Form of Beauty, and can be known, says this wise woman Diotima, when someone

> "*rises by these stages . . . using beautiful things like stairs from one body to two and from two to all beautiful bodies, then from beautiful bodies to beautiful customs, and from customs to learning beautiful* [ideas]. *This is how to arrive at knowing Beauty Itself. When you behold that, then you will not measure beauty by gold or clothing or boys and youths*" (211b6–d5).

---

26. Plato, *Symposium*, 210b1–3. All passages here in the text numbered 210–212 are from the *Symposium*.

The Forms and the Tao

KYDES: You will not measure it, in other words, by luxuries—what motivated Glaucon and Adeimantus to move us from the healthy city to the fevered city.

DEMETRA: That seems to be the case. To use such measurements is to fail to see *"the Beautiful Itself, divine Beauty itself in its one Form, absolute, pure, unmixed, not polluted by human flesh or colors or any other great nonsense of mortality"* (211e1–212a1).

What's the lesson from all of this, the upshot of all of this? Having seen the Form of Beauty, only then is it possible, according to Diotima, to give birth not to images of virtue—because at the level of the Forms there are no images—but to true virtue (212a5–6).

KYDES: And that is so, because we come to know the virtues as they are, the virtues in themselves, by themselves, with themselves. That is, we come to know the virtues as not dependent on anything for their essence, an essence that is always and everywhere eternal, unchanging, and absolute. Each absolute essence, as Socrates said in the *Phaedo*, "exists by itself, remains the same, and never in any way admits of any change."[27]

All of the virtues arise from the Good, which can be known, but can't be named. So, is this the point of knowing the Good?

PLATO: Ah, a very good question, Kydes. And it brings us not only to our second question—How can the Good be known?—but also to a third: What is the value of knowing the Good? Answers to these questions can help us understand, then, why a society can only be virtuous or moral when kings and queens are philosophers or philosophers are kings and queens.

Still, before we get to these questions, consider this from the *Tao*:

> *If* [persons] *could remain centered on the Good*
> *All things would be in harmony.*
> *All people would be at peace,*
> *And the law would be written in their hearts.*[28]

DEMETRA: But can all persons ever come to know the Good, let alone remain centered on it? If they could, then we do not need philosopher kings or queens to rule us. We can rule ourselves.

---

27 Plato, *Phaedo*, 78d.
28. Lao Tzu, *Tao Te Ching* (trans. Mitchell), verse 37.

KYDES: I'm not clear on how you can start with one beautiful body and from that proceed upward to the Forms and the Good. How do we find these stairs, as Diotima describes these stages, let alone climb them and come to know Beauty itself?

PLATO: Socrates might help with that in what he offers next in our dialogue: the metaphor of the Divided Line.

10

Up the Divided Line and Out of the Cave

THE DIVIDED LINE

PLATO: Imagine a line, and, to match Diotima's stairs, we'll make it a vertical line. We shall divide that line into two unequal sections. The smaller section represents what we can know through our senses. The larger section represents what we can grasp intellectually, what we can know with our minds. Socrates describes these two sections as "*that which is visible and that which is intelligible*" (509d7). The intelligible section is larger because it is more real, closer to the Forms—that is, closer to the perfect and the ideal.

Next, using the same proportions, we shall divide each unequal section into similar unequal sections. There are now two sections of the visible world and two of the intelligible world. So, our line is divided into four unequal sections reflecting the same ratio.

In the visible sections we have what we can perceive through our senses, phenomena that are physical, empirical, and changing. In the lowest section of the visible, on the lowest stair, we find what we call the "least real"—that is, shadows of things; reflections of things, say, your face as reflected in water; and images, maybe something drawn or painted.

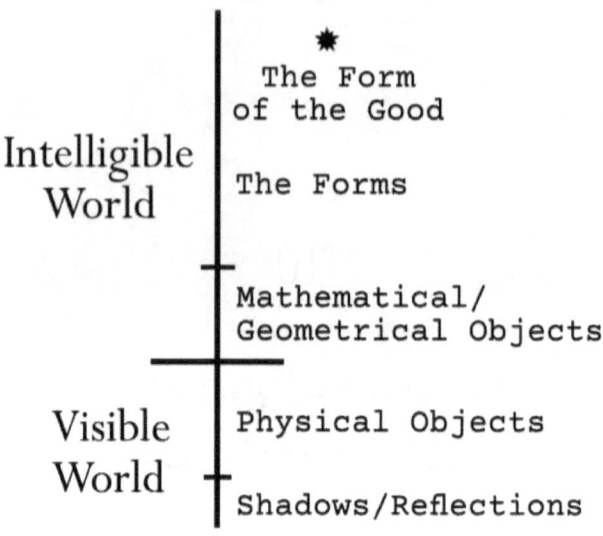

HERMIAS: Just to be clear, Plato, although the sections in the visible world refer to what we perceive through our senses, nevertheless this still involves us in using our minds, right?

PLATO: Say more, Hermias.

HERMIAS: Well, I can think of an image as well as see an image. I can imagine a smell as well as actually smell an odor.

PLATO: That is correct, and the mind is engaged to that extent. But only to that extent. When we hold an object, we learn about that object through our senses—how it feels, how it smells and tastes, an orange, for example. Based on this sensory information, we form beliefs about this object. Those beliefs may well be accurate, but they are limited to only sensory information.

KYDES: So, to return to the beginning of the analogy, if I draw a circle in the dirt, this would be an image and at the lowest visible level, since it is lower or less real than, say, an actual discus.

HERMIAS: And the subsection within the visible realm right above this level of shadows, the next stair above, would be the actual physical objects, like the discus.

PLATO: Correct.

HERMIAS: When we move above the visible section to the intelligible section, we get into the realm of ideas or thoughts about circles. We think in terms of definitions of a circle—a round shape where any point around its curve is equidistant from its center.

KYDES: That's the universal property of a circle, because it is what all circles have in common.

DEMETRA: Another way of saying this is that we now have a concept. This intelligible section is the realm of concepts or intellectual understanding.

PLATO: Correct, again. Socrates refers to the lowest subsection on the line as the realm of imagining (*eikasia*) and conjecture. The subsection above it, the realm of actual physical objects, he calls "belief" (*pistis*). You will not be surprised to hear, then, that the first subsection in the intelligible realm Socrates calls "thought" (*dianoia*).

DEMETRA: Not "understanding"?

PLATO: No. He reserves that term, *noēsis* or direct apprehension through intuitive insight, for the highest subsection on the Divided Line. This highest subsection is the realm of the Forms, which we understand as essences that are real but are independent of our minds, of our thoughts.[1]

Unlike the realm of the Forms, the level below, the level of thought, is the realm of mathematics and hypotheses. Mathematics and hypotheses can help us reach conclusions about what is seen within the visible world. Yet, mathematics and hypotheses can also help us ascend to first principles, toward the Forms.

HERMIAS: It depends, then, on which way you look—whether up the Divided Line or down the Divided Line. Are you trying to use mathematics to understand how to design and forge a better discus for the Olympics, or are you thinking about the nature of circles, about circles themselves?

KYDES: Let me try an example to see whether I'm grasping how the Divided Line works. Let's say I see a sculpture of a woman. I think that she is beautiful, and I ask the sculptor whether he used a living model.

---

1. *Epopteia* is another term for the direct apprehension of truth through the contemplation of the Forms.

He says that he did, and I meet her. To me she is even more beautiful than her image, the sculpture.

I see that there are other models who are beautiful too. I begin to think about what makes them all beautiful to me. Are they beautiful, as beautiful, to others as they are to me? I look at persons whom others think are beautiful, and I wonder what qualities make them beautiful. That leads me to ask whether beauty can reside outside of people. Landscapes can be beautiful; sunsets can be beautiful. What about ideas? Aren't ideas, aren't words in poems, described as beautiful?

What about ideas that underlie our laws and customs? If all of those can be described as beautiful, what are the qualities that constitute beauty in such diversity? Now I might think about proportionality or symmetry of features, whether in a face or a landscape or an idea. Then I begin to wonder about the beauty in these concepts of symmetry and proportionality themselves. Am I on my way to the Form of Beauty?

HERMIAS: I'd say that you are, Kydes. Let me use another example, but this time, it's an example of someone who doesn't do as you did. Let's take a carpenter as an example. He sets out to make a table, and not any ordinary table, but one that is beautiful and can serve as a magnificent centerpiece in any room. He makes drawings first, the images he will work from.

Of course, measurements and calculations are important in his work. He uses math to build his table. Because he wants it to be beautiful as well as functional, he makes exact cuts in the wood and takes precise measurements for the tongue-and-groove fittings so that they will be not just snug but also flush and flawless. He studies the best temperatures of hot water for bending wood. He experiments with methods for clamping and curving the wood for the table and the elegant, ornate, beautiful accompanying chairs.

As he becomes more experienced and skilled in his trade, he sees more and more the usefulness of math for his craft and in his business. But that insight, the thought about math's usefulness for business and his craft, doesn't take him beyond his woodwork. His interests in his business trap him on the Divided Line. The carpenter does not think of beauty beyond what he perceives in his table; his measurements and calculations do not take him into examining mathematics itself. He does not see the usefulness of math to move him toward first principles.

KYDES: Why doesn't he? Why doesn't this carpenter, as Plato says, reach beyond his hypotheses and use those hypotheses instead to travel up to a first principle, toward the Forms (511a2–4)? Why doesn't he turn his intelligible gaze and move up the Divided Line?

HERMIAS: Practice. He lacks practice in dialectic, in asking and answering questions, in inquiring, in arguing and refuting. That is the method, is it not, for ascending up the Divided Line?

PLATO: It is the method, Hermias, and Socrates agrees with you. He says that *"the power of dialectical discussion could reveal itself only to someone experienced in the subjects we described"* (533a7–8), such as mathematics and hypotheses. But if one uses those subjects only with a concern for

> *"human beliefs and appetites, with growing or construction, or with the care of growing and constructing things . . .* [then although] *they do dream about what is, they cannot see it while wide awake as long as they make use of hypotheses that they leave undisturbed and for which they cannot give any argument. After all, when the first principle is unknown, and the conclusion and the steps in between are put together out of what is unknown, what mechanism could possibly turn any agreement reached in such cases into knowledge?"* (533b34–c5)

KYDES: No mechanism could do this, for the dialectic is absent.

PLATO: Just so. It is only the power of dialectic that shows us that hypotheses are not first principles, but are stepping stones to take off from to reach

> *"the unhypothetical first principle of everything. Then having grasped this principle, it reverses itself and, keeping hold of what follows from it, comes down to a conclusion without making use of anything visible at all, but only of Forms themselves, moving on from Forms to Forms, and ending in Forms."* (513b3–c1)

HERMIAS: And this is understanding or knowing beyond thought. Thought, the activity of our minds, is intermediate between opinion, which is the visible world, and understanding, which is the world of the Forms.

DEMETRA: If I grasp the Socratic tetralogy, and we move down the Divided Line from the top, then at the highest realm, we know the Forms through our soul; that knowledge is direct apperception or *noēsis*. Going down the Line we arrive at thought or our minds. Below that is the visible world of sense perceptions housed in our bodies. The mind can take us up the Line or down the Line.

Nothing is lost by exercising philosophical education—that is, dialectic—to move up the Divided Line. We can still move down to the visible world and function within that world using our five senses and our minds. We don't lose imagination; indeed, because of what we have learned and seen in the intelligible realms, we might actually imagine better, more widely. Using dialectic enables us to transcend the visible realms but also include the visible realms, since we can return to them.

Our carpenter, as Hermias said, is stuck at the level of mind. He cannot move up the Divided Line to the eyes of the soul, because he uses hypotheses only to operate in and on the visible world, not thinking to turn his attention, to turn his mind, to the world of Being, of what is transcendent, eternal, and immutable. He could benefit from instruction in and the practice of dialectic.

PLATO: Socrates tells us, *"When the eye of the soul is really buried in a sort of barbaric bog, dialectic gently pulls it out and leads it upward . . . turning the soul around"* (533d2–4).

Recall what Socrates told us in the *Phaedo* about how dialectic operates: The soul learns best when none of the senses distracts it: *"neither hearing, nor sight, nor pain and pleasure, but when it is most by itself, taking leave of the body and as far as possible having no contact or association with it in its search for reality."*[2]

If thinking is itself an activity of the body—a kind of sense activity, as Hermias mentioned—then there must be a special kind of thinking connected to the soul freed of the body that brings us knowledge of the Forms. This is pure thought, which is our clumsy way of describing noetic knowing beyond our reasoning minds. Using this *"pure thought alone,"* we can track down *"each reality pure and by itself."* In this way, we can come to grasp *"a thing* [such] *as the Just itself . . . and the Beautiful and the Good."*[3]

DEMETRA: But isn't Socrates suggesting here that our carpenter could turn around, could use his understanding of mathematics and geometry to ascend the Divided Line and know the Forms? He's already thinking

---

2. Plato, *Phaedo*, 65c4–7.
3. Plato, *Phaedo*, 66a2–3, 65d4–7.

in terms of the universals of things, the definitions or abstractions that unite them. Why can't that thinking get him moving up the Line beyond conclusions to first principles?

KYDES: And if he can do that, if there is nothing phony like the Noble Lie to pretend that he's incapable, then why can't he come to practice dialectic? After all, as Deme said, if his soul can move into the intelligible section of the Divided Line and into the world of thought, why can't his soul move as well into the world of understanding, into the realm of the Forms?

PLATO: You are correct in your deduction or intuition that the Divided Line represents the four conditions of the soul. Understanding is its highest condition, thought is the second, belief the third, and imaging the last (513d6–e1). The carpenter seems to have at least three of those conditions and lacks only practice in dialectic to examine the fourth—understanding beyond thought.

KYDES: Yes, Plato, we can see the truth of that. And the introduction of the Divided Line does address the question that you left us with: How can we know the Forms? But in the city only the guardians have an education that prepares them for using dialectic. What about our carpenter, who seemingly has the wherewithal but not the impetus to ascend up the Divided Line? He has the capability to use arithmetic and calculation for his business, but he's denied the education that could lead the soul upward and compel him to investigate numbers themselves.

PLATO: I see the dilemma, but we are hardly at the end of our story. Socrates continues the dialogue with an allegory that might help us.

ALLEGORY OF THE CAVE

> "Imagine human beings living in an underground, cave-like dwelling, with an entrance a long way up that is open to the light and as wide as the cave itself. They have been there since childhood, with their necks and legs fettered, so that they are fixed in the same place, able to see only in front of them, because their bonds prevent them from turning their heads around. Light is provided by a fire burning far above and behind them. Also behind them, but on higher ground, there is a path stretching between them and the

> fire. Imagine that along this path a low wall has been built, like the screen in front of puppeteers above which they show their puppets.
>
> "Also imagine, then, that there are people along the wall, carrying multifarious artifacts that project above it—*statues of people and other animals, made out of stone, wood, and every material. And as you would expect, some of the carriers are talking and some are silent.*" (514a1–515a2)

HERMIAS: So, these people can see only what is projected as shadows on the wall in front of them. They can't even see their neighbors?

PLATO: That's correct.

KYDES: But they can hear one another, right?

HERMIAS: Still, the conversations will only be about what they see before them, what are cast as shadows. Since they cannot move their heads at all, any sound may seem to be coming from the shadows.

PLATO: Then, what these human prisoners would take for true reality is only the shadows of the artifacts passing by (515c1–2).

Now further imagine that one of these prisoners is freed from or breaks his bonds and

> "is suddenly compelled to stand up, turn his head around, walk, and look up toward the light. He would be pained by doing all these things and would be unable to see the things whose shadows he had seen before. What do you think he would say if we told him that what he had seen before was silly nonsense, but that now—because he is a bit closer to what is, and is turned toward things that are more—he sees more correctly? And in particular, if we pointed to each of the things passing by and compelled him to answer what each of them is, don't you think he would be puzzled and believe that the things he saw earlier were more truly real than the ones he was being shown?" (515c6–d7)

KYDES: Having spent so much time with the shadows, he would surely think that they were more real.

PLATO: And if someone compelled him to look at the fire itself, the light itself, would he not shield his eyes from the pain? Would he not then turn back toward the shadows—the things he can see and with which he is familiar—believing them to be really clearer than what he has been shown (515e1–4)?

HERMIAS: I see what's going on here. This freed prisoner is headed up the Divided Line. First, he only sees shadows, mere images, of what is carried past him, shadows cast by the fire onto the wall. That's the first level or section of the Divided Line. Then, he turns around and sees the fire that casts the shadows and the actual objects paraded by. If his eyes could adjust, he'd see the fire and the actual objects. He'd still be in the visible world, but in the realm of belief rather than below in the subsection of only images.

DEMETRA: What Hermias says seems clear enough. But who is doing all of this "compelling"—compelling him to stand up and turn around, compelling him to look at the fire directly?

PLATO: An interesting question, Demetra, and we will come to it. But, for now, let us go along with Socrates. Imagine now that someone drags him away from the cave, compels him up the rough, steep path to the entrance,

> "and does not let him go until he had dragged him into the light of the sun outside the cave. Wouldn't he be pained and angry at being treated that way? And when he came into the light, wouldn't he have his eyes filled with sunlight and be unable to see a single one of the things now said to be truly real?" (515e7–516a3)

KYDES: I'd say so! If his eyes pained him when he looked at the fire burning in the cave, imagine how they feel in sharp sunlight. He's in a world now where he is blinded by the sunlight.

PLATO: Of course. He is going to need time for his eyes to adjust to the bright light.

> "At first, he would see shadows most easily, then images of men and other things in water, then the things themselves. From these, it would be easier for him to go on to look at the things in the sky and the sky itself at night, gazing at the light of the stars and the moon, than during the day, gazing at the sun and the light of the sun." [After some time,] "he would be able to see the sun—not reflections of it in water or some alien place, but the sun just by itself in its own place—and be able to look at it and see what it is like." (516a4–b5)

Over time, he would be able to see that the sun governs everything in the visible world "*and is in some way the cause of all the things he and his fellows used to see*" (516b10–c2). At this point, do you think our prisoner would be relieved to be free of the cave and that vision of reality? In the cave one received prizes and honors for being the

> "sharpest at identifying the shadows as they passed by; and was best able to remember which shadows usually came earlier, which later, and which simultaneously; and who was thus best able to prophesize the future. Do you think that our man would desire these rewards or envy those among the prisoners who were honored and held power? Or do you think he would feel with Homer that he would much prefer to . . . go through any sufferings rather than share their benefits and live as they do?" (516c8–d6)

KYDES: This prisoner is up the Divided Line now, into the realm of thought, because as we saw with the analogy of the sun, the sun is to the things in the visible world as the Good is to the things in the intelligible world. Although our former prisoner is seeing the physical sun, it is a metaphor for what's up the Divided Line. He would much prefer, I think, to have the knowledge gained by moving up the Line—that is, outside the cave—rather than continue living in and among shadows only.

PLATO: Well said, Kydes. But we are not yet finished with the metaphor. Now imagine that

> "this man went back down into the cave and sat down in his same seat. Wouldn't his eyes be filled with darkness, coming suddenly out of the sun like that? [And] if he had to compete once again with the perpetual prisoners in recognizing the shadows, while his sight was still dim and before his eyes had recovered, and if the time required for readjustment was not short, wouldn't he provoke ridicule? Wouldn't it be said of him that he had returned from his upward journey with his eyes ruined, and that it is not worthwhile even to try to travel upward? And as for anyone who tried to free the prisoners and lead them upward, if they could somehow get their hands on him, wouldn't they kill him?" (516e2–517a6)

KYDES: They would treat him like the stargazer on the ship. But he is far more dangerous. He is not simply minding his own business. He is trying to free the prisoners and turn them around. He is threatening their whole way of seeing the world.

HERMIAS: He is trying to force people up the Divided Line when they are not ready.

PLATO: You three have already gleaned Socrates's meaning. He says:

> "This image, my dear Glaucon, must be fitted together as a whole with what we said before. The realm revealed through sight should be likened to the prison dwelling, and the light of the fire inside it to the sun's power. And if you think of the upward journey and the seeing of things above as the upward journey of the soul to the intelligible realm, you won't mistake my intention—since it is what you wanted to hear about.
>
> "This is how these phenomena seem to me: in the knowable realm, the last thing to be seen is the Form of the Good, and it is seen only with toil and trouble. Once one has seen it, however, one must infer that it is the cause of all that is correct and beautiful in anything, that in the visible realm it produces both light and its source, and that in the intelligible realm it controls and provides truth and understanding; and that anyone who is to act sensibly in private or public must see it." (517a8-c5)

HERMIAS: When Socrates says "see the Form of the Good," given what we said about it earlier, including what is written in the *Tao Te Ching*, he can only mean that one sees it with the eye of the soul, not even the mind's eye. Socrates said that the sun is the "*offspring of the Good*," not the Good itself, which is "*not being, but prior and superior to being*" (509b8).

PLATO: That is so. They see the Form of the Good. Such a "sight," let us call it "insight," captivates the former prisoners such that

> "the ones who get to this point are not willing to occupy themselves with human affairs, but that, on the contrary, their souls are always eager to spend their time above. I mean, that is surely what we would expect, if indeed the image I described is also accurate here." (517c8-d1)

Nor should we be surprised if having seen divine things like the Forms, a person who turns back to human affairs should appear completely ridiculous. With his sight well beyond the darkness around him, he is compelled either in the courts or elsewhere to compete within the shadows of morality and to dispute how things are understood by people who have never seen, say, the Form of Justice itself (517d3-e1).

KYDES: We must be careful here, Plato, because one needs to discern whether a person appears completely ridiculous because he is ignorant of the city's justice and its laws, because he is ignorant of logic and reason. Or is he ridiculous because he has seen the Forms of Justice and Wisdom and Beauty and cannot translate that adequately to those who do not know them?

PLATO: Exactly so, Kydes. Socrates says, *"Education isn't what some people declare it to be, namely putting knowledge into souls that lack it, like putting sight into blindness"* (518b7–c1). No. *"Education takes for granted that sight is there, but that the soul isn't turned the right way"* (518d5–6).

KYDES: So, the soul must be turned the right way, just as the freed prisoner turns to look first at the fire in the cave and then moves outside the cave and turns toward the sun.

HERMIAS: Then, an educator's role is to find those souls who can be turned the right way.

PLATO: Not quite, Hermias. Socrates says that our whole discussion *"shows that the power to learn is present in everyone's soul"* (518c4–5).

DEMETRA: YES! Thank you, Plato. I've been saying this practically from the very beginning: The foundation of this fevered city is a lie that your brothers should have challenged from the start. The idea that there are gold souls and silver souls and bronze souls is nonsense. Every soul can learn, because every soul has the three parts that Socrates outlined—reason, emotions, and needs and desires. There are no artisans who have only bodily desires and physical tasks, auxiliaries who only express a spirited nature and controlled emotions, and guardians alone who have the wherewithal to learn and rule. No. Every soul can learn and grow. Every person. No one is excluded.

PLATO: And Socrates tells us that education turns more than a part of the soul. Education turns body, mind, and soul:

> *"Just as an eye cannot be turned around from darkness to light except by turning the whole body, so this instrument cannot be turned around from that which is coming into being without turning the whole soul, until it is able to study that which is and the brightest thing that is—namely, the one we call the Good."* (518c6–d1)

If we can free a person's soul from its fixation on becoming, *"which has been fastened to it by feasting, greed, and other such pleasures and indulgences and which pulls the soul's vision downward, if we can turn the soul toward truly real things..."*

KYDES: ... turn the soul up the Divided Line, not down it ...

PLATO (nodding): ... then being rid of these lower things, if the soul turned to look at true things, to look up and move up the Divided Line as Kydes says, then this same soul will see truly real things most sharply (519a7–b4).

DEMETRA: All of that is a further indictment, I'm sorry to say, Plato, of both of your brothers and of the fevered city, because it is the desire for lavish living that launched this whole discussion in the first place.

KYDES: And that diverted us from talking of what Socrates described as the healthy city. Adeimantus and Glaucon are like the prisoners facing the wall, seeing only shadows.

DEMETRA: That's right. Plus, when they can turn and see the fire, then Plato's brothers are those fixated on feasting, greed, and pleasures.

HERMIAS: So, when Socrates introduces the healthy city, Glaucon and Adeimantus can turn from the shadows, but only so far as the fire in the cave. Thus, they insist on the fevered city, the luxurious city. What is missing, what is necessary to turn the whole soul around and head to the light outside the cave, is education leading to dialectic.

PLATO: As Socrates has said,

> "Eyes may be confused in two ways and from two causes: when they change from the light into the darkness, or from the darkness into the light. If anyone kept in mind that the same applies to the soul, then when he saw a soul disturbed and unable to see something, he would not laugh absurdly. Instead, he would see whether it had come from a brighter life and was dimmed through not having yet become accustomed to the dark, or from greater ignorance into greater light and was dazzled by the increased brilliance." (518a1–b4)

HERMIAS: Plato's brothers are confused in the second way: Socrates is moving them from *"greater ignorance into greater light."* Because they are at first dazzled by the increased brilliance, they seek refuge in what they already know, in the dim light of the cave. In this case, they dismiss the healthy city as a city fit only for pigs and seek refuge in the luxurious city, one that they already know. Socrates's mission is to turn their souls, their whole souls, around.

DEMETRA: Notice where this whole dialogue is taking place. Socrates goes with Glaucon to, and meets Adeimantus in, the Piraeus, which one might call a dark and shadowy part of Athens. The first line Socrates utters is "I went down to the Piraeus." Socrates, Glaucon, and Adeimantus are down the Divided Line, and the dialogue is Socrates's way of showing us how one might through dialectic be pulled up the Divided Line.

KYDES: That's a good way to phrase it, Deme. Socrates is not lecturing Glaucon and Adeimantus about the intelligible world and the Forms. He is guiding them along through the discussion, based on the questions he introduces and the responses they give.

HERMIAS: Just as Socrates has said, he isn't "*putting knowledge into souls that lack it, like putting sight into blindness*" (518b7–c1). No. Socrates takes "*for granted that sight is there, but that the soul isn't turned the right way.*" As a philosopher and educator, Socrates is simply turning their souls around.

KYDES: So, Glaucon and Adeimantus had not yet turned their souls enough, early on, to see the flaws in the fevered city and the Noble Lie.

DEMETRA: This is the role of the true philosopher and true teacher, one who helps us turn our souls around. This reflects what we cited earlier from Socrates in the *Phaedo*: Philosophers help us turn "*away from the body towards the soul*" (64e). As Plato reminded us, Socrates goes on:

> "The soul reasons best when none of the senses trouble it, neither hearing nor sight, nor pain nor pleasure, but when it is most by itself, taking leave of the body as far as possible having no contact or association with it in its search for reality."[4]

KYDES: May I try, Plato, to recapitulate from the perspective of this evening's dialogue what this allegory of the cave is showing us?

PLATO: Please do, Kydes.

KYDES: What we have in the allegory is a depiction of the fevered city and how it operates. The chained prisoners represent the artisan class, those with bronze in their souls. They work only at their crafts or occupations and see nothing but shadows.

Some few of them strain against their chains and are freed by guardians. These few are those Socrates describes as having souls that belong

---

4. Plato, *Phaedo*, 65c.

in a higher class, the silver souled. They then join with the silver souls, the auxiliaries. These are the persons in the cave who carry the artifacts and objects that cast the shadows that the prisoners see. By fulfilling such duties, the auxiliaries help the founders and guardians, the gold souls, who rule the cave.

Some few among the silver souls are able to walk the steep, rocky path out of the cave. Here those few see the actual sun, the Forms, and then bring that knowledge back down into the darkness and become "complete guardians" to rule over the cave, which is the city.

HERMIAS: Your description fits well, Kydes, with much that Socrates has said and has described. But it runs counter to what we have been saying just now; namely, that the mission is to turn attention away from the body to the soul. As Demetra has pointed out, Socrates himself says that the majority is capable of learning and thus of "turning the soul around." So, I don't think the allegory is so much about ruling the city, though that fits. It is more about education, about philosophers freeing the prisoners and turning their souls around.

KYDES: Explain that, Hermias.

HERMIAS: I'll try. The prisoners are all of us. We start out at the bottom of the Divided Line, seeing only reflections and shadows. We start off as children. Then, as we age and grow, teachers help us break free of the needs and desires of only the body and help us develop our minds. When we can do so, we turn around from the shadows and begin to study objects as they appear to our full senses. We operate on these objects by using concepts, mathematics, and other skills of thought. The fire burning in the cave is really the flame of inspection. More than that even, it is the flame of introspection or self-examination. This is the real fire that Prometheus brought to humans.

PLATO: Perhaps a recapitulation of that story would be welcomed here? (All nod, including Hermias.)

Prometheus and Epimetheus had been given the task of distributing the various powers and capacities to the animals created by the gods. But Epimetheus did so without any advice or ideas from Prometheus. When Prometheus looked at the distribution, he saw that the animals were adequately equipped to survive, but that humans were *"naked and unshod, without bedding and weapons."*[5]

So, to compensate the humans Prometheus *"stole from Hephaestus and Athena their technical wisdom, together with fire . . . ."*[6] Notice, here, that fire is not necessarily highlighted more than technical wisdom, but is separated from it. This fire is not just physical fire, as exists in the metaphor in the cave. As Hermias suggests, it is also the fire of self-reflection, and it is this fire that enables the person to use his mind to move up the Divided Line, to move in the cave from shadows to physical objects.

It could be, then, that this firelight ignites in the person the intuition that there is something more, much more, than what is illuminated in the cave. Indeed, as Socrates said earlier, that intuition comes like the spark when *"rubbing fire-sticks together"* (435a1–2). Then, like that spark, the sticks are ignited in a sudden flame. That spark, an internal spark, springs to life and brings forth an insight that perhaps there is something more. Insight born of intuition is a remembrance of the Good. Then . . . up the steep and rough road out of the cave itself and into the sunlight to know the Good.

The spark is born, then, in the soul of the person. But his soul is not fully awake. He must know the Forms. His soul yearns for that, to turn the internal spark into a fire, into an internal sun.

KYDES: In your account, Hermias, who are the persons carrying the artifacts and objects, who are aiding in the charade that the shadow world is the only reality?

HERMIAS: Well, they could be, like the auxiliaries, apprentice teachers meeting the prisoners or children where they are—those who can process at this point only shadows and reflections. Nevertheless, these apprentice teachers are available to free from their chains those who are ready.

But keep in mind that many adults, especially those in luxurious cities, are like the chained prisoners only able to see and work with shadows and images—needs and desires of the body. They aren't ready to turn around, and those carrying the objects that cast shadows are bringing them along slowly, for they are carrying real physical objects that could be seen when the prisoners finally turn.

---

5. Plato, *Protagoras*, 320d–321c.
6. Plato, *Protagoras*, 321d.

KYDES: Or these auxiliaries help keep them chained by perpetuating the charade.

HERMIAS: We don't know that this is a charade. We don't know that this isn't the best way to educate persons chained by their own physical needs and desires. Perhaps there is a significant order in which the objects that cast shadows are presented. Maybe there is some ascending order of complexity to them that spurs the prisoners up the Divided Line.

KYDES: Fanciful, Hermias.

HERMIAS: Perhaps. But let me go on.
   Having now traveled up the Divided Line into the intelligible realm, those apprentice teachers who can see and use the fire in the cave present the physical objects and artifacts that the prisoners can now see. This might be the best kind of education for stimulating some prisoners to try to turn around.
   Regardless, some of these freed prisoners, call them silver-souled if you like, are then compelled to move toward and up the steep path to the entrance of the cave. Having gone outside and experienced the Forms, the highest section of the Divided Line, these persons return to the cave, adjust to the darkness, and use their insight to oversee the operations within the cave. In short, those who exit the cave and return to it have reached the pinnacle not just of knowledge but also of education. They are dialecticians. They are philosophers who know how to introduce and use dialectic.

KYDES: So, for you, Hermias, Socrates isn't talking at all about ruling the city. He is talking about philosophers who, first, rule themselves and, second, "rule" by educating the people.

HERMIAS: Yes. Something along those lines.

DEMETRA: Both interpretations have merit, I think. But I'd like to offer one more interpretation, which, I acknowledge at the outset, might be a stretch.

PLATO: Please do, Demetra.

DEMETRA: I want to build on what Hermias said, especially on his point about the philosopher and self-rule. A philosopher who escapes the cave and sees the sun knows the Forms, yes, but he also knows his Being, knows the reality of his true Soul.

Why is this important? I think that the cave represents not the city and not pupils or even people. The cave is the philosopher's soul. Philosophers are ruling or governing their own souls.

Chained within the cave are the person's perceptions. Tap into one such perception, and the only insight that you can gain is shadowy and mute and shallow images. That is all the person can see and process. But at some point, the person's intellect comes awake. She wants to turn. Her attention, if only as and through one perception, breaks free from the chains.

Her attention, as that perception, then turns to the fire, which, as Hermias said, is the fire of self-examination. That perception now unchained is an actual object for her that her intellect, her cognitive powers, stimulated by the fire can examine and know. At this point, however, this perception is the examination only of physical properties and their extrapolations, since so much of her perception remains tied to her senses only.

Her mind is absorbed, first, in exploring physical objects and then in exploring the concepts underlying and surrounding physical objects. She is now moving into greater and greater abstractions and into deeper levels of thought. Her mind now compels her to even greater depths, which is symbolized by the rocky path, because, as we all know, thinking is hard work. She is now headed even further up the Divided Line.

Her thinking moves beyond *dianoia* into *noēsis*, as her soul, which is in charge of perceiving and conceiving, ascends the rocky path out of the cave. Once out and adjusted, she sees Reality as it is, Being as it is. The soul knows herself now to be not just her bodily senses bound to shadows and images, bound to the visible world. Nor does she know herself to be only the mind that can think noble and glorious thoughts, that can work through theorems and equations, work with philosophical concepts and dilemmas. The soul knows herself now to be eternal, unchanging, and transcendent.

KYDES: But who are those prisoners who remain in the cave? If the soul has freed herself and come to know the Forms, then who remains in the cave?

DEMETRA: Those could be aspects of herself that are not yet freed. Those could be additional images, perceptions, and impulses buried deep inside her that need to be released, examined, dropped, or integrated if the person hopes to grow into a flourishing, whole, and fulfilled person.

We don't develop all parts of ourselves at the same time. Our physical bodies develop before our intellects. Olympian athletes, especially gymnasts, have bodies that develop before their intellects. They can move in space gracefully and powerfully long before they can solve mathematical problems.

KYDES: So, what are these aspects or parts of the soul that remain chained inside the cave?

DEMETRA: That might depend on each individual. Some people's musical abilities show way before their cognitive abilities. Perhaps for that person the first awareness that turns is one's musical awareness, while other aspects of living remain hidden or chained. Or maybe someone's social and interpersonal skills develop first, are freed first. Turning and looking at the fire is how one then hones those skills. Or maybe it is one's self-awareness that matures first.

KYDES: So, according to you, what is chained are not persons but someone's ideas. The philosopher returns to the cave, the darkness, to free his ideas, turn them around, and examine them in the light of the fire, the light of introspection. Those that are judged worthy are then "thought" up the Divided Line to the pinnacle of the idea's very Form.

DEMETRA: I like that, Kydes. It reminds me of what Diotima said to Socrates: Some persons are pregnant not in body but in soul. What are they pregnant with? Diotima says that they are pregnant with the virtues, which they can bring forth. She says that they "*teem with ideas and arguments about virtue*," about what qualities constitute a virtuous man. The practice of such persons, then, is to educate others about the virtues.[7]

Regardless, we all have aspects of ourselves that don't develop in concert. Some precede others. Or we hold some ideas that are more worthy of pursuit and development than others. What the person does on returning to the cave from the outside is to use her knowledge and discernment to examine which aspects of her soul deserve to be further developed. This might be especially true of the virtues. They don't all arise simultaneously. Ideas about them must first be examined. Then, if found worthy, those ideas must be developed by habit and practice into a morality we can better live out. These are ideas, divine ideas maybe, that cannot be transmuted without divine insight.

---

7. Plato, *Symposium*, 208e3–209c3.

The "prisoners" that she is freeing are not persons of a city, but the captured and chained impulses and desires that live in the dark. These need to be freed, brought out of the world that is only shadows, into the light of recognition and reflection, the fire inside the cave. When impulses and desires are brought forth in this way, then they are seen in the same light—the fire within the cave or mind—that the very objects that cast the shadows are seen. They are, that is, examined and reflected upon by the light of our minds.

So the "people" carrying the objects whose shadows are projected onto the cave wall are not themselves people. They are instead our power of reflection. At first, when we are toddlers, the power is incipient, and we can only attend to images and shadows of objects. Then, as the power grows, we become restless, as our minds are chained to examining only superficial aspects of objects. We then turn and examine the physical objects themselves. Our minds continue to turn, and we move up the Divided Line toward the intelligible realm.

HERMIAS: That doesn't seem to be the way that Socrates describes the process. He says that the whole soul is turned, not parts of the soul.

DEMETRA: That's a good point, Hermias. So, maybe it's the whole soul that turns, but parts of the soul must still be worked on? Something like that?

PLATO: And what is it that initiates and perpetuates all of this turning?

11

Returning to the Cave

PLATO: Have you forgotten your concern from earlier, Demetra?

DEMETRA: My concern? I think that I have, Plato. Please remind me.

PLATO: You wanted to know who inside the cave is doing all of this "compelling."

DEMETRA: That's right! I did forget. Who is freeing the prisoners? Who compels them to turn around and see the fire? Most important, who compels them to travel up the steep and rocky path to get outside the cave?

KYDES: And why must they be compelled at all? Isn't each turn a move up the Divided Line, a move to greater insight and knowledge? Isn't that something they want?

HERMIAS: Yes, but remember, Kydes, each turn is painful and scary, so different from what one had experienced up to that point.

PLATO: Socrates reminds us that the task of the city's founders or philosophers is to compel the best natures to learn what was said to be the most important thing; namely, to make the ascent and see the Good. And when they have ascended and looked sufficiently, we must not allow them to do what they now have the ability to do (519c7–d2).

KYDES: What is that, Plato?

PLATO: To remain outside the cave and to refuse to act, because they thought that they were settled *"while still alive, in the faraway Isles of the*

Blessed (519c4–5) . . . [t]o stay there and refuse to go down again to the prisoners in the cave and share their labors and honors . . ." (519d4–5).

KYDES: You can understand their reluctance to return to the darkness from the land of brilliant sunlight and knowledge of the Forms.

PLATO: Indeed, Kydes, this is the very point that Glaucon makes: You mean to treat them immorally by forcing them to live a worse life when they could live a better one, when they could remain outside the cave (519d7–8).

KYDES: Glaucon certainly has a point. Besides, this raises the issue that we talked about earlier: Isn't it a violation of the city's morality to make the philosopher do two jobs? Recall that morality in the city was to have each class of person—gold, silver, or bronze—do their own jobs and no other jobs. Do your job, and don't meddle in other people's business (433a7). But here the ruler has two jobs: to govern or rule the city and to philosophize. Socrates says that there is a *"philosophic way of life"* (497e) and that philosophers in most cities live a quiet life *"and do their own work"* (496d), which is to philosophize.

HERMIAS: Then there is no problem if philosophizing is the sole job. This helps make my point: "ruling" the city means the philosopher educating the citizens.

DEMETRA: Or ruling over one's own soul.

PLATO: Here is how Socrates explains this compulsion to return to the cave: We will say to them, when we compel them to take care of the others and guard those others, that

> *"for your own sakes and for that of the rest of the city, we have bred you to be leaders and kings in the hive, so to speak. You are better and more completely educated than the others, and better able to share in both types of life. So each of you in turn must go down to live in the common dwelling place of the other citizens and grow accustomed to seeing in the dark. For when you are used to it, you will see infinitely better than the people there and know precisely what each image is, and also what it is an image of, because you have seen the truth about fine, just, and good things. So the city will be awake, governed by us and by you; not dreaming like the majority of cities nowadays, governed by men who fight against*

one another over shadows and form factions in order to rule—as if that were a great good.

"The truth of the matter is surely this: a city in which those who are going to rule are least eager to rule is necessarily best and freest from faction, whereas a city with the opposite kind of rulers is governed in the opposite way." (520b4–d4)

KYDES: This seems to support my view that the cave is, as is most obvious, the city. Yes, the philosopher returns to rule over it, which seems quite different, Hermias, from educating the populace. Even though Socrates says that all souls are capable of learning and growing, this city needs to be governed by those who know the Forms, even if the philosophers doing the governing must be compelled to rule.

And the compulsion seems to be persuasion—that is, these philosophers have been raised and educated by the city, by persons such as themselves. So, the philosophers have a moral obligation to return and give back to the city and to those who raised them. Besides, there is self-interest involved here as well. The philosophers don't want to live in a city—and they must live somewhere—where they are governed by those inferior to them.

HERMIAS: This sounds logical, Kydes, but I think there is a fundamental problem here.

KYDES: Oh? Do tell.

HERMIAS: Remember what it is that the philosopher comes to know once outside the cave. Recall what Socrates said in the *Phaedrus*: He sees what is real and what is true. He has

> "[a] view of Knowledge—not the knowledge that is close to change, that becomes different as it knows the different things which we consider real down here [in the cave]. No, it is the knowledge of what really is what it is. And when the soul has seen all the things that are as they are and feasted on them, it sinks back inside heaven and goes home."[1]

KYDES: You see, Hermias, "goes home." He goes back down into the cave.

---

1. Plato, *Phaedrus*, 247d7–e4.

HERMIAS: I don't dispute that part, Kydes. I acknowledge that he is compelled to return to the cave. But to do what? That is where we differ.

KYDES: To govern the city.

HERMIAS: I don't think so. Let's start here: Can the philosopher on returning to the city, going down into the cave, now throw the javelin the distance of an Olympic champion? Can the philosopher now write better plays than the greatest poets? Can he solve all the mathematical problems stumping our best mathematicians? Has his knowledge of the Forms provided those skills?

KYDES: No, but we don't expect him to do any of that.

HERMIAS: Precisely. Nor should we expect him to know the best laws for governing a city. We should not expect him to know how best to settle divorce and inheritance cases, which buildings to tear down and which to repair, or which taxes to levy this year. For the philosopher, ruling isn't about creating the perfect sewer system or even a better sewer system. That isn't the knowledge that the philosopher has. At the most, applying morality as it is might mean knowing how to create the right circumstances and identifying the right people to make the judgments necessary to get good answers, proper answers, to those kinds of issues.

The philosopher's knowledge is about the nature of Reality and Being. Therefore, his applicable knowledge pertains to dialectic and how to instruct about and lead persons to virtue, true virtue. That requires knowledge of how to use dialectic, and that requires philosophy and requires teaching.

DEMETRA: Recall what Socrates says in this dialogue:

> "For surely, Adeimantus, the man whose mind is truly fixed on eternal realities has no leisure to turn his eyes downward upon the petty affairs of men, or be filled with envy and hatred by competing with people. Instead, he fixes his gaze upon the things of the eternal and unchanging order . . . and tries to become as like them as he can." (500b7–c3)

"Tries to become as like them as he can." That is to be "as ordered and divine as a human being can become" (501c6–8).

PLATO: In the dialogue, Socrates now asks this: How do we lead people up to the light? It is not a matter of flipping a coin, but is, as we have said, "*of turning a soul from a day that is a kind of night in comparison to the true day—that ascent to what is, which we say is true philosophy*" (521c2–6).

HERMIAS: That's what I've been saying—to turn souls around and lead them up the Divided Line toward the Forms, just what Socrates in the dialogue is doing with Glaucon and Adeimantus. That's what their ruling would be. Their obligation to the city is the same: to use dialectic to turn as many souls as they can toward the light.

KYDES: Is that obligation really the compulsion that brings them back down into the city? After all, the city is based on the Noble Lie and the myth of the metals. The last thing the founders of the city want is for philosophers to come down into it and start turning souls willy-nilly toward the light. That could result in uncovering the Lie. That would be disruptive to the functioning of this city, to the classes on which its functioning depends. Look at the price Socrates paid for practicing philosophy in Athens. Why, then, would the city compel philosophers to return to the city at all if it isn't to fulfill the obligations to govern?

HERMIAS: How is a philosopher, one who has come to know the Good and the Forms, supposed to govern the city as it is depicted in the allegory? Is his duty now to perpetuate this charade of trapped people and shadows cast on the wall, which is what your position amounts to, Kydes?

Finally, how can any of that be moral—keeping some or most chained, freeing a select few, and marching objects along the parapet so that shadows are cast? Are thousands to be relegated to a permanent shadow world for the sake of a lie about metals in the soul?

DEMETRA: I don't think it's the rulers of the city who compel the philosophers or even their sense of duty to the city that compels them. It may not even be fellow philosophers. It is philosophy itself that compels them. They are "lovers of wisdom." It is that love, *philia*, that compels them. *Philia* is a sublimated, even a sublime, form of passion, one that relies strongly on mental stimulation, curiosity, satisfaction, and pursuit—the love of thinking, creating, and problem-solving.

KYDES: You mean *eros*, don't you, Deme? Not *philia*. Socrates states clearly in the *Symposium* that it is *eros* that drives us up the ladder of love to the Form of Beauty.[2]

---

2. Plato, *Symposium*, 210–12.

DEMETRA: It might be *eros* that drives us toward Beauty itself and even to see the Beauty of the Forms themselves, but I follow Socrates in the *Phaedrus* where he describes humans as driven by two principles. The first is the innate desire for pleasures; the second is "*our acquired judgment that pursues what is best.*"[3] When these two principles clash, then sometimes "*desire takes command in us and drags us without reasoning toward pleasure.*"[4] That desire is *eros*. Yet at other times, "*judgment is in control and leads us by reasoning toward what is best.*"[5] This is *philia*.

If it is *eros* that drags us up the rocky path out of the cave, then would we not be captured by the pleasure of what is seen rather than by coming to a recognition of and knowledge about what is "the best"? *Eros* is centered in and directed toward the body. It is the crudest and easiest form of love. *Philia*, on the other hand, is centered in the mind and pursues what is best.[6]

So, first *philia* compels the philosophers to turn their souls and to head up the path out of the cave. Then it is the insight that the Good is not separate from the world of thoughts and objects. The Good is found there as much as it is found on the Isles of the Blessed. It is simply easier to live on the Isles, to be absorbed in and by the Good.

Nevertheless, the Good cannot be fully lived by one who continues to live in the body and live with her mind unless she returns to integrate her insights into all aspects of her life. Her knowledge of Being, of Reality, of the Good, compels her, then, to return to the rougher path, the path of humans living in the world, for she is one of them. After all, even a philosopher who knows the Good cannot exist without food, shelter, and sleep. For those goods, we may well need to rely on others. Philosophers still live in the world and need to learn to live in the world that they had just left and now know to be false. What compels them back down into the cave? It is the need to live in the world and to do so sanely. For the sake of that sanity they need to clear their caves of bad ideas, of false ideas, and bring to their minds the clarity, beauty, and compassion that the Forms bestow.

So, the philosopher returns to integrate the Good into all aspects of her life. If the cave is indeed her own soul, as I have suggested, then she

---

3. Plato, *Phaedrus*, 237d7-8.
4. Plato, *Phaedrus*, 237e2-4.
5. Plato, *Phaedrus*, 238c4.
6. *Philia* could also be conceived as *eros* transformed, from sensory passion (even lust) into the pull and push toward wisdom and supra-sensible knowledge.

seeks to live her life in the body as an expression of the Good integrated within her soul. She lives her life as the embodiment of that which is both beyond all forms and simultaneously in and of all forms. And, if we follow Hermias, the philosopher returns not just as a model for others of an integrated soul, but also as an educator to integrate the Good into the thoughts and lives of others.

HERMIAS: And if we follow Deme, and it is *philia* that compels them, if it is the philosophers' passionate love of wisdom that drives them, then it might be a transformed *philia* that compels them back into the cave. This transformed *philia* is a combination of passion and insight. It is compassion for those persons still in the cave and a need to help those persons escape from their chains.[7]

KYDES: But Socrates is clear that it is someone who compels the person up the steep path and outside the cave, someone who drags him by force and drags him into the sunlight (515e5–6). It isn't *eros* or even *philia* or something internal that does the work.

DEMETRA: *"Drags him by force."* What do you think that force is, Kydes? Do you think that the philosopher, who might be short like you and slight like me, physically drags everyone up the slope and into the sunlight? Isn't it more likely that the force that does the compelling is dialectic? Isn't *philia* the force that first draws the soul to dialectic?

PLATO: In the *Tao Te Ching*, Lao Tzu asks: *"Can you love people and lead them without imposing your will?"*[8] If so, how can that be done? If not, then are you even a teacher if you must impose your will?

True philosophy, we can agree, is what turns the soul and then draws the soul from the realm of becoming to the realm of being, the realm of what is. Certainly, love has a significant role to play in a person's education. Notice that we begin education with movement and physical development. Some persons' love or passion remains focused on that level. Next, we introduce music and poetry. These subjects also capture some students' love, and they may exhibit little if any interest in the next subjects such as mathematics. Even those who do love

---

7. In the Middle Ages, Christians described this love as *agape*, brotherly love or spiritual love, love in its most sublime form and a counter to *eros*, sensual or sexual love. It is love of the soul by the soul, a kind of universal love. From *agapâō/agápi*, Greek for "to love."

8. Lao Tzu, *Tao Te Ching* (trans. Le Guin), 13.

mathematics, like our carpenter, may fail to use it as a system for moving toward Being. Is the love involved in the pursuit of knowledge and the virtues a form, as Demetra says, of *philia*, a passionate and intimate type of love?

HERMIAS: Perhaps the answer lies in combining my view with Deme's view. The philosophers see and feel their duty through their compassion for those trapped in the shadows and the dim light of the fire inside the cave.

Compassion creates an internal bond between teacher and student, and the teacher sees that teaching the students in the cave is a kind of liberation for both teacher and student. No hike from the cave to the light is possible without *"winged steeds,"* and here those steeds are the teacher (external) and *philia* (internal) that drive the student up the rocky path, up the Divided Line: *"The natural property of a wing is to raise that which is heavy and carry it aloft to the region where the gods dwell."*[9]

DEMETRA: If the philosopher comes to know the Form of morality and the Forms of the virtues—that is, know these as they are in essence—then how can that knowledge be used or expressed or made real unless it is exercised? Dialectic does not seem complete until the philosopher has returned to the cave. The dialectical method transcends but retains all below it, and now that which is below—that which is visible and becoming—is understood in the light of the Forms.

Hence, now knowing the realm of the Forms, integrating insight concerning the realm of Being into one's understanding of the world of becoming is the dialectical task. The task is no longer just to bring oneself to the realm of the Forms. It is to use that knowledge in the visible world below. Only the philosopher who knows the Forms can now know that there is a cave and that the visible world, the physical world, is a world only of shadows and physical objects. Those in the cave, not knowing the Forms, cannot see the cave and its shadows for what they are. Indeed, they cannot see the cave at all. Only the philosopher, having stepped outside the cave, can help them see the light, and that help is an act of morality. Give people their due by helping them see that the sensible world is not Real, not really Real.

KYDES: So, dialectic is not complete until the philosopher has returned to the cave. Hermias's "compassion" enters here. When *philia* or passion

---

9. Plato, *Phaedrus*, 247c.

transforms through knowledge of the Forms into com-passion, then *philia* goes back down the Divided Line for the purpose of bringing others up that Line to the light, the sun, the transcendent. This makes the philosopher's return to the cave a selfless act.

HERMIAS: I think that it is both selfless and self-interested. The philosopher returns knowing the virtues and morality, and he wants to exercise both. Morality looks both ways—inside oneself and outside to behaviors toward others. Justice, for example, is an interactive virtue. As such, it cannot be exercised in isolation. The philosopher cannot be just, therefore, without returning to the cave, to the visible world.

DEMETRA: To turn this idea even more transcendental: When someone knows the Forms, then she sees that what we are in essence, our Being, is no different from what others are. We are all the same Being. Therefore, returning to the cave is not to be absent from the grand Soul, the single Soul, the universal Soul, the Form of the Soul, that we all are. Helping to bring others to the light, to the realm of the Forms, is helping free none other than ourselves—manifestations of our Self, the one universal singular Self.

KYDES: So, the act of returning to the cave is nothing but an act of self-interest. In helping others, we help ourselves?

DEMETRA: Yes, depending on how you understand the idea of "self" in "self-interest." There are no singular isolated selves parading about the shadow realm as individuals, even individuals within the social ethos of the polis. Instead, this is an insight from the Absolute, the Good: There is only one Self, and the philosopher's duty is to help people awaken to that realization, that Reality. Therein lies the excellent life for all of us.

What Socrates says in the *Timaeus* is, I think, reminiscent of this:

> "[The] *motions that have an affinity to the divine part within us are the thoughts and revolutions of the universe. These, surely, are the ones which each of us should follow. We should redirect the revolutions in our heads that were thrown off course at our birth.*"[10]

By this I think he means that our souls must remember and thereby know the Forms and the divine that are now entombed in the body. Socrates goes on to say that we redirect our thinking in the right direction

---

10. Plato, *Timaeus*, 90c8–10.

> "*by coming to learn the harmonies and revolutions of the universe, and so bring into conformity with its objects our faculty of understanding, as it was in its original conditions. And when this conformity is complete, we shall have achieved our goal: that most excellent life offered to humankind by the gods, both now and forevermore.*"[11]

What kind of excellent life is this?

> "*If a man has seriously devoted himself to the love of learning and to true wisdom, if he has exercised these aspects of himself above all, then there is absolutely no way that his thoughts can fail to be immortal and divine. And to the extent that human nature can partake of immortality, he can in no way fail to achieve this.* [By] *constantly caring for his divine part as he does, keeping well-ordered the guiding spirit that lives within him, he must indeed be supremely happy.*"[12]

On one level, then, the philosopher doesn't have to return to the cave, because his happiness is found in communing with the Forms, with what is immortal and divine. On another level, he must return to the cave, because his happiness is now seen to be linked always and deeply with the happiness of all others, because those others can have the same harmonies within them that align with the divine. All others have the same immortal origins and are an aspect of the divine Self, just as the philosopher is.

The philosopher's task is to help others redirect the revolutions in their heads toward the divine so that they, too, can recognize the immortal divinity within them and live happy lives. That is the compulsion: The philosopher cannot be happy unless he is bringing others to that happiness. This is a love of or for humanity, which is a love for the one Self that is all of us. Recall what Socrates said in this dialogue: The task is not to make any single person happy, but to make the whole city happy. What is a city but its population?

KYDES: But why should there be only one Self, even one Soul? We are all different in appearance, in interests, in goals, in thoughts. Why think we are all the same Self or Soul?

---

11. Plato, *Timaeus*, 90d3–8.
12. Plato, *Phaedrus*, 90b6–c6.

DEMETRA: We are different only in what we see and think within the cave. But in the sunlight outside the cave, where we know and commune with the Forms, we are all divinely the same. We are the Form of Soul.

HERMIAS: Do you know that there is such a Form?

DEMETRA: We know that the soul is such a Form. Socrates certainly discusses that enough. It is what ascends the Divided Line; it is what the dialectic turns around. We all have souls. Those souls are descended from the Good, the Absolute Unmanifest, and must manifest first as an archetype, as a Form. How can we not, then, all be constituted as part of the single, perfect, universal, eternal, unchanging Soul? If we have souls and we are constituted by the Good, by all of that, how can we not share in or be the same Soul?

Recall what Socrates said in the *Phaedrus*: When raised up, the soul can see "*what is outside heaven. The place beyond heaven . . . is without color and without shape and without solidity, a being that really is what it is.*"[13] This is the essence of being, prior to content. The first "content" that we see is when our soul's gaze moves from what is outside heaven to what is first apprehended. This is knowledge of what is "*true*" and "*real.*" This knowledge of seeing things correctly permits us to be "*as perfect as perfect can be . . .* [as one] *draws close to the divine*" (249c8–d5). How is this not true of every soul? That perfection, manifested in flesh, is multifarious and also expressive of one Soul. In the Forms we find real Beauty and Wisdom and Being. How is there not also Soul, the singular Form of Soul?

KYDES: What we see here in the visible world, then, is the content of individual souls or our experiences gained through living in this changing world?

DEMETRA: I think so. Is your soul perfect for you, or is it perfect, period? In the *Phaedo* Socrates claims that "*just as the* [Forms] *exist, so our soul must exist before we are born.*"[14] If our souls exist before we are born, then they must exist in the same reality as the Forms themselves, which makes our souls eternal and perfect. In the realm of the Forms is there a Form for Kydes's soul or for Soul? Once an individual soul steps

---

13. Plato, *Phaedrus*, 247c2–d1.
14. Plato, *Phaedo*, 76e2–4.

down from the Form and enters the body, then perfection is hidden and eternity is forgotten.

PLATO: Let us get back to the dialogue, for I think that Socrates addresses your concerns both about compulsion and about what ruling might mean. He says that our rulers, however you now interpret that term, must undergo strenuous and dedicated practice in dialectic. When they have had sufficient exercise in that endeavor, then

> "you must make them go down into the cave again and compel them to take command in matters of war and the other offices suitable for young people, so that they won't be inferior to the others in experience. And in these offices, too, they must be tested to see whether they will remain steadfast when they are pulled in different directions or shift their ground." (539e3–540a1)

KYDES: If Socrates isn't talking about the actual city and its political matters, then what is he talking about when mentioning "*matters of war and these offices*"?

HERMIAS: He's talking about going into the world of desires and luxuries and temptations to see whether the philosopher, in light of them, can maintain his focus on dialectic and the Forms. Men inside the cave have only a meager vision, say, of justice. They are content to argue in the cities, the courts, and the assemblies about the shadows of justice that this meager vision casts. Can the man of true knowledge, now back in the cave, transcend these chains of conventional thought and abstraction and maintain his vision of the sunlight?

The "*matters of war*" refer to civil war, a war between those who want luxuries, like Glaucon and Adeimantus, and those who have different, and I would say "loftier," values and goals.

DEMETRA: Or Socrates could mean an internal civil war—that which within pulls the philosopher toward the material life or that pulls her up the Divided Line to the transcendent.

KYDES: And compulsion? Who do you think is making them go down again into the cave? Who compels them to take command? We're back to that question.

HERMIAS: And I'll repeat what I said earlier. It is their teachers who compel them. Remember, those who have exited the cave wish to remain in the sunlight, not in the shadows. They must be forced to return to the cave to test themselves to see whether they are ready to teach philosophy and dialectic.

DEMETRA: In one aspect, I agree with Hermias. Those outside the cave must be compelled to return. But like the internal civil war, compulsion is an internal drive, their *philia*, that compels them back down. Only when they have settled the civil war, when they have integrated their insights from the sunlight into their physical life, are they ready to withstand the stresses and challenges of those who are committed to the luxurious life and all that that entails.

PLATO: I wonder whether Socrates doesn't agree with all three of you. He says,

> "And once they have seen the Good itself, they must use it as their model and put the city, its citizens, and themselves in order throughout the remainder of their lives, each in turn. They will spend most of their time doing philosophy, but, when his turn comes, each must labor in politics and rule for the city's sake, not as something fine, but rather as something that must be done. In that way, always having educated others like themselves to take their place as guardians of the city, they will depart for the Isles of the Blessed and dwell there." (540a7–b7)

KYDES: You're right, Plato. He says all three—city, citizens, and themselves. The philosopher works on all three simultaneously. In addition, Socrates says, "Each must labor in politics and rule for the city's sake." What could be clearer than that?

HERMIAS: What do you imagine the philosopher is going to do when he returns to this city now knowing the Good? Is he going to plop down next to those who are chained and help people understand the shadows, how they move, and what they say? Will he help organize the objects as they pass along the parapet? Is either of those ruling? Both simply reinforce the shadow world, which the philosopher now knows is false, nothing but images and phantoms. Instead, the philosopher returns to liberate his people. Manipulating and expatiating on the shadows won't do that. And all aspects related to political ruling are related to that kind of manipulation and ordering.

Unless the repetition of "city" is an ongoing test of Plato's brothers, I don't see how that formulation, Kydes, gets us anywhere. We have already argued, and I think agreed, that this fevered city is immoral from the beginning and remains so. Can the philosopher transform this immoral city into a moral one by laboring in politics? Perhaps laboring in politics means, as Socrates himself shows, that philosophers must operate as gadflies and try to turn the souls of citizens away from the world of corruption and luxuries and temptations—all of which he summarizes by one word, the "city"—and toward the Forms. After all, Socrates himself never held political office.

DEMETRA: Or if the term "city" stands in for "soul," then the philosopher is navigating and guiding himself through these distractions and temptations and corruptions that reside within him. That is labor. Internal harmony must be attained and maintained. As Socrates said, *"He regulates well what is really his own and rules himself"* (443d3–4).

KYDES: Still, he is clear: Those who know the Good educate others like themselves to take their place as guardians—as philosophers—of the city. When they've educated other philosophers in dialectic, then they can retire to the Isle of the Blessed. So . . . I guess I'm persuaded by our discussion that the city itself, immoral from the outset, can't be the true setting. I'm with Hermias. Socrates must be referring to the obligations of those who know the Good to instruct others to turn their souls.

And I guess I agree with Demetra that those philosophers must also continue to work on their own souls. Turning souls, then, is necessary but not sufficient. More work needs to be done, and part of that work is internal as well as external, as well as teaching others. Philosophers do both—help others to learn to rule themselves, to balance and harmonize their souls, as the philosopher himself continues to balance and harmonize his own soul.

PLATO: Now what do you think about what Socrates says next?

> *"When one or more true philosophers come to power in a city—people who think little of present honors, regarding them as illiberal and worthless, who prize what is right and the honors that come from it above everything, and who consider morality as the most important and most essential thing, who serve morality and foster it—then they will set their city in order."* (540d3–e3)

KYDES: I think this is just what we have been saying. But if Socrates has in mind here the fevered city that he's been discussing, then the philosopher committed to morality, truth, and the Good is going to meet the same fate as those philosophers in the allegory who returned to the cave and were torn to pieces by those enslaved to pleasures and luxuries. He'll meet the same fate as Socrates did in Athens.

HERMIAS: But that can't be the city that Socrates has in mind, because it is a corrupt city, built on the myth of the metals and all the wobbly elements that follow from it, as we've discussed. He says "*a city*," not "the city we've been discussing."

KYDES: Yet, what if Socrates means that city, the fevered city? Can it be set in order?

PLATO: Socrates continues by telling us how that might happen. To set the city in order by those who serve morality and the Good requires sending

> "everyone in the city who is over ten years old . . . into the country. They [i.e., philosophers] *will take over the children, and far removed from current habits, which their parents possess, they will bring them up in their own ways and laws, which are the ones we described before. And with the city and constitution we were discussing thus established in the quickest and easiest way, it will itself be happy and bring the greatest benefit to the people among whom it comes to be.*" (540e5–541a6)

(All three students burst out laughing.)

PLATO: Why do you laugh?

KYDES: It's a giveaway, Plato! This is a firm admission that the city as presented has failed. All of that talk about classes of citizens assigned by their metals obviously didn't result in a settled city, a moral city. Otherwise, why the need to send everyone out of it and leave only the impressionable children? And will these children follow the metal classifications, or are all now considered equal? I could live with the latter.

HERMIAS: You know who can't live with the latter, Kydes? The artisans, the bronze souls who have raised their families themselves. They aren't going to stand for someone removing them from their children. Even the auxiliaries, the silver soldiers ordered to exile everyone over ten, won't stand for that, since their mission is to protect all the children of the city as if they were "*fathers and mothers*" (457b–466d) to them all. Also, every level of person over ten, child or adult, is removed from the city. So, of what value now is this mythic classification of people? The Noble Lie is overturned. There will be outright resistance. It's an invitation to rebellion, because the parents will fight to keep their children and restore their families. Talk about civil war!

DEMETRA: This won't be much of a civil war. The auxiliaries aren't going to remove the children. They're exiled themselves. Socrates says that only the philosophers remain. Who's left to defend the city when those over ten organize to take the city? Only the philosophers? Or are all of the adults, including the auxiliaries, so entranced by the philosophers that they won't rebel?

PLATO: Socrates tells us in the dialogue that this is not the only way to or reason for civil war.

KYDES: What is another way or another reason?

PLATO: As with everything finite, the constitution of this city must decay. Socrates says that it will happen in the following way:

> "The people you have educated to be leaders in your city will, by using rational calculation combined with sense-perception, nonetheless fail to ascertain the periods of good fertility and of infertility for your species. Instead, these will escape them, and so they will sometimes beget children when they should not. . . . Geometrical numbers control better and worse births. And when your rulers, through ignorance of these births, join brides and grooms at the wrong time, the children will be neither good natured nor fortunate. The older generation will choose the best of these children, but they are unworthy nevertheless. . . . Hence rulers chosen from among them won't be able to guard well the testing of the golden, silver, bronze, and iron races. The intermixing of iron with silver and bronze with gold will engender lack of likeness and unharmonious inequality, and these always breed war and hostility wherever they arise. Civil war, we declare, is always and everywhere 'of this lineage.'" (546a1–547a3)

KYDES: The philosopher kings and philosopher queens, with all their education and breeding, get the math wrong. What kind of education is that? As we've been saying, not much of an education at all.

Also, they certainly haven't retained much of what they were supposed to learn about the Divided Line. They are mired in the quotidian and use mathematics only to fiddle with the functioning of the city and not with bringing the higher knowledge of the Forms into the city. An emphasis on math alone cannot save the city. Missing here is philosophy, the pull of dialectic up the Divided Line. It's not through math that we attain knowledge of the Forms. That path is beyond math and into *noēsis*.

HERMIAS: Don't get pulled into trying to rationalize any of this, Kydes. As we've been saying, this fevered city is diseased and troubled from the outset, with its crazy myth of the metals. Here Socrates is pointing out the obvious to Glaucon and Adeimantus: The city can't survive regardless of how clever at mathematics the rulers are. It's all nonsense, start to finish, and here Socrates is offering a splendid gloss on its collapse. The foundation of the city rests on a Lie. Where is that Lie on the Divided Line?

DEMETRA: Hermias is right. The fevered city fails because it never was a moral or just city. It cannot be reformed and thus cannot be saved from the Noble Lie. Even if you tried to save it by starting anew with those under ten who can all be raised the proper way, in the end the failures of rulers will always bring it down. Nothing can save the fevered city, because it is diseased from the beginning. But as Hermias said, the parents will organize and fight against this regime. Besides, what kind of people would countenance abandoning their children in this way?

KYDES: Plato, how did Glaucon and Adeimantus react to all of this?

PLATO: Glaucon says, removing everyone over ten is *"the quickest and easiest way"* (541a7) to create a city ruled by philosopher kings and queens.

(The three look at one another.)

KYDES: Seriously? What kinds of students of philosophy are your brothers?

DEMETRA: And what kinds of people would accept this plan? Don't your brothers recognize that Socrates is telling them, in the most convoluted fashion, that nothing can be done? Not even complex mathematical formulas and rational calculation by trained philosophers can save a diseased city from its inevitable collapse.

PLATO: This is where Socrates goes next: *"Haven't we said enough, then, about this city and the man who is like it? For surely it is clear what sort of person we will say he has to be"* (541b2-3).

KYDES: It is clear what sort of person would accept and resemble this city, and that isn't good.

12

Are the Forms a Noble Lie?

DEMETRA: It is good that Socrates is returning us to the original questions posed by Glaucon and Adeimantus: What is morality in itself, and what is the moral person? After all, Socrates moved us toward morality in a city, because he claimed that it was easier to see morality there than in an individual. But it's become clear, I think, throughout our discussion that this city was a failure from the beginning. Besides, in this dialogue Socrates isn't after the souls of states. He is concerned about the states of souls, of individuals, and how they can be moral.

KYDES: Yet, based on your interpretation of the allegory of the cave, Deme, Socrates has not really taken us into a city. For you, isn't the fevered city really just a single person, a fevered man or woman in pursuit of and even fixated on luxuries?

PLATO: According to the *Chandogya Upanishad*, a foreign sacred text, the city could be a metaphor for the body, and a house within that "city" would be the heart. "*Within it are heaven and earth, the sun, the moon, the lightning, and all the stars. Whatsoever is in the macrocosm is in the microcosm. All things that exist, all beings and all desires, are in the city of Brahman*" or the Good, as we have referred to it. The heart of each person is where Brahman, the Good, resides within all persons. That is, the Hindu seers say, "*the true city of Brahman*."[1]

KYDES: What is this, Plato?

---

1. Prabhavananda, *Upanishads*, 119–20.

DEMETRA: I love the metaphor, of course, but what text are you quoting?

HERMIAS: Before you divert us onto this new path, if, indeed, you are doing that, I want to ask you a question, Plato.

PLATO: By all means, Hermias. If that is acceptable to Demetra and Kydes? (They nod.)

HERMIAS: How do we know that the entire theory of the Forms and of the Good isn't just another Noble Lie?

KYDES: Why would you think that?

HERMIAS: Because on its face the ideas sound preposterous—an actual realm of perfect "types" that are immutable and eternal—which some can come to know first hand but not by reasoning or language.

PLATO: You mean such ideas as this, Hermias: The Good is "*an invisible and characterless sort of thing . . . and* [yet] *in a most perplexing way is intelligible*"?[2]

HERMIAS: Just like that Plato. We've heard several such ideas tonight, and before tonight. It sounds like the Noble Lie and the myths of the metals—some fanciful tale to anoint a select few as rulers based on special knowledge that they allegedly have that others do not and, perhaps, cannot have.

KYDES: So, Socrates is lying, Hermias?

HERMIAS: Well, he's done it before.

DEMETRA: When he's done so, he has told us so, as with the Noble Lie. That's not the case with the Good and the Forms. Indeed, he's told us how we can know the Forms, and some of that corresponds to experiences that each of us has already had. Plus, it helps to make sense of Socrates's own experiences and behaviors.

PLATO: That is a good point, Demetra, but let us pursue for just a little Hermias's very good question.

Is it fair to say, as Socrates does, that "*virtue is a kind of knowledge*" and that "*virtue is itself something good*"?[3]

---

2. Plato, *Timaeus*, 51b.
3. Plato, *Meno*, 87c4, 87d2.

DEMETRA: I think it is, Plato.

PLATO: Good. Then we want to know what kind of knowledge virtue is and how we can come to know it. To this point in our dialogue this evening, Socrates has told us that we can come to know virtue-in-itself through dialectic. We can come to know the Forms of virtues.

Hermias questions whether there is any such thing as the Form of Beauty or Justice or Wisdom. We might agree that these are qualities or virtues that we wish to know. These are qualities or virtues that we can know as they relate to thoughts and behaviors that we see in our everyday lives, or we can know them as ideals that we pursue or try to model our behavior after. Such a position, of course, does not rely on anything related to the Forms.

On the other hand, if there is a realm known as the Forms, and if someone did know the Forms of Virtues, should we expect them to behave virtuously in all their acts? In other words, to know the Good is to do good.

KYDES: That seems to follow, Plato.

PLATO: Then how would we test that?

KYDES: We would observe their actions, and we would examine the thinking behind those actions.

DEMETRA: We could do so just as Socrates did in Athens, by examining teachers and philosophers, politicians and artisans, to see what they knew and whether they were wise.

KYDES: And observe and interrogate their actions.

HERMIAS: Couldn't they fool us, though? They could introduce a lot of fancy rigmarole, maybe about transcendence, the Good prior to and superior to Being, and the like.

DEMETRA: So, we would want them examined, especially by fellow philosophers, fellow dialecticians who could cut through the rigmarole and seek out consistency in behavior and accuracy in thought. That is how we verify knowledge, whether the Forms exist or not—a public examination of claims to see what those claims rest on.

PLATO: Here is how Socrates responds in our dialogue to such a line of inquiry: How do we know whether someone understands dialectic and knows the Forms?

> "Don't you call someone a dialectician when he is able to grasp an account of the being of each thing? And when he cannot do so, won't you, too, say that to the extent that he cannot give an account of something either to himself or to another, to that extent he does not understand it?"

KYDES: That is just what we have been saying, Plato.

PLATO: You have. Socrates goes on:

> "Then the same applies to the Good. Unless someone can give an account of the form of the Good, distinguishing it from everything else, and can survive all examination as if in a battle, striving to examine things not in accordance with belief, but in accordance with being; and can journey through all that with his account still intact, you will say that he does not know the Good itself or any other good whatsoever. And if he does manage to grasp some image of it, you will say that it is through belief, not knowledge, that he grasps it; that he is dreaming and asleep throughout his present life." (534b2–c7)

KYDES: That is Deme's point. We expect to see consistency in both thought and action. Even when that account is about something as ineffable as the Good, something beyond language and logic, we expect it to be consistent, like what we heard from the *Tao Te Ching*. It will be an attempt to put into words what itself goes beyond words, and it goes beyond logic and argument into the realm of the intuitive or of direct apprehension.

DEMETRA: Kydes brings up another way to refute Hermias's charge that the theory of the Forms and the Good are lies.

HERMIAS: Hold on! I didn't say they were lies. I raised the question whether they could be distractions or distortions like the Noble Lie.

DEMETRA: Fair enough. But Plato has introduced a document from a distant place echoing Socrates's account of the Forms and the Good. Dialecticians, let's call them, from *Seres* and *Sinae*, have said much the same thing in the *Tao Te Ching*. Isn't that evidence that the Forms and the Good are real?

HERMIAS: That is certainly corroborating evidence, I grant you that.

KYDES: But is it corroborating evidence? Just because philosophers from faraway places have similar phrases and writings about transcendental subjects doesn't necessarily mean that they are any more valid than the theory of the Forms.

HERMIAS: You think that other cultures are lying, too? Besides, these insights arose independently of one another.

KYDES: Plato told us that the *Tao Te Ching* came to him through the travels and work of Ladmon. Why couldn't such transactions be going on all the time and across the world? People copy other people. We need to hear that these faraway scholars undergo the same kind of test that Socrates describes—that is, providing a consistent account of what they have written about and experienced.

PLATO: Here is what I have learned from Ladmon on this subject. Those from *Seres* and *Sinae* agree with Socrates. They acknowledge that their insights and experiences aren't visible to us and can't be tested in the physical world. As we have discussed the topic, these insights and experiences are trans-linguistic and trans-logical. Nevertheless, they are public.

DEMETRA: What does that mean, Plato?

PLATO: It means that what they claim must be tested by those who have the expertise to examine those claims. Such tests are the means by which we establish epistemological validity. That is, how do we verify that what these mystics experience is genuine knowledge? How do we separate genuine transcendental insight from a delusion or an emotional outpouring? We do so just as Socrates suggested: We require a public accounting of what they have seen. "Public" means that a large number of seemingly private experiences are presented to and validated by others. That is why the *Tao* can be considered a public announcement of the kinds of experiences also described by Socrates, and that is why it can be used as evidence to corroborate what Socrates tells us.

Perhaps an example will help. According to Ladmon, Taoist monks will examine their students in intense interactions with their elders to determine the nature of the students' experiences. All claims to direct apprehension of the *Tao* are measured by the facts as understood by the acknowledged masters within the Taoist community. No one within the community is asked to accept anything on faith. They are told, instead, to record in some fashion what they themselves have experienced and then to bring that experience to the community. In other words, make that experience public so that it can be communally verified or refuted. As Socrates says, can one who claims to know essential reality run the gauntlet of all tests without tripping in his explanations and insights (534b8–d2)? That is what the community is looking out for.[4] Without such public tests, we can be trapped within our own interior, thinking that our personal fantasies, visions, and delusions are really reflections of the divine.

At this juncture, also in response to Kydes's concern about corroborating evidence, it is worth pointing out that references to and insights into knowing the transcendent are not unusual across the world. In addition to the *Tao Te Ching*, which I introduced tonight, I have heard mention of such teachings from *Indoi*[5] involving one they call "the Buddha," which means "the awakened one." Similarly, from Persia come the transcendental teachings of *Zōroastris*.[6] These teachings exist prior to those of us in Hellas hearing about them. This suggests that they developed independent, at least, of our own such teachings and are parallel to one another.[7]

HERMIAS: Is the foreign text that you cited earlier, Plato, one of those? Something from the Buddha, perhaps?

PLATO: The text is from *Indoi*, but it is not from the Buddha. It is the *Chandogya Upanishad*, which represents a different lineage.

DEMETRA: What is that lineage, Plato? What sort of texts are these?

PLATO: They are called the Upanishads, of which *Chandogya* is one of these sacred texts referred to as "Vedanta." (Here he reaches beneath his

---

4. Such public testing is a key part of mystical traditions. In Zen Buddhism, for example, a student's transcendental breakthrough, called *satori* or *kensho*—both meaning "direct seeing into spirit" or "intuitive apprehension"—must be examined for authenticity through *dokusan*, intense interaction with the Zen master, and through *shosan*, tests undertaken under the scrutiny of the community of practitioners. "Inward" insights must be turned "outward" in deliberation with others to establish their epistemological validity.

5. The ancient Greeks used the term to refer to the "region of the Indus River" and its people, what we today refer to as "India."

6. This is the Greek rendering of Zoroaster or Zarathustra.

7. See Jaspers, *Origin and the Goal*; and Eisenstadt, *Origins and Diversity*, for more information.

couch and pulls out two more scrolls.) The oldest written sacred texts from *Indoi* are the *Vedas*. The parts of the *Vedas* that deal with knowledge, especially knowledge of God, are called the Upanishads, also known as Vedanta or "end of the *Vedas*." The word "Upanishad" means, literally, "sitting near devotedly," like a student at the feet of a teacher or a philosopher. But it can also mean "secret teaching"—whose secrets, presumably, are available only to those ready to receive the teaching, like students of dialectic.

The Upanishads vary in length from a few hundred words to many thousands of words; some are in verse, some are in prose, some reflect both. As with the *Tao Te Ching*, no one is certain of the authors or when they were written. What is clear is that they were written by *rishis*—saints and seers of the Hindu religion, whom we might call their dialecticians. The writers are all reporting on what they have seen and learned, what knowledge they have gleaned, about the nature of Reality and Being and what we have been calling the Good.

In keeping with what we have just been saying about testing persons about the Forms, the rishis taught the scriptures, but, equally important, taught by their example of living in the world with this sacred knowledge. Studying the *Vedas* is not just about reading to inform the intellect. It is about absorbing and meditating on the texts to cleanse and enrich the soul and take that soul into the world. That is perhaps the greatest test of the validity of these experiences: How does the person who "knows" live in the world, act in the world, and interact with others? As Socrates says, show us in your life that you know not just beautiful things but Beauty itself. Let us see how Beauty and Truth and Goodness are brought forth and lived out (476c2–4, 507b1–6).

These scrolls were copied and presented to me by Critocles. Like Ladmon, Critocles went in search of wisdom in faraway places, distant from Hellas, that he had learned about from foreign merchants and traders. Critocles told me that, with regard to the *Vedas*, one does not accept the texts because they are declared sacred or authoritative. They are accepted because they can be "*verified, immediately, at any moment, in one's own experience*" and by the community of rishis.[8] If it is not verifiable, the text is then rejected.

Following this perspective would mean for us that what is said about the Forms can be verified by one's own experience. In the meantime,

---

8. Prabhavananda, *Upanishads*, xxi.

absent such experience, we rely on the reports from those who purport to have had such experience. Even more important, we should look at the lives of those who claim to have had these transcendent experiences to see how their experiences have influenced their lives.

What I cited earlier is, as I said, from the *Chandogya Upanishad*, thought to be one of the earliest. Yet the one I wish to focus on tonight is one of the shortest—the *Mandūkya Upanishad*, for it offers not only a description of the transcendent, but also a way to know it. The name "Mandūkya" comes from the Sanskrit word—the language of *Indoi*— "manduka," which means "teacher." Although brief, the *Mandūkya* is considered more profound than any other Upanishad.[9]

Consider, first, these stanzas and compare them with what Socrates has been saying and what we heard from the *Tao Te Ching*:

> "OM, the imperishable Syllable, is the Universe. Whatsoever has existed, whatsoever exists, whatsoever shall exist hereafter, is OM."[10]

KYDES: It is a syllable, Plato. So, is it also a word like Tao or the Good?

PLATO: I think that that will become clearer as we proceed.

According to Critocles, at the origin, in the beginning, OM is supposed to have been the first vibratory sound that emanated as the seed of creation, emanated out of the Unmanifest, as you have been calling it. In the beginning was silence. From silence emerged a sound. The sound had a vibration. That vibration was precise and ordered, geometrical, mathematical, harmonious, and it created a pattern, a perfect form.[11]

But OM is not merely a syllable or sound. It exists independent of anything and everything. It exists not because it refers to anything else or exists with reference to anything else. Instead, it is something by itself.

---

9. Rama, *Mandūkya Upanishad*, 8. Some date the authorship of the *Mandūkya Upanishad* to sometime between 800–500 BCE. Others, however, suggest that it was written much later, perhaps in the first or second century of the Common Era. Thus, the *Mandūkya* might not be old enough to have been familiar to Plato's peripatetic students and, thus, to Plato himself.

10. Prabhavananda, *Upanishads*, 73.

11. From string theory in physics we learn that vibrations give rise to particles. Beyond or below or before those vibrations there are no things. There are only patterns of excitation, vibrations or ripples without space or boundaries. The micro-instant before even the ripple is the unmanifest, the quantum void, the realm of pure potentiality pregnant with possibilities, that is the ground of all that manifests. As we have been describing it, this is formless emptiness, out of which any manifestations, however infinitesimal, arise or sing into existence.

Repetition of OM, of the syllable, takes you beyond the verbal, the visible, beyond all manifestation. It takes you to Brahman.

Brahman is the name (*nama* in Sanskrit, the language of *Indoi*) of the Form (*rupa*) of the Supreme Absolute or Ultimate Reality. By chanting OM, we summon into our awareness the Being or the Form of Brahman or what we call the Form of the Good. Brahman is not a particular form. It is a Universal Form not particularized in any language or as any object—nothing and everything, not here or there, but everywhere.

When you chant OM, its vibration melts all other vibrations and creates only a desire for the Supreme Absolute, for the Universal Form that has no form. Nor does the Universal have time; it is beyond time, beyond the past, the present, and the future:

> "And whatsoever transcends past, present, and future—all else that may exist beyond the bounds of Time—that too is OM."[12]

KYDES: So, when you chant OM, you concentrate on it and nothing else? That takes you into the transcendent.

PLATO: Not quite. When you chant OM, you don't focus on OM, but you don't not focus on OM. You don't try to hold it in mind. You take it as it arises. Sometimes it is there; other times, it is not there. When you realize that you have been thinking of something else, you simply reintroduce OM to your awareness. There will be times when you will be thinking nothing at all.

HERMIAS: As if stung by Socrates's, and your, stingray.

PLATO (smiling): Something like that, yes. At this point, when we are thinking nothing, then we are the very space in which thoughts arise. We are not there thinking. "We" are no longer; "we cease to be" at that moment. We are the Good, the thing-in-itself.

KYDES: Here we go again: We disappear. Nothing is everything. Pure existence without object or content.

PLATO: Well said, Kydes.

KYDES: I don't know what I said!

HERMIAS: You cannot express it, Kydes. It is transcendent, beyond words or sound or thought.

---

12. Prabhavananda, *Upanishads*, 73.

DEMETRA: Remember the time in the gymnasium when you were wrestling, and every move was effortless?

KYDES: I do. It was like I wasn't the one wrestling. I was just watching moves unfold. Every move was perfect, and I wasn't doing anything. The moves just flowed out of me, and I wasn't doing anything.

DEMETRA: You weren't thinking of moves; the moves just came and went. You were there, but you weren't there. As Plato just said, "You are not there thinking. You are no longer."

KYDES: Yes, I see. It was just like that. The moves just were. It's all puzzles and paradoxes, trying to explain the ineffable.

PLATO: And paradoxes and contradictions are our means of expressing what is beyond expression. OM is a syllable, is a sound. But in its eternal form, OM has no form, but is *"formless, durationless, and spaceless."* OM therefore *"is name and form; form and the formless, vibration and awareness, creation and being and bliss. All of that is OM."*[13]

KYDES: Okay, so like the Good and the Tao, whatever we can say about Brahman and even *OM* cannot be what they really are.

HERMIAS: That's right.

KYDES: And somehow, though they cannot be named, they can be known. (Kydes now shakes his head.)

PLATO: Perhaps this will help anchor us somewhat:

> "All of this Universe is the Eternal Brahman, the Eternal Self. This Self, which is one with OM, has three aspects, and beyond these three, different from and indefinable—the Fourth."[14]

KYDES: Well, this isn't anchoring me. Help me here, Plato. Are these three aspects—leaving aside the indefinable fourth, which may or may not be an aspect at all—in any way related to our idea of the three-part, or tri-partite, soul?

PLATO: Yes, you can think that. Through chanting OM repeatedly and writing it out as it sounds, we spell it O-M. But the more accurate spelling

---

13. Prabhavananda, *Upanishads*, 26.
14. Prabhavananda, *Upanishads*, 73.

is A-U-M. These are the three components of the syllable OM and are identical to the four aspects of the Self or Soul.

KYDES (with a deep sigh): The three components, which may or may not relate to our tripartite soul, have four aspects?

PLATO (smiling): That's right. Bear with me, Kydes. The first component called, *Vaiśvānara* or A, relates to desirable objects, material objects, and thus to appetites and desires. *"This aspect of Soul is aware only of external objects."*[15] This is associated with our waking state and the appetitive part of our tripartite soul. M, the third or *Prājña*, is wisdom and the departure point into the Eternal. This aspect is what we might think of as our individual mind and the reasoning part of our soul. Here the mind is at rest in the state of deep or dreamless sleep. U, the second or *Taijasa*, is the dream state. It is less identifiable, but does contain the qualities of the other two, and so may be likened to the spirited part of the soul.

HERMIAS: And the fourth aspect, Plato?

PLATO: The fourth aspect—*Turīya*—as you can guess, is letterless. Thus, the confusion that you felt, Kydes. The fourth aspect is also soundless, the end of all manifestations. They call it an "aspect" or "state," but it is really the condition underlying all three states. As the *Mandūkya Upanishad* says, it is

> "beyond the senses, beyond understanding, beyond all expression . . . wherein awareness of the world and of multiplicity is completely obliterated. It is ineffable peace. It is the supreme good. . . . He who knows this merges his soul into the Soul."[16]

The rishis refer to this fourth aspect as "*unutterable and beyond mind . . .* [in which] *the manifold world disappears*"; it is eternal and unchanging, beyond comprehension by the mind, beyond comparison with anything. It cannot be perceived, inferred, thought, or described.[17]

HERMIAS: Then, can we say that *Turīya* is like our Good, superior and prior to Being?

PLATO: I think that we can.

---

15. Prabhavananda, *Upanishads*, 73.
16. Prabhavananda, *Upanishads*, 75.
17. Prabhavananda, *Upanishads*, 76.

KYDES: And so through OM/A-U-M the person who chants it transcends all manifestation, moves into the eternal, immutable, perfect Soul, which is our Unbounded Unmanifest, the Good before Being and including all Being. It is a meditative method of dialectic.

PLATO: I think that you have said that very well, Kydes.

KYDES: But, again, I don't know what I've said!
(The other three laugh.)

PLATO: Oh, I think you know more than you are letting on. There are many ways to the Good. Dialectic is one such way; meditating with OM is another. They might not be that different.

KYDES (laughing): I have a difficult time imagining Socrates sitting and chanting *OM*.

PLATO: Why is that difficult to imagine?

KYDES: Socrates seems so active and talkative, moving about Athens interrogating everyone, philosophizing all day long. He seems so ... ah ... gabby.

PLATO: That is true. But you would not deny, would you, that Socrates has his contemplative side as well? Recall what he says in the *Phaedo*:

> *"For as they say in the* [Eleusinian] *mysteries, 'the thyrsus-bearers are many, but the mystics are few'; and these mystics* [Bacchoi] *are, I believe, those who have been true philosophers. And I in my life, so far as I could, left nothing undone, and have striven in every way to make myself one of them."*[18]

Socrates knew, as we are learning, that there are many ways up the steep and rocky path to get into the sunlight. The goal is to know the Forms, knowledge that is nourishment for the soul and not simply abstractions.

When the Good first manifests, as I understand the *Māṇḍūkya*, it condenses into a universal Name and a universal Form. This creates one Being. This one Being can be thought as Universal Soul.

KYDES: Do you mean God?

---

18. Plato, *Phaedo*, 69c–d.

PLATO: Many might call it that, but this Being or Reality or Good or Soul is beyond any name, description, or form that corresponds to a label. Its nature transcends our language and logic. We may provide it a name and form so that we can conceive of it when we undertake to recognize or remember it. Although Being is beyond description, something must be said to convey a sense of it. Expression is necessary to prepare one for its realization, the realization of Being, of Reality.

How do we describe a light that shines but does not shine on anything, a light beyond any manifestation of any kind, but that is? We call it the Absolute, as the rishis do; we call it, as Socrates did, the Good prior and superior to Being. Its offspring Socrates calls the sun; we might also call it the Soul.

HERMIAS: I must say, Plato, that the evidence from the Far East shows me that the theory of the Forms at least has independent, collaborating evidence. But, now, here is what I wish to know: When you come to know the Good, the Soul, is that then reflected in your everyday actions and behaviors?

PLATO: As we have been told, the rishis studied the Upanishads and the Vedas to cleanse their souls, to attain this knowledge of Soul, and to carry that into their everyday experiences. And if we attach this view to our own understanding, as Socrates said, *"by consorting with what is divine and ordered"*—the Forms—*"we will become as divine and ordered as a human being can"* (501c6–8).

Live the knowledge that you have remembered and recognized. Bring it into your daily life so that you may, as Socrates said, be as divine and ordered as a human can be. Then your life and your contemplation will display no separation. Bring the Isles of the Blessed into all that you do, and all that you do will be a lesson and a blessing to all those you encounter. As is written in the *Māṇḍūkya Upanishad*: "He who knows Brahman becomes Brahman."[19] That is also the message of the *Māṇḍūkya Upanishad*.

KYDES: Is this what Socrates is telling us in the dialogue? When you know the Forms you become the Forms? When you know what morality is in itself, when you know pure or perfect morality, then you become purely moral yourself? That's what the philosopher king or philosopher queen brings back down into the city, into the cave.

---

19. Prabhavananda, *Upanishads*, 69.

HERMIAS: I don't think that the knowledge operates on that level, on the level of walking the streets of Athens. Brahman is the equivalent of our Good. The Good is beyond all qualifications and categories, beyond all description. It is Absolute Reality, Supreme Being, and every one of those labels is wrong because it is bounded and limited. Knowing the Good can't translate into anything we can imagine or conceive as affecting our lives, for whatever we imagine or conceive can't be the Good itself.

DEMETRA: *"To be as divine and ordered as a human being can be."* I think of that phrase this way: In the *Apology*, Socrates claims that his reputation around Athens and Greece as the wisest man rested on a kind of wisdom, *"human wisdom"* he called it.[20] Those who slandered him, he thought, if they were right, might well have access to a *"wisdom more than human."*[21] Well, is Socrates simply being sarcastic or mischievous here? Or is he serious that there is such a wisdom and others might have it? Socrates goes on to say that whatever this wisdom is, those he interrogated throughout Athens—politicians, poets, soldiers, craftsmen, and the like—didn't have it. They didn't even seem to have human wisdom, which Socrates concluded was *"worth little or nothing."*[22]

So, the wisest person in all of Greece acknowledges that he is wise only because he has "human wisdom," which for him, after years of searching for wisdom among Athenians, amounts to this: I am wise because *"I do not think I know what I do not know."*[23] But how would one be wise, Socrates included, if he had divine wisdom, *"wisdom more than human"*?

It was, perhaps, for this reason that Socrates said that men *"should make haste to escape earth to heaven."* Escaping earth *"means becoming as like God as possible; and a man becomes like God when he becomes just and pure, with understanding."*[24] This is what we have been saying—come to know the Forms and become like God in purity and justice. The person most like God *"is the man who has become as just as it lies in human nature to be. . . . [I]t is the realization of this that is genuine wisdom and goodness."*[25]

20. Plato, *Apology*, 21d6.
21. Plato, *Apology*, 21e2.
22. Plato, *Apology*, 23b1.
23. Plato, *Apology*, 21d6–7.
24. Plato, *Theaetetus*, 176b1–3.
25. Plato, *Theaetetus*, 176c5–7.

This, to me, is what Socrates meant by divine wisdom, and this suggests that we can know it. Human wisdom can become divine wisdom; it is the pinnacle of our wisdom. We can become *"as like God as possible."* That is consorting with the divine.

Of course, such wisdom is hard to come by, as we saw with the trip up the Divided Line. It requires turning our soul's focus from what most people cherish—wealth, household affairs, the position of public orator, holding political office, and participating in political clubs, all of which Socrates criticizes in his defense.[26] In their place, Socrates wandered about Athens trying to convince people to eschew these interests and pursue the elevation of the soul—becoming *"as good and wise as possible"* or divinely wise. *"My art is midwifery,"* he said. *"I watch over the labor of their souls."* Young minds then *"discover within themselves a multitude of beautiful things, which they bring forth into the light."*[27] This is also the labor that Diotima talked about:

> "Once getting near what really is and having intercourse with it and having begotten understanding and truth, he knows, truly lives, is nourished, and—at that point, but not before—is relieved from the pains of labor."[28]

Knowing the Forms makes us as like God as possible, and that means liberating us from thinking the shadow world or even the world of objects seen in the physical fire is the real world. Knowing the Forms enables one to help clear out one's own cave, one's own soul, and to help liberate others by introducing them to, and guiding them according to, dialectic.

KYDES: So, those who know the Forms aren't going to be unjust to others or unwise in their words or cowardly in the face of a bully. They know what justice and wisdom and courage require in each situation, because they know the Form of each of those.

HERMIAS: I don't think it's that clear-cut. It sounds to me more like an ongoing process. We come closer to being like God, but we don't attain that. Socrates said, *"becoming as ordered and divine as possible."* That doesn't mean that we ever attain divinity. We aren't going to be pure or

---

26. Plato, *Apology*, 36b9–10.
27. Plato, *Theaetetus*, 150b7–8, d7–9.
28. Plato, *Symposium*, 490b4–6.

perfect. We move toward that. As we said earlier, we won't know how to solve every mathematical problem once we know the Form of Wisdom.

So, what is it we would know? We'd know the nature of wisdom, and perhaps that resonates within us so we know intuitively, as Deme intimated, how to bring others closer to its Form. Philosopher kings radiate wisdom, and that might mean that they never judge or decide for you, but bring you as close to wisdom in a situation as they can by using, as Socrates does, dialectic to awaken you to Wisdom itself.[29]

DEMETRA: A doctor gives you medicine for an illness so that your body can use that medicine to heal. The medicine doesn't heal; it enables the body to heal itself. That's what the philosopher does. She provides the medicine, in this case dialectic, to help you heal yourself, liberate yourself from the shadows that are stifling you.

KYDES: So, philosophers are doctors of the soul.

HERMIAS: Yes! I like that. They operate on the soul level, not on the walking-around level.

DEMETRA: Well, don't they operate on both levels? Don't they help orient your soul away from the shadows and out of the cave, and do so by helping you learn how better to navigate and understand the cave itself?

The doctors of the soul help us awaken to self-control and help us learn to temper our desires so that they don't overwhelm and bury the mind and the soul.

KYDES: Don't let *eros* overwhelm *philia*.

DEMETRA: Exactly. Doctors of the soul help us learn to balance the three aspects in the tripartite soul.

HERMIAS: Philosophers see the shadows as shadows. They see through illusions and false ideas and beliefs. They are up the Divided Line looking back down to the realm of images and beliefs from the perspective of knowledge. To those in the cave, the illusions, the shadows, are real. These doctors of the soul work to disturb, disrupt, and dispel illusions, as Socrates does, through *elenchus* and dialectic—undercut through

---

29. "*But when the soul investigates by itself it passes into the realm of what is pure, ever existing, immortal and unchanging, and being akin to this, it always stays with it whenever it is by itself and can do so; it ceases to stray and remains in the same state as it is in touch with things of the same kind, and its experience then is what is called wisdom.*" Plato, *Phaedo*, 79d1–5.

discussion and questions, answers, and more questions what people hold as reality yet is only partial or even untrue.

KYDES: So, the philosophers are driving people up the Divided Line. Could we return to our earlier discussion and say compelling people up the Divided Line?

HERMIAS: As we concluded, not compelled physically; no one is compelled to engage with Socrates. Instead, once engaged, he is compelled by the force of the discussion, by the questions and answers themselves.

KYDES: And if our doctors of the soul were to narrow their focuses to politics, to issues such as the city's plumbing system or finances or its markets, then, like our carpenter, the ruler's focus moves down the Divided Line and his insights are lowered or narrowed to serve the functions of politics rather than as a stimulus for moving up the Line toward virtues and the Forms. Then, before you know it, virtue could come to mean the ability to use the crowd or manipulate the legal system and not respect people as you find them.

HERMIAS: Our model for all things philosophical—namely, Socrates—didn't participate in Athens's politics. He even said that he did not know how to vote when elected to the Council of five hundred.[30]

KYDES: He seemed to disrespect the rule of the Thirty Tyrants, when he defied their orders for him to help bring Leon of Salamis to court. Instead, in a quietly defiant act, Socrates simply peeled off from the guard sent to arrest Leon and went home.[31]

HERMIAS: Which tells us what, Kydes? That Socrates was no friend of oligarchy and no admirer either of Athenian democracy?

DEMETRA: It tells me that an act that on the surface appears to be a violation of law—Socrates's defiance of a direct order—is nevertheless moral. How could a philosopher who, we assume, knew the Forms and the Good, defy the lawmakers of Athens? That can only be so, if Socrates's act is the just act and the order was itself unjust. To understand that, we must explore with Socrates the reasons for his action, and that must entail engaging with him in dialogue.

30. Plato, *Gorgias*, 473e.
31. Plato, *Apology*, 32a–d.

HERMIAS: Is Socrates responsible for his own morality?

KYDES: What can you possibly mean by that?

HERMIAS: Socrates sometimes refers to his *daimon*. The *daimon*, he says, is "*my familiar prophetic power, my spiritual manifestation*," which opposes Socrates when he is about to do something wrong.[32] So, is Socrates reasoning about what is right and good? It seems not to be the case. It is the *daimon* that knows what is virtuous, not Socrates. He believes the *daimon*; he trusts the *daimon*. But it is not Socrates doing the work of coming to know what is virtuous in each situation.

KYDES: Or is the *daimon* simply his inner knowing, a kind of intuition? We speak sometimes of a "voice of reason," speaking to us. This could be Socrates's "voice of virtue" or "voice of morality" that he attributes to his power.

DEMETRA: Yes. He refers to his *daimon* as a "*prophetic power*," but also as "*my spiritual manifestation*." It is the manifestation of what he is essentially—a spiritual being that is different from his human manifestation.

When the universal Soul, as opposed to the individual's soul, manifests within the person, it might do so as the *daimon*. The *daimon*'s voice arises, then, out of knowing the Forms, out of awakening within oneself what is fundamentally and essentially true about Being—that we are spirit within as we have a physical body without.

Remember how we talked earlier about coming to know the Forms and the Good? It wasn't through intellect or logic or reasoning. It was through dialectic that brings us up the Divided Line to and through a kind of divine intuition whereby we realize that we are Being beyond manifestation itself.

HERMIAS: This doesn't help us, for Socrates might trust his inner self, his true self, his *daimon*, but we can't. In trusting Socrates on a matter on which his *daimon* has spoken, we are not ourselves encouraged to reason. Reason, indeed, seems circumvented. We're trusting Socrates, not reasoning—his or our own.

DEMETRA: Isn't that the point? We might be bothered that Socrates defied the legal order. We think it unjust and immoral. So, we engage with him to understand his reasons. We don't accept at face value what he tells

---

32. Plato, *Apology*, 40a3–4.

us about his behavior. We investigate, just as a philosopher would want us to do.

KYDES: But he just says, "My *daimon* wouldn't let me do it." End of discussion.

DEMETRA: No, Kydes; it's the beginning of the discussion. Push beyond his easy answer by questioning and probing about the nature of the *daimon* and how, or why, Socrates, the great philosopher, attends to an inner voice. Whenever Socrates mentions his *daimon*, why isn't that an immediate challenge or invitation to interrogate him, just as are his questions that he directs to his interlocutors? Why assume that he simply wants to be believed? If, as you suggested a bit ago, that the *daimon* is really Socrates's intuition, his intuitive inner voice, then even that doesn't steer us away from interrogation. Instead, it leads us right into interrogation.

HERMIAS: Perhaps intuition, after experiencing the transcendent, is nothing but an unrecognized amalgam, almost an abbreviation, of a lot of reasoning. Intuition, then, is a shortcut of sorts. It's what we might call "reason in a hurry."[33]

DEMETRA: I guess intuition could be like that, racing in a second through a series of logical moves or steps. But to me, it seems to be more a kind of instantaneous seeing—that is, seeing all at once a series of perspectives or insights, seeing the totality of these perspectives or insights in a single view. Intuition, then, can hold contradictions and opposites in mind and seek out the unity behind them so as to integrate them.

KYDES: So, Socrates should be able to explain that, right, how intuition works to unify or integrate perspectives, especially contradictory ones? That's a moment to engage in dialectic.

HERMIAS: But isn't the whole point about intuition that it can't be explained? We know something automatically without thinking and thus without an explanation. We feel it more than we think it. So, we know something, but we can't demonstrate it.

---

33. My friend Debi Campbell shared this phrase with me. She's not sure that it's hers, but she conveniently can't recall where she heard it or whether she heard it elsewhere. So, as far as I'm concerned, she's responsible. Any gripes with the formulation, take them up with her.

DEMETRA: That seems right, Hermias: "We feel it more than we think it." Intuition seems to defy the tyranny of "straight-line" thinking—that is, getting from point A to point B and beyond. It is a direct and immediate knowing of whatever is experienced. It is a knowing in the blink of an eye.

Does intuition need to be, can it be, demonstrated? Socrates's *daimon* told him that it was wrong to arrest Leon. Could Socrates explain why the *daimon* told him that, why it was wrong, and why Socrates should instead walk home? Perhaps explaining it is an invitation for Socrates himself to understand the line of reasoning that made the arrest wrong. But feelings, the body itself, are involved here as well. So, intuition could be an integration of feelings and reason, the harmonious cooperation between the mind and body, reason and emotion.

Did Socrates sort all of that out? Maybe through experience he had confidence that his *daimon* never steered him wrong. But those of us on the outside need to know why those decisions of his *daimon* are, as Socrates intimates, always right.

HERMIAS: In your view, Deme, Socrates needs a dialectical moment to do more than recognize the wisdom, divine wisdom, of his *daimon*. He needs that moment to understand that wisdom.

DEMETRA: I don't want to speak for Socrates. I can't speak for Socrates. Plato probably can, but he is remaining silent. (And Plato smiled.) So, I'll speak for myself. I think that we three need dialectical moments designed to develop within us our own *daimon*, to hear our intuitive voice, to recognize its wisdom, to know that what it says is so because we know that what it is is nothing less than our own divine Being giving expression to Truth and Reality.

KYDES: I'm curious: Do you think when Socrates stood transfixed for twenty-four hours, that he would give us an account of how he remained upright? Would he explain to us how he then went about his day without a night's rest? Or would he avoid an account and instead twist us around through some dialectical exercise?

PLATO: Do you think that his *daimon* told him that sleeping was wrong? What would you think if Socrates told you that, when standing, he had rested beyond sleep, that he was in fact fully rested? He had rested in the Absolute. Do you think that anything would be more refreshing?

13

Political Character and the Nature of the Soul

PLATO: Earlier, Hermias, you asked Kydes—well, you asked all of us, really—whether Socrates, being no friend of oligarchy, was an admirer of democracy. Having just discussed his *daimon* and the need for engagement to understand Socrates's motivations and reasoning, are you closer to an answer? Does exercise of dialectic favor democracy over other types of regimes?

HERMIAS: Since democracy put him to death, I doubt that he is much of an admirer.

KYDES: Athenian democracy put him to death. Maybe that didn't represent what Socrates thought was a proper democracy.

HERMIAS: Fair enough. But what would a "proper democracy," then, look like for him?

PLATO: First, however, recall where we ended an earlier part of our conversation. That, I think, can lead us to an answer to your question.

KYDES: Remind us, Plato.

PLATO: Socrates asked, "*What sort of person will we say reflects this city?*" (541b2–3).

DEMETRA: So, that is where we are now: Back to examining the character of persons raised in and groomed for leadership in the fevered city?

Don't we already know what sorts of persons they are? They are immoral and unjust, living under and by a lie, however noble your brothers, Plato, think it might be.

PLATO: But more specifically, Demetra, what kinds of persons will we see? When the rational calculations by the rulers fail and marriages and births result in mixed metals and chaos among the classes, then, as we saw, civil war ensues. Then

> "two races, the iron and the bronze, pull the constitution toward moneymaking and the acquisition of land, houses, gold, and silver. The other two, by contrast, the gold and silver races—since they are not poor, but naturally rich in their souls—lead the constitution toward virtue and the old political system. Striving and struggling with one another, they compromise on a middle way: they distribute the land and houses among themselves as private property; enslave and hold as serfs and servants those whom they had previously guarded as free friends and providers of upkeep; and take responsibility themselves for making war and for guarding against the ones they had enslaved." (547b6–c4)

KYDES: Oh, you mean like today's cities. After all of this discussion with your brothers, Plato, Socrates brings us back to what we see today—that is, a society ruled by *eros* and not *philia*, one dominated by a desire for material wealth and for physical intimacy, for comfort and security, but not for knowledge.

HERMIAS: So, if one's character or one's soul is ruled by a desire for wealth—for exercising *eros* in that sense—then this person is plutocratic and interested in wealth and luxuries. He is ruled by the appetitive part of his soul. But if he is ruled more by the spirited part—that is, if he pursues not luxuries but honor—then he would have or would be a timocratic or honor-loving person.

DEMETRA: And when there is honor in making money, when one is judged as honorable not so much by how he spends his money but by how much money he has to spend, then money-making and not virtue becomes the motivation.

PLATO: Socrates says as much, Demetra: *"When wealth and the wealthy are valued and honored in a city, virtue and goodness are valued less"* (551a1–2).

DEMETRA: Soon what is honored becomes the practice, and the virtues, which are not honored, fade.

PLATO: Quite so. Socrates observes:

> "In the end, victory-loving and honor-loving men become lovers of making money and money-lovers, and they praise and admire the wealthy man and appoint him as ruler, and dishonor the poor one." (551a6–8)

KYDES: In short order, there will be two classes in this city—the rich and the poor—forever at war with each other. The result must be tyranny, for only a strong man can end this enmity.

HERMIAS: Why not a democracy?

KYDES: A democracy? The rich don't trust the poor to rule. The rich fear that the masses will seize power, strip the rich of their wealth, and distribute that wealth to themselves. The poor cannot be trusted with power.

PLATO: Perhaps democracy could arise out of this mixture in the city of rich and poor. Socrates suggests that the youthful offspring of the wealthy spend and waste their wealth because they are undisciplined. The young, who want to grow richer, borrow on credit, but then, because of their profligate spending, cannot repay their loans and lose their money (555c1–6). Now, having never known poverty before, these young debtors

> "sit around in the city, I suppose, armed with stings or weapons—some of them in debt, some disenfranchised, some both—hating and plotting against those who have acquired their property, and all the others as well; passionately longing for revolution." (555d7–e1)

What kind of revolution might that be? These young debtors side with the poor in seeing how their needs and desires should be met. Could this not lead to a desire and demand for democracy?

KYDES: I suppose it could, Plato. So, democracy arises from the disgruntled masses who are joined by disaffected and impoverished youth. That's the basis of democracy—disaffection and poverty?

PLATO: But as Socrates tells us, at the same time isn't this democratic city *"full of freedom and freedom of speech? And doesn't everyone in it have the license to do what they want?"* (557b3–5).

HERMIAS: License, Plato? That doesn't seem healthy or right.

PLATO: Explain what you mean, Hermias.

HERMIAS: "License" implies having no restrictions, regulations, or restraints. That isn't freedom. That's chaos and an absence of control.

PLATO: Yet is this not the way in which people can arrange their own lives in whatever manner pleases them?

HERMIAS: But "whatever manner" allows for all sorts of arrangements that might come at the expense of the well-being of others. There must be some regulations of behavior, some gestures toward the virtues, and not simply "anything goes."

PLATO: Socrates agrees with you. Some of our pleasures and desires "*seem to me to be lawless. They are probably present in everyone, but they are held in check by the laws and by better desires in alliance with reason*" (572b4–6).

KYDES: The soul of each person must be ruled by reason to whatever extent that is possible within the individual.

PLATO: That is right. Socrates reminds us that many desires

> "*are awakened in sleep, when the rest of the soul—the rational, gentle, and ruling part—slumbers. Then the savage and beastly part, full of food or drink, comes alive, casts off sleep, and seeks to go and gratify its own characteristic instincts. You know it will dare to do anything in such a state, released and freed from all shame and wisdom. In fantasy, it does not shrink from trying to have sex with a mother or with anyone else—man, god, or beast. It will commit any foul murder, and there is no food it refuses to eat. In a word, it does not refrain from anything, no matter how foolish or shameful.*" (571c3–d3)

And so we need, as you two suggest, some guiding rules and regulations for democracy. Nevertheless, under democracy one finds people of all varieties, and this helps make it

> "*the finest or most beautiful of the constitutions, for, like a coat embroidered with every kind of ornament, this city embroidered with every kind of character type, would seem to be the most beautiful. And many people would probably judge it to be so, as women and children do when they see something multicolored.*" (557c3–7)

KYDES: Assuming, of course, there are those rules and regulations. Otherwise, license will leave people doing whatever they please whenever they please. Such action can be costly to others and can lead to all sorts of licentious behavior.

PLATO: Because, for one reason, democracy "*distributes a sort of equality to both equals and unequals alike*" (558c5–6).

HERMIAS: Democracy, then, requires vigilance, for there is always the danger that *eros* will run unabated both within the individual and among the citizenry.

DEMETRA: Diversity allows for that vigilance, even demands it somewhat. Democracy also allows for, but doesn't guarantee, the possibility of philosophy. This is what we said is missing from the healthy city, what Glaucon called "*the city for pigs*" (372d3).

Can we have philosophy without the entanglements of democracy? I don't think that we can. In any other system it is someone dictating those rules and regulations. They might dictate the need for philosophical education, but then, again, as with the fevered city, the dictates might limit such education to a select few. Those few will be the sons and daughters of the aristocrats or oligarchs who rule, who issue the orders. In democracy everyone has a chance to express her talents and develop the virtues as expressions of the city's multi-colors.

KYDES: The freedom of democracy also sets *eros* loose in many ways to pursue many things.

DEMETRA: I agree, and all people in the city are free to learn from their experiences, some of which will be mistakes. But "learn from them" is the key phrase for me. This is why deliberation and judgment are so important, for without that to differentiate our types of pursuits, we lose *philia* in the miasma of erotic pleasures and desires that democracy can unleash.

HERMIAS: Without that judgment, without philosophical education, appetites can overwhelm reason, and democracy itself is then lost.

PLATO: Socrates says something similar:

> "*Seeing the citadel of the young man's soul empty of knowledge, fine ways of living, and words of truth (which are the best watchmen and guardians of the thoughts of those men whom the gods*

love), the citadel is occupied with [560b6–9] insolence, anarchy, extravagance, and shamelessness. . . . They praise the returning exiles and give them fine names, calling insolence good breeding, anarchy freedom, extravagance magnificence, and shamelessness courage." (560b6–e5)

Because this person in democracy has freedom and variety:

"He lives from day to day, gratifying the appetite of the moment. Sometimes he drinks heavily while listening to the flute, while at others he drinks only water and is on a diet. Sometimes he goes in for physical training, while there are others when he is idle and neglects everything. Sometimes he spends his time engaged in what he takes to be philosophy. Often, though, he takes part in politics, leaping to his feet and saying and doing whatever happens to come into his mind. If he admires some military men, that is the direction in which he is carried; if some moneymakers, then in that different one. There is neither order nor necessity in his life, yet he calls it pleasant, free, and blessedly happy, and follows it throughout his entire life." (561c6–d7)

HERMIAS: This person lacks discernment, Plato. Notice that Socrates says that he spends his time *"engaged in what he takes to be philosophy."* But philosophy is determined by its results or effects; in other words, as we have been discussing, does the practice move the person up the Divided Line? That is our measure. It isn't just thinking thoughts that are pleasurable and that might sound profound.

KYDES: Not everyone is interested in philosophy, Hermias. Besides, even those who are don't always show aptitude for it.

HERMIAS: I don't begrudge those who have no interest in it. No one should be forced to think philosophically. But all citizens should be exposed to it and, at the least, should learn to form ideas and to argue for and against positions. Everyone should listen to positions with which they disagree, so that they can better understand what they think and what other people think and why they think it.

Those who show an inclination for philosophy don't have to be great thinkers. People pursue it to the best of their abilities. Likewise, as Socrates has told us, the free person must not be compelled to learn, . . . no compulsory learning can remain in the soul.

Regardless, I think that everyone is a philosopher at heart. As children, we begin by asking "Why?" endlessly. We are naturally curious about what we experience around us. Isn't that all that philosophy is, showing curiosity about people and the world and asking questions about them?

KYDES: So, if we added philosophy as you have described it—that which elevates our thinking, moving us up the Divided Line—would that make democracy the best constitution, because it marries freedom with diversity of perspectives within a context of philosophy?

DEMETRA: Does Socrates's healthy city, the one he first described, offer sufficient freedom and diversity, even if we add philosophy to it? If so, then even with philosophy, where within the lifestyles described in the healthy city do you see diversity? If not, then are freedom and diversity more important than even philosophy? Are they the footholds for moving toward or into philosophy?

HERMIAS: But if you add philosophy to the healthy city, the city for pigs, would it by necessity bring increased freedom and diversity? Otherwise, how is moving up the Divided Line going to reflect increased discernment and judgment? We're arguing, Deme, about which comes first—diversity and freedom or philosophy.

KYDES: Don't they come in at the same time? Can you be philosophical if you don't have the freedom to investigate as you choose? And how strong is philosophy if you don't have diverse perspectives and ways of life to investigate?

HERMIAS: That seems right, Kydes. Gaining insight and knowledge comes from interrogating our own thoughts and experiences, as well as the thoughts and experiences of others. To understand our own positions, we need to see and be able to explore differing thoughts and positions, different ways of life. So that requires freedom and diversity.

It appears that freedom, diversity, and philosophy cannot be separated. They are of a piece. To know requires examining what we like and dislike, love and hate, fear and yearn for. In short, we must understand what we think and why we think it, and that means hearing opposing perspectives as well as congruent ones. Even if everyone in the healthy city ends up living and loving the same simple life that reflects little diversity, the city can't start off that way or continue that way if philosophy is valued and available. Citizens must question and evaluate ways of living.

DEMETRA: I agree with you, Hermias, that there is no movement up the Divided Line without philosophy and that knowledge along the way up requires us to hear a variety of perspectives, especially perspectives of those who disagree with and challenge us. That is how we exit the cave and move into the sunlight. But once having visited the Isles of the Blessed, once established in Being and in the Forms, is not the simple life, the gentle and quiet life, the best life?

KYDES: Why does that follow? If you are fully established in Being, as you say, why not the fast-paced life of Athens rather than the slow drone of rural life?

DEMETRA: Because rural life would not have a slow drone. What is it that the hustle of Athens offers? Isn't it amusement? Isn't it distraction? Isn't it anything to take our minds off of our own existence and worries and angst? Isn't it what drives timocrats toward honor, oligarchs toward riches, and tyrants toward power? Isn't it what turns people away from the soul?

What is it that we are striving for when everything is right here within us always? I think in that circumstance we might prefer the peace of the slow pace of the river through the Academy to the dust and noise of the Agora. If Being is never absent from us, because it is the ground of all that we do, of everything and anything we do, then is it not refreshing to rest in the sound of the river rather than the din of the market? What else is there, when Being is fully with us?

KYDES: That's your preference, Deme, but it doesn't have to be everyone's. If Being is never separate from us, if Being is always here, then it doesn't matter where you live or even how you live. I think that I might well prefer the bustle of Athens, even the wildness of the Piraeus, to the bucolic life. Besides, Socrates, our exemplar, did quite well coming to know the Good and sharing his knowledge of the Forms by staying put in Athens. You can chant *OM* anywhere, no?

DEMETRA: I suppose you're right, Kydes. It is a preference to live a quiet rustic life, and it might not matter what circumstances you find yourself living in. If you think philosophically and exercise dialectic to move up the Divided Line, then you can be anywhere. Plato has given us a rich philosophical life here in this idyllic setting of the Academy, but I suppose that he could have set it up in the center of Athens just as well.

KYDES: And I could happily live here, too, provided he keeps these comfortable couches. (Fingering the material.) By the way, what is this, Plato? Finely rendered leather?

DEMETRA: Perhaps we have differing views on what is the measure of happiness and success. Those who chase power or riches or honor, can they ever have enough? Is there a point at which they stop and say, "That's enough; I need no more"? I've never met such a person who had those ambitions and sated them.

But if your measure is loving your family and friends and being loved in return, if success for you is doing your best work—whether that work is with your hands or your mind—keeping quality always in the foreground, and if you seek to learn and to share that learning, to be open to all who come to you for help and advice, then I think that any life, quiet or busy, is a good life. After all, what did Socrates tell us? *"All I do is go about Athens trying to persuade . . . both young and old . . . not to care for your bodies or your monies first, and to care more exceedingly for the soul, to make it as good as possible."*[1]

PLATO: But is not Socrates also warning us that every city, no matter how grand its constitution and how idyllic its way of life, will decay and thus decline? No city is perfect or permanent, because no human is. We all decay and decline.

DEMETRA: That is so, Plato, though those who come to know the Good and the Forms understand the perfect and permanent part of them— their part in the Universal Soul. Not all persons will attain that knowledge, and so the best that the philosopher king and philosopher queen can do is show people the path to the Good and help them walk it. They will be models or examples of a healthy soul immersed within the universal Soul, trying within a world and a life of opposites and flux to find the perfect and permanent where neither exists. Not all will want to walk that path.

PLATO: The rishis in *Indoi* have a saying for what you are describing, Demetra: *Yogastha Kuru Karmani*. It means, "Established in Being, perform action." Immersed in the universal Soul, take your mind and body into the world. We shall return to this idea later tonight.

---

1. Plato, *Apology*, 30a6–b.

Political Character and the Nature of the Soul

HERMIAS: Perhaps it is in the simple life, the life in the healthy city, where decline can best be postponed. A society focused on the virtues might be one that can delay the decline into oligarchy or tyranny or a democracy of unbridled freedom.

KYDES: And bear in mind that not many people are or will be "established in Being." Even for the philosopher king or queen, until that point, every person has this tension, this strife, between the virtues and the lure of wealth, honor, and power going on inside of them. Civil war exists within each person between the appetites and reason, spirit and reason, like the horses pulling the chariot in different directions.

HERMIAS: Which is all the more reason to focus on education throughout the city, and not just in schools, to focus on philosophy and the virtues and not on material or even psychological rewards.

DEMETRA: Do the auxiliaries of the fevered city have knowledge?

KYDES: Of course they do. They engage in philosophy, and those worthy of higher philosophy move on to be guardians and even philosopher kings or philosopher queens.

HERMIAS: I think I see where Deme is going here. Recall that earlier tonight in our discussion Socrates said that the city, to protect the souls of the young, must purge those poets who told stories about the gods that put them in a bad light. Are those stories not the very ones that the guardians need to hear and deal with if they are to adopt critically for themselves perspectives that are not simply a set of opinions and beliefs inculcated by the rulers?

DEMETRA: Congratulations, Hermias. That is just what I was suggesting. If the auxiliaries do not have the discernment and skill to think independently and critically, then the rulers can bamboozle them into accepting a different set of opinions and beliefs, meanwhile rejecting the former set as outdated or obsolete.

PLATO: Socrates asks, *"How are we to know . . . how are we to judge things if we want to judge them well? Isn't it by experience, reason, and argument"* (582a1–4)? If so, then is not the philosopher in the best position to judge? Has she not tasted physical and sensual pleasures? Has he not experienced the pleasure of being honored in some fashion for some exploit or achievement? *"But the pleasure of studying the things that are cannot be tasted by anyone except a philosopher"* (582c1–8).

KYDES: So, it follows that the philosopher has experience and knowledge of all sorts of pleasures that others taste, but only he has the experience, and therefore the pleasure, of knowledge up the Divided Line. He, then, is the best judge.

HERMIAS: Yes, he has the most experience with an array of pleasures. But, as we have been saying, he needs to hear and see that which opposes his own proclivities.

DEMETRA: There is another point here as well. The pursuit of philosophy is the greatest pleasure, because through philosophy one ultimately comes to know about Being. Being is permanent, stable, and perfect. All other pleasures—money-making, food, honor, eroticism—change, decay, and are lost. All other pleasures can be taken away. None of that is true of Being.

PLATO: Here is what Socrates says:

> *"That which is related to what is always the same, immortal, and true is itself of that kind* [i.e., of pure being] *and comes to be in something of that kind. And does the being of what is always the same partake any more of being than of knowledge?"* (585b13–c5)

KYDES: What does that mean, *"partake any more of being than of knowledge"*?

HERMIAS: It seems to me that Socrates is saying that those things associated with or close to Being are more real and more satisfying than those associated with the body.

DEMETRA: And Socrates might be going even beyond that. Perhaps coming to know Being not only brings us into the experience of Being itself, but also aids in our becoming more like Being itself. If you are filled with Being and Truth and Reality, will you not be more like Being and Truth and Reality in action?

KYDES: *"By consorting with what is divine and ordered . . .* [we] *will become as divine and ordered as human beings can"* (501c6–8).

DEMETRA: What was that Hindu aphorism, Plato, that you earlier recited? Isn't that the idea?

Political Character and the Nature of the Soul

PLATO: *Yogastha Kuru Karmani*. "Established in Being, perform action." As divine and ordered as human beings can be. Put that "being" into the world. I think you have captured the idea nicely, Demetra.

Now let us hear Socrates on the other group—those who lose the civil war within that Kydes talked about:

> "So, those who lack experience of knowledge or virtue, but are always occupied with feasts and the like, are brought down, apparently, and then back up to the middle state; and wander in this way throughout their lives, never reaching beyond this to what is truly higher up, never looking up at it or brought up to it, never filled with what really is, and never tasting any stable or pure pleasure. On the contrary, they are always looking downward like cattle and, with their heads bent over the earth or the dinner table, they feed, fatten, and fornicate. And, in order to do better than others in these things, they kick and butt with iron horns and hooves, killing each other, because their desires are insatiable. For the part that they are trying to fill is like a vessel full of holes, and neither it nor the things they are trying to fill it with are among the things that are." (586a1–b4)

KYDES: Yes! This is the life of those living in the fevered city, the lives of those, like your brothers, who long for and need luxuries and pleasures of the body. They rise up the Divided Line to "*the middle state,*" but "*never reach beyond this to what is truly higher up.*"

PLATO: "*Therefore when the entire soul follows the philosophic element and does not engage in faction, the result is that each element does its own work and is just; and, in particular, each enjoys its own pleasures, the best pleasures and—to the degree possible—the truest*" (586e4–587a1).

HERMIAS: Here we are, then, Plato, at the end of our inquiry. The moral person is one whose parts of his soul stick to their own elements and don't try to meddle in the elements of other parts of the soul. All of this rests on the philosophical part organizing and leading the whole soul. So, parts of the soul have "metals" and that has nothing to do with classes within a city.

DEMETRA: And every soul has these three parts, and every soul has the capacity to organize and be led by the philosophical part. As we learned from the *Mandūkya Upanishad*, the true city is Brahman, and Brahman resides in each person's heart. All souls, then, are souls of gold.

PLATO: Socrates points out:

> "It is better for everyone to be ruled by a divine and wise ruler—preferably one that is his own and that he has inside himself; otherwise one is imposed on him from outside, so that we may all be as alike and as friendly as possible, because we are all captained by the same thing." (590d2–6)

HERMIAS: Here is room for rule by a philosopher king or philosopher queen—someone who rules over others and themselves in the city.

KYDES: Correct me if I have misunderstood, but wasn't the earlier talk about diversity and freedom and democracy about souls ruling over themselves, about all of us, as Deme said, being souls of gold?

HERMIAS: Yes, and that clearly seems to be Socrates's preferred choice. But sometimes that can't or doesn't happen because of the nature of the city.

DEMETRA: Thus, this very exercise tonight! We are trying to see how to structure a city, a good city, so that people can rule themselves by ordering their own souls. The laws of the city create the conditions by which people can develop themselves, learn to think critically, and can rule the city as they rule themselves. But, of course, laws cannot be substitutes for education and philosophy, for laws can structure behavior—to encourage us or restrain us—but laws cannot create virtuous souls.

PLATO: Have you anticipated Socrates, Demetra? He says next:

> "This is clearly the aim of the law as well, which is the ally of everyone in the city. It is also our aim in ruling our children. We do not allow them to be free until we establish a constitution in them as in a city. That is to say, we take care of their best part with the similar one in ourselves and equip them with a guardian and ruler similar to our own to take our place. Only then do we set them free." (590e1–591a2)

KYDES: This is the educational system we've been talking about. Parents equip their children with an education that addresses character and judgment and critical thinking to ensure that their rational part, what Socrates called "*the divine and wise ruler within themselves,*" rules their souls. Notice here that the parents have not given up their children to be raised by others, though they would have teachers as well.

DEMETRA: Don't forget, Kydes, that philosophy and dialectic constitute character and the soul. Education, then, is interactive. It is a combination of the constitution of the city that provided the laws and structures by which citizens learn and grow and of the use of philosophy by students and citizens alike that structures the soul. *Paideia* is the responsibility of the entire society. Every citizen, regardless of his craft or responsibility, is a kind of teacher, for everyone in the city, and the city itself, is a setting for the ordering of lives—internal and external—and the development of greater virtue.

HERMIAS: Through such a system, a person develops a healthy soul, takes care of his soul, and lives a life in balance.

PLATO: So, Socrates asks:

> "Won't anyone with any sense, then, give everything he has to achieve [such a soul] *as long as he lives? First, won't he honor the studies that produce it and not honor the others? Second, as regards the condition and nurture of his body, not only will he not give himself over to bestial and irrational pleasure, and live turned in that direction; but he won't make health his aim nor give precedence to the ways of becoming strong or healthy or beautiful, unless he is also going to become temperate as a result of them. On the contrary, it is clear that he will always be tuning the harmony of his body for the sake of the concord of his soul."* (591b9–c9)

KYDES: As Socrates said earlier, take care of your soul and don't dwell on and worry about your body and its needs and pleasures.

PLATO: What we have been saying just now about the soul is true as it appears within the body and within the city. But we know from our examination to this point that the soul has an even higher nature.

KYDES: A nature that we come to know through philosophy and moving up the Divided Line to the Forms and to the Good.

PLATO: Precisely so, Kydes. To understand its true nature, we must realize through our love of wisdom what the soul grasps and longs to have intercourse with, and that is what the soul is akin to—that is, the "*divine and immortal and what always is.*" We must also "*realize what it would become if it followed this longing with its whole being, and if the resulting effort lifted it out of the sea in which it now dwells*" (611e1–5), the sea that is our human life.

KYDES: We know now, do we not, what that soul would become?

HERMIAS: The soul would be pure gold, as divine and ordered as it can become.

KYDES: But we live in that sea, Plato. We can't escape it.

DEMETRA: That's right; we can't escape that sea as long as we have bodies. And so, as Plato told us, *Yogastha Kuru Karmani*—Bring your soul of gold, your transcendent light, into that sea.

HERMIAS: Through our love of wisdom, we move out of the cave and into the sunlight, up the Divided Line to the Good. Then we return to the cave, to the sea, and live as best we can, having brought back with us what we have come to know of the Good and of the Forms.

DEMETRA: We are the reverse Gyges.

KYDES: Meaning what?

DEMETRA: Gyges, or his cousin, goes down into the earth and discovers buried there a human body with a ring. Gyges comes back up out of the earth, out of this "cave." Now back in his regular life, he discovers that this ring enables him, the wearer, to become invisible upon turning it. Having moved up and out of the cave, Gyges is fixed in the middle portion of the Divided Line, where his focus is on the goods and trappings of this life. He uses his new power of invisibility to secure riches, kill the king, seduce the queen, and accrue power, all of which is manifestly deceitful and immoral.

So, Gyges feeds his appetites, feeds his inner beasts, and uses his power, his spirit, to gain wealth and influence at the expense of his reason and philosophy, which he ignores. He turns the ring to become invisible, but he does not use that power to turn his soul and move out of the middle portion. He is content to make his visible life invisible, but he does not move up the Divided Line to know the invisible, the intelligible, and bring that back down to his physical life.

But we have established tonight through Socrates and Plato that the moral soul, and the happy soul, is one in balance and led by the rational part within us. We know this, or could, by using philosophy and dialectic to move up the Divided Line and thereby commune with the Forms.

We then return to the cave to order our souls and to instruct others as best we can according to what we know. We do so by trying to bring the invisible down to the visible. Whatever power we have, we have accrued through the love of wisdom and use that love to transcend the visible world and come to know the invisible.

The invisible world, the realm of the Forms, is the source of the true nature of our soul, which is good and immortal and unchanging. We are, then, the reverse of Gyges. Where Gyges used the power of the ring to turn himself invisible and thereby commit nefarious acts, we use the power of dialectic to turn souls, ours and others', from focusing on the visible to the invisible, to head up the Divided Line toward the Good to keep our souls in balance and true.

PLATO: So, says Socrates, *"haven't we found that morality itself is the best thing for the soul itself, and that the soul, even if it has the ring of Gyges, should do moral things?"* (612b1–3).

KYDES: Yes, we have found that. Then we have answered Glaucon's and Adeimantus's concern about the moral man being happy, even if he is thought immoral.

PLATO: Well, it must be true, says Socrates,

> *"that if a just man falls into poverty or disease or some of the other things that seem bad, it will end well for him during his lifetime or even in death. For surely the gods at least will never neglect anyone who eagerly wishes to become [moral] and, by practicing virtue, to make himself as much like a god as a human being can."* (613a4–b1)

KYDES: We have said as much ourselves, Plato: Knowing and communing with the Forms enables us, following Socrates, to be *"as divine and ordered as a human being can."* The more we learn about the invisible realms, the more we practice virtue and morality and the more we can taste the bliss and happiness of the Isles of the Blessed.

HERMIAS: And the more our souls will radiate transcendent light to live a moral life and guide others toward it.

DEMETRA: *Yogastha Kuru Karmani*, my friends, *Yogastha Kuru Karmani*. My new favorite catchphrase!

14

Imitation and the Myth of Er

PLATO: There is a final aspect of our inquiry that we need to address.

HERMIAS (yawning with fatigue): What aspect, Plato?

PLATO: Earlier in our evening's discussion, Socrates suggested banishing certain kinds of stories and poems from the city. Given your recent comments about the need for diversity, perhaps we ought to revisit the topic.

KYDES: Banished from the fevered city, Plato.

PLATO: Indeed, Kydes. This raises the issue of whether poetry and especially imitative arts should now be permitted in the city, the city that you three have constructed tonight.

DEMETRA: I think I see where this is headed, Plato. Are you asking whether artists should be permitted to add to the shadows cast on the wall seen by those chained before it? Should imitation, especially if that deepens their imprisonment, be allowed?

KYDES: Because what they present through "imitation" isn't real.

PLATO: Socrates says that imitation is *"likely to distort the thought of anyone who hears or sees it, unless that person has the knowledge of what it is really like"* (596b3–5). Let us consider as an example a couch of a kind that each of us is lying on. First, there is the nature of the couch. Following Socrates, I presume we would say that a god makes that (597b5–6).

Next is the carpenter who makes the couches we lie on. Third would be a painter who paints a couch as part of his art. The painter is the furthest from the nature of the couch, would you not agree? (They nod, all yawning now.) We might say that the painter is an imitator of both the nature of the couch and the object we call "couch." He imitates what the others make (597d11–e3).

The same can be said of poets as well. Good poets, Socrates tells us, are also imitators. They

> *"do not realize, when they see their works, that they are three removes from what is, and are easy to produce without knowledge of the truth. For they produce illusions, not things that are. Or whether there is something in what they say, and good poets really do have knowledge of the things about which the masses think they speak so well . . . . (598e7–599a4)*
>
> *"Let's not demand an account, then, from Homer or any other poet. Let's not ask if any of them is a doctor or only an imitator of what doctors say; or which people any of the poets, old or new, has reportedly made healthy, as Asclepius did; or which students of medicine he left behind, as Asclepius did his sons. And let's not ask them about the other crafts either, but leave them aside. When it comes, however, to the most important and most beautiful things of which Homer undertakes to speak—warfare, generalship, city government, and a person's education—surely, it is fair to question him as follows: 'My dear Homer, if you are not third removed from the truth about virtue, and are not the sort of craftsman of an image, which is what we defined an imitator to be, but if you are even in second place and capable of knowing what practices make people better or worse in private or in public life, tell us which cities are better governed because of you, as the Lacedaemonians are because of Lycurgus, and as many others—big and small—are because of many other men. What city gives you credit for having proved to be a good lawgiver who benefited it? Italy and Sicily give it to Charondas, and we give it to Solon. Who gives it to you?' Will he be able to name one?'" (599b9–e3)*

HERMIAS: I do not think that he could name one.

PLATO: If Homer had really been able to educate people and help them be better,

> *"if Homer had been able to help people become virtuous, [would] his companions have allowed either him or Hesiod to wander around as rhapsodes? Wouldn't [they] have clung far tighter to*

them than to gold and compelled them to come home and live with them? And if persuasion failed, wouldn't they have followed them wherever they went until they had received sufficient education?" (600d3–7)

HERMIAS: Yes, they would, just as we do with you!

PLATO: Then can we conclude, as Socrates suggests,

> "that all poets, beginning with Homer, imitate images of virtue and of all the other things they write about, and have no grasp of the truth? (600e4–6) ... [T]he poet uses words and phrases to paint colored pictures of each of the crafts, even though he knows only how to imitate them; so that others like himself, who look at things in terms of words, will think he speaks extremely well about shoemaking or generalship or anything else, provided he speaks with meter, rhythm, and harmony. That is how great a natural spell these things cast." (601a4–b1)

Therefore, continues Socrates, an imitator will keep imitating, even though he has "*no worthwhile knowledge of the things he imitates*" (602b4–5). Because imitation is so far from the truth, from the nature of the object or subject, "*imitation really consorts with a part of us that is far from reason*" (60b3–4). This is true of all imitators, whether a poet or a painter.

> "So, we would also at last be justified in not admitting him into a city that is to be well governed. You see, he arouses and nourishes [the appetitive part] *in the soul and, by making it strong, destroys the rational one—just as someone in a city who makes wicked people strong, by handing the city over to them, ruins the better ones. Similarly, we will say an imitative poet produces a bad constitution in the soul of each individual by making images that are very far removed from the truth and by gratifying the element in it that lacks understanding* . . . ." (605b1–c1)

DEMETRA: This seems to be a severe penalty, Plato. Here Socrates is arguing to banish all storytelling, which is really what poetry broadly defined is. So, Socrates wants to ban poems and plays and tales of all sorts.

PLATO: This position does seem harsh, I grant that. Socrates offers, then, this stipulation: If poetry and the rest of the imitative arts have "*any argument to bring forward that proves that they ought to have a place in a well-governed city, we at least would gladly welcome them back*" (607c3–5).

HERMIAS: What did your brothers say in response, Plato?

PLATO: They did not offer an argument.

KYDES: I have an argument, Plato. Let's say, for example, that a friend paints a picture of the couch that I am lying on tonight. He does not see it or touch it; he does not lie on it. I describe it to him. In observing his painting I am then brought to ask whether it is a close approximation of this couch or a poor rendering.

I have some knowledge of what the couch "is really like," because I have experience of it in physical life. Whether the painting is close to or far from the physical couch, it reminds me of that couch and gets me thinking about it—how comfortable it was, how high off the ground, how soft the material—though Plato refuses to reveal whether it's leather. Ah, it is a great couch.

But then I ask, "Is it?" What makes a great couch, and is this one an example of it? This gets me thinking about the "couchness" of all couches and about the Form or essence of a couch, the one *"we'd say that a god makes"* (597b6). So, the imitation has gotten me to move up the Divided Line toward the Forms. That is one reason for permitting imitation in our city.

HERMIAS: Or how about this example? Let's say that Pheidias sculpts a statue of Athena. People marvel at its dimensions and symmetries and the overall beauty of the statue. Is it an imitation? Nobody I know, nobody we know, has seen "the real thing,"—that is, the goddess—so do we know whether the statue is a good or bad imitation? Should it then be excluded from the city because, regardless of its qualities, it imitates the goddess Athena whom no one has seen? Or can that statue, with its magnificence and beauty, lead us to think about, as Kydes suggests, the realm of the gods and the Forms themselves? If so, then imitation serves a truly significant function.

DEMETRA: Or how about this angle? I see a fresco of a seascape where the mountains come down to the sea and form a perfect beach and idyllic cove. I find it moving and restful at the same time. I ask the painter, "Where is this cove?" He responds, "I don't know. I've never seen it or anything like it. I made it up." I ask, "What do you mean you 'made it up'?" He says, "It comes from my imagination."

Is this an imitation? The painter didn't try to represent in his painting anything he knew or had seen or had even heard about in real life.

Instead, he "presented" something never seen. Would Socrates think this better or worse than imitation itself—something that doesn't reflect that which is found in physical life? But like Pheidias, the artist is bringing to life something for us that we do not see. Both are making the invisible visible. At the very least, this could get us thinking about whether something unseen in this life—the goddess Athena and this idyllic cove—itself has a Form.

So, even as a distortion, imitation can get us thinking about the "real thing." That, in itself, is worthwhile, because it can take us to and through the physical object to the Forms, just as Diotima described moving from one beautiful person to wondering about beauty in all persons. Or, in the case of the statue of Athena and the imaginary cove, to think about that which is in the art compared to that which is ideal that might stimulate the depiction or idea.

Finally, we must also consider what we have discussed tonight. Plato, you have introduced us through Socrates to the analogy of the sun, the allegory of the cave, the ship of state, and other such examples. These are metaphors and images related to real items—the sun, caves, ships, and the like. All of them are, therefore, imitations of those real items. But you used them to move us to think of how they relate to something above and beyond them as physical objects. Likewise, you yourself in introducing these ideas have imitated the voices and persons of Socrates and your brothers. This can only mean that the entire dialogue on which our evening's conversation is built would have to be banned from the city.

But, of course, the description and inner workings of the "city" itself, whether the fevered city or the healthy city, would have to be banned, since no such city exists except in imitation of elements of real cities. I cannot think that you believe that this entire discussion tonight has been a fruitless exercise and should not be permitted. We certainly don't.

HERMIAS: Of course, the Divided Line starts somewhere. We begin with images and then proceed up the Line to symbols—words and numbers—and then to concepts. Although we transcend images as we move up the Line, we don't discard them. We transcend but retain them. When we reach the level of understanding, we can look down the Line to see the value and even the importance of using images to get our thinking going, as in the word "imagination."

The same holds, it seems to me, for imitation. The higher up the Divided Line we go, the better we can see the usefulness and even importance of imitation, at least for initiating movement up the Line. We start instruction where people are, even at the level of images, and move them along from there. Imitation can be the initial and important first step, whether that involves the poems of Homer or the sculptures of Pheidias.

KYDES: I agree completely. For all the reasons that Deme and Hermias and I have mentioned, we can see that there is value in imitation. The *Mandūkya Upanishad* says that *OM* is a representation of the primordial sound of the universe from which all sounds are derived. Should we not chant *OM*, because our version would be an imitation of the sound of the universe? No! Of course we should chant it, because that can transport us to the realm of Being, of Truth, of Reality. As Hermias just said, imitation has value as a vehicle for taking us up the Divided Line. Imitation has the ability to turn the soul up the Divided Line.

HERMIAS: I think that we have offered decent philosophical arguments for why stories of all sorts, even those that portray the gods in a bad light, ought to be permitted in the healthy city. They challenge people's perspectives and thereby help strengthen and balance the soul.

KYDES: I have to say, Plato, that I find it surprising and disappointing that your brothers offered no defense at all of poetry and no argument for admitting it into the city. After all of this discussion and all that Socrates offered, after all of the talk of philosophy and dialectic, how could they not offer something at least similar to what we provided earlier?

PLATO: I cannot answer for them, Kydes. Socrates does lead them after this to what we ourselves have concluded this evening—that is, that the soul is immortal when it is pure, untainted by the body that limits, even maims, it (611b9–c2).

HERMIAS: What those in the Far East are calling "the Soul," as opposed to the soul enveloped within our physical bodies.

PLATO: That's right. We need to look in that direction . . .

KYDES: . . . up the Divided Line . . .

PLATO: Yes. Through our physically encased soul's love of wisdom. Remember what Socrates says of that soul:

> "We must keep in mind what it grasps and the kinds of things with which it longs to associate, because it is akin to what is divine and immortal and what always exists, and what it would become if it followed this longing with its whole being and if that impulse lifted it out of the sea in which it now is. . . . And then you would see its true nature, whether multiform or uniform . . . ." (611d9–612a4)

Socrates concludes that we have at this point already provided "*a pretty good account*" of the condition of the soul, its form, and what it longs for.

KYDES: We have, Plato. The soul strives to realize its true nature as Soul, as the Universal or Singular Soul, as we ascend the Divided Line to become as godlike as is humanly possible. It does so when the soul encased within the body is led by the rational part, exercised and expressed through its love of wisdom, to the Forms.

PLATO: Well said. Socrates reminds my brothers that the gods never neglect anyone who eagerly wishes to become just and who makes himself as much like a god as a human can by adopting a virtuous way of life (613 6–b1).

KYDES: This takes us back to the beginning of this evening, doesn't it, when Glaucon and Adeimantus put the challenge to Socrates? Then they wanted reassurances that morality was good in and of itself and not simply for gaining rewards from the gods. But here deep in the discussion, Socrates's statement about the gods never neglecting one who seeks virtue returns us to the idea that pursuing morality has an instrumental effect—what the gods will do for us. Might as well, then, do what your brothers suggested at the beginning: while living a life of immorality, make sacrifices to the gods as expiation for all the injustice and immorality one had caused in his lifetime and hope for rewards in the life to come.

HERMIAS: This turn seems to neglect or abandon the idea that regardless of our circumstances, even when we are moral but thought to be immoral, morality has a deep effect on our soul. We do moral things, just things, because it is in the nature of the healthy soul, the balanced soul, to do so. We know this when we come to know the Forms and the Good. Established in that knowledge . . .

DEMETRA: . . . *Yogastha Kuru Karmani*, right?

HERMIAS (rolling his eyes): Yes, Deme, we get it. But you're right: Established in this knowledge, we go out into the world, or come back into the world, to do what is right and good. As we were reminded earlier, the soul is moral, even when we possess Gyges's ring. Virtue is undertaken for its own sake, not for some reward while living or dead. Health is good for its own sake, and so is the health of the soul.

PLATO: Perhaps my brothers are hard cases, needing more persuasion, for Socrates ends the dialogue with another tale—the myth of Er.

KYDES: Ah, something else to ban from our city, Plato.

DEMETRA: And banned maybe it should be, since a myth is not any form of argument and thus not persuasive to those using philosophy and dialectic. Nevertheless, the myth as a contrast with argument and dialectic can be a nudge in the right hands to move us along up the Divided Line.

KYDES: Yes, maybe Plato's brothers need something other than dialectic and philosophy at this point to get them moving?
(And Plato smiled.)

THE MYTH OF ER

PLATO: Er was a brave warrior killed in battle. Ten days after the battle, those who collected the corpses from the field found Er's body. Unlike the other dead bodies that were putrefying, Er's body was quite fresh. This did not deter them, however, from placing Er with the other corpses on the funeral pyre. As the funeral was about to begin, Er suddenly came back to life and told them of his trip to the world beyond.

His soul traveled with many other souls, and all of the souls arrived at a place with four openings—two into the earth and two into the heavens. In this region, which Er described as "*mysterious*" or "*sacred*" and "*awesome*,"[1] sat the judges who would send those judged as moral through one of the openings up to the heavens and those judged immoral down through an opening into the earth.

When Er's turn came, the judges told him that he was to be a messenger to human beings about the things taking place there, and so he

---

1. The adjectives used to describe this region vary with the translation.

should watch and listen to everything happening in this place (614b4–d3). In addition to the souls departing through the openings, he saw souls descend from the heavens through the second opening. These "*souls came down pure*" (614d7–e1). Meanwhile, other souls arose from the other opening in the earth and arrived covered with dust and dirt.

Like a crowd to a festival, these arriving souls gathered in a meadow, where they exchanged tales of what they had experienced in the heavens or below. Someone asked about Ardiaius, a tyrant in Er's city of Pamphylia from a thousand years before. Ardiaius had killed his father and older brother and had committed many other horrid deeds as well. The person queried about whether Ardiaius had himself come up from the earth. He responded:

> "*He has not come here and never will. For in fact this, too, was one of the terrible sights we saw. When we were near the mouth, about to come up after all our sufferings were over, we suddenly saw Ardiaius together with some others, almost all of whom were tyrants—although there were also some private individuals among them who had committed great crimes. They thought that they were about to go up, but the mouth would not let them rise. Instead, it roared whenever one of these incurably bad people, or anyone else who had not paid a sufficient penalty, tried to go up. At that location, there were savage men, all fiery to look at, standing by, paying attention to the roar, who grabbed some of these people and led them away. But in the case of Ardiaius and others, they bound their feet, hands, and neck and threw them down and flayed them. They dragged them along the road outside, lacerating them on thorn bushes. They explained to those who were passing by at the time why they were being dragged away, and said that they were to be thrown into Tartarus. He said that of the many and multifarious fears they experienced there, the greatest each of them had was that the roar would be heard as he came up, and that each was very pleased when it was silent as he went up. Such then were the penalties and punishments, and the rewards that were their counterparts.*" (615c5–616b1)

After seven days in the meadow and four days of travel, the group arrived at the spindle of Necessity. Sitting at equal distance from the spindle were the three Fates, the daughters of Necessity—Lachesis (past), Clotho (present), and Atropos (future). Each soul went immediately to Lachesis. A "spokesman" of sorts arranged the group of souls in ranks,

Imitation and the Myth of Er

took a number of lots and models of lives from Lachesis's lap, mounted a large platform, and spoke to the group:

> "Ephemeral souls: This is the beginning of another death-bringing cycle for mortal-kind! Your daimon or guardian spirit will not be assigned to you by lot; you will choose him. The one who has the first lot will be the first to choose a life to which he will then be bound by necessity. Virtue knows no master: each will possess it to a greater or lesser degree, depending on whether he values or disdains it. Responsibility lies with the one who makes the choice; the god has none." (617d6–e5)

KYDES: I am sorry to interrupt, Plato, but I must ask in case this is not covered in the myth: If terrible tyrants like Ardiaius are never to come up out of the earth, if they can never escape this cycle of punishment, then is it possible that a virtuous person, moral through and through, might never return from the heavens and never be reborn in physical form?

HERMIAS: What exactly are you asking, Kydes?

KYDES: It seems straightforward enough to me. *Megiston mathema*! The "most important subject" is knowing the Good (505a1). If we come to know the Good, the Tao, Brahman, can we escape the cycle of birth-death-and-rebirth?

DEMETRA: Could you live forever on the Blessed Isles?

KYDES: Yes.

DEMETRA: That would seem to follow logically, as you pointed out, from what has been said.

HERMIAS: Follow logically? This is a myth. It isn't real.

PLATO: Of course, that does not mean that the myth lacks a point. Perhaps we are not there yet.

KYDES: Well, it's already made a point for me.

PLATO: That is good, Kydes. But let us finish.

After this speech, the spokesman threw the lots he was holding out among the group of souls. Each soul picked up the lot closest to him—all, that is, but Er, who was forbidden to select one. The number on the lot indicated the order in which each soul would pick from the models of lives that the spokesman next placed on the ground, models that vastly outnumbered the number of souls in the group. Among the models were all kinds of lives:

> "All animal lives were there, as well as all human lives. There were tyrannies among them, some life-long, others ending halfway through in poverty, exile, and beggary. There were lives of famous men—some famous for the beauty of their appearance or for their other strengths or athletic prowess, others for their nobility and the virtues of their ancestors, and also some infamous in these respects—and similarly for women. But the structure of the soul was not included, because with the choice of a different life it would inevitably become different. But all the other qualities were mixed with each other and with wealth or poverty, sickness or health, or the states in between." (618a3–b5)

The challenge, of course, is to take care, as Socrates tells us, so that "*above all else be a seeker and a student of that subject that will enable you to learn to distinguish a good life from a bad, to always in any circumstances choose the better life from among those that are possible*" (618b6–c4).

HERMIAS: To be a student of philosophy. To be able to reason on the basis of the nature of the soul, as we have been discussing tonight, which life is better and which worse.

KYDES: A good life being one that leads the soul to be moral; a bad life, one that leads toward immorality.

DEMETRA: So, choose to balance appetites, emotions, and reason where the soul is led by *philia* to and into wisdom and harmony.

PLATO: The spokesman then announced to the group, "*Even for the one who chooses last, if he chooses wisely and lives earnestly, there is a satisfactory life available, not a bad one. Let not the first to choose be careless, nor the last discouraged*" (619b3–5).

Then the one who drew the first lot came forward to choose his life and immediately chose the greatest tyranny. "*In his folly and greed he chose it without adequate examination and didn't notice that, among other evils, he was fated to eat his own children as a part of it*" (619b6–c1). He then blamed everyone but himself. He had come down from the heavens, and even though he had lived under an orderly constitution, he had participated in virtue through habit and not through philosophy.

KYDES: We could have warned him. He's just like the guardians in the fevered city—raised with virtue instilled through the founders and rulers, not through philosophy.

PLATO: In like manner, with more or less or equal examination as with the first chooser, souls made their selections. Those who had suffered or had seen others suffer were in no hurry to make their choices. Many who had come down from heaven, having not tasted suffering, often chose a life similar to the first soul who chose. Not surprisingly, then, most of the souls reversed their previous lives—from bad and evil lives to good ones and vice versa.

On the other hand, those who had practiced philosophy in their lifetime, as Er reported, chose lives in which they would be happy and for whom the *"journey from here to there and back again"*—from the afterlife to the earthly life and back again—*"won't be along the rough underground path, but along the smooth heavenly one"* (619e3–5).

Odysseus made the last choice of all. He spent a long time looking for *"the life of a private individual without interest in political affairs"* (620c5–6).[2]

When all the souls had finished choosing lives, they turned to Lachesis, who then assigned them each the *daimon* or guardian spirit that would be with them all their lives and help them fulfill their choices.

Finally, all souls drank a certain measure from the River of Forgetfulness and soon forgot everything. Some, however, lacking wisdom, drank more than the measure. Such souls would have a difficult time recollecting the knowledge of what occurred before they were born. Er was forbidden to drink at all.

A clap of thunder and an earthquake at midnight interrupted their sleep, and all the souls, like shooting stars, were carried this way and that up to their births. How Er returned to his body he did not know. He woke up suddenly at dawn lying on the funeral pyre (620d6–621b6).

---

2. The life chosen by Odysseus seems uniformly translated as "the life of a private individual," but translators differ on the second clause. Reeve uses the phrase "who did his own work" (620c5). Emlyn-Jones and Preddy write "with no interest in public affairs" (Plato, *Republic* [trans. Emlyn-Jones and Preddy], 620c7–8). I follow Waterfield and use something akin to his "looking for a life as a non-political private citizen" (Plato, *Republic* [trans. Waterfield], 620c7–8). I do so to separate, say, the active public life of Socrates in the Agora from his avoidance of serving in political offices.

What has Socrates shown us in this tale of Er? If he has been persuasive, we shall see that the soul is immortal and able to endure every evil and also every good. And we should

> "always hold to the upward path, practicing morality with wisdom every way we can, so that we will be friends to ourselves and to the gods, both while we remain here on Earth and when we receive the rewards of justice, and go around like victors in the games collecting prizes; and so both in this life and on the journey we have described, we will fare well." (621c3–9)

KYDES: Well, that was disappointing.

PLATO: For whom?

KYDES: For Socrates. After a lengthy dialogue on morality and philosophy, he ends with another "myth of the metals," a story without arguments or reality. How is the myth of Er not the worst embodiment of "imitation," since it purports to be about the afterlife, which cannot in any way be verified, and about rewards and prizes as an inducement to behave morally?

HERMIAS: But why would Socrates be disappointed? He offered to Glaucon and Adeimantus a lesson in dialectic, permitting Plato's brothers to guide the discussion as they reacted to what Socrates said and presented.

KYDES: But ending like this, with another questionable tale, doesn't persuade. It isn't an argument about morality for its own sake. Indeed, it seems that Socrates uses the myth of Er to frighten Glaucon and Adeimantus into philosophy. According to the spokesman in the afterworld, if someone who has pursued philosophy chooses, then he won't go down in the afterlife along the rough underground path, but will stay along the smooth heavenly one. Socrates is warning the brothers: Stick to philosophy if you don't want to experience the tortures and miseries of the underworld.

Glaucon and Adeimantus seemed to have missed so much of the lesson if Socrates has to end by appealing to a myth! It means that these interlocutors couldn't follow the dialectic and now must be frightened into staying with philosophy. It's as if he's telling them: "Believe this myth, lads, and it will inspire you to live lives of philosophy and virtue so that you can escape the worst of the afterlife."

HERMIAS: That's what you think, Kydes. For them, as students of philosophy, Glaucon and Adeimantus had opportunities through this dialogue to think about so much of life and social order and education. Every twist they took that we might not like or agree with, that we might even ridicule, was a chance for them to look into and think about something significant in how and why we order our lives and souls. They did follow the dialectic as much and as far as they could. Isn't that also what Socrates is showing us?

KYDES: Yes, maybe so. But you'd think that they'd have a better grasp of philosophy, even if they just walked around Athens all day with Socrates.

DEMETRA: I think that Glaucon and Adeimantus are just placeholders.

KYDES: They're what?

DEMETRA: Placeholders. For us. I don't think that this evening's dialogue is really about Plato's brothers. The dialogue tonight was our opportunity to think about these lessons, and part of that thinking was to challenge where Glaucon and Adeimantus went in the conversation and why we would go in a different direction. It seems that they needed to hear the myth of Er. From where they were on their own dialectical journey up the Divided Line, this tale was important for them to react to.

Remember Alcibiades's metaphor for Socrates's arguments? He said that Socrates's arguments are like

> "those hollow statues of Silenus. If you were to listen to his arguments, at first they'd strike you as totally ridiculous. . . . He's always going on about pack asses or blacksmiths or cobblers or tanners; he's always making the same tired old points in the same tired old words. . . . But if you see them when they open up like the statues, if you go behind their surface, . . . they are freely worthy of a god, bursting with figures of virtue inside. They are of . . . the greatest importance for anyone who wants to become a truly good man."[3]

Think of the profundity of this observation: Socrates is hollow, empty, without content save for the same old tired phrases and points. He spins out these same arguments, which appear worn and even ridiculous. Until you realize that behind what he is saying lies something else, something richer and deeper. But that realization depends upon you, what you bring to the discussion.

---

3. Plato, *Symposium*, 221e1–22a1–6.

In his discussions, Socrates goes where his interlocutors take him. Most often they don't take him very far, and so his arguments seem to be repeats—using the same examples of tanners and bakers and the like. Only until the interlocutors themselves can see below the surface do the arguments then burst with figures of virtues.

Socrates's arguments are like a mirror in which we see ourselves, because there is nothing definitive in Socrates. He is without a content to press. There is nothing inside him, no-thing inside him, but his full presence is focused on you and what you argue. So, the arguments tonight say more about us than about anything definitive Socrates is trying to impart.

KYDES: Certainly one aspect to note immediately that Socrates makes clear through the Myth of Er is a point we have made throughout the night—that the myth of the metals is no way to structure a city. Philosophers are made, not born, and made through education. You cannot assign people to classes based on some fanciful view of the metal in their soul. The myth of Er tells us that individuals, when in the afterlife, choose the kinds of lives they will lead. *"Virtue knows no master; each will possess it to a greater or lesser degree, depending on whether he values or disdains it"* (617e). Can that valuing be taught? Of course it can. So, cannot the absence of philosophy in one's life be attributed to the deprivation by society of an adequate education because of the class to which one is assigned?

DEMETRA: Even if the fevered city didn't follow the Noble Lie, even if it had a sophisticated educational system for all of her citizens, the end point is no less unsatisfying. Rule in the city by philosopher kings and philosopher queens, even those who follow dialectic and know the Forms, would reduce citizens to subjects. Socrates told us as much earlier this evening: *"Don't you think it is a disgrace, and a sign of poor education, to be forced to rely on morality imposed by others—that of masters and judges—for want of a sense of morality on one's own"* (405b1–4)? And if we are to rule ourselves and rely on our own sense of morality, is not each citizen, then, to be a philosopher to whatever extent possible?

Philosophizing to the best of your abilities is already an expression of your desires and values. Using philosophy to guide your life is already an expression of your discernment, of your desire to live an examined life, and even of inner harmony, the balance of parts within your soul.

HERMIAS: Deme is giving us one positive use of the myth of Er. Each of us, as students of dialectic and philosophy, gives our own interpretation of the meaning and place of the myth at the end of the dialogue. Whether we judge it meaningful or disappointing, it seems surprising, because, as Kydes said, it's a story, an imitative story by Socrates, that ends a dialogue where arguments and reason have supplanted habits, rituals, and incantations. "Believe it or be punished! Do it and receive a reward!" Can the myth of Er, then, be construed as another aspect of Socrates's argument for the external prizes of morality, which seems the least significant challenge of the dialogue? If so, we have to recognize, as Kydes pointed out, that it succeeds, if it does, through assertion, since nothing in it can be independently verified.

15

Inner Harmony Through the Transcendent Light

KYDES: So here we are at the end with a final myth, which returns us to the beginning of the evening's dialogue when we asked whether morality has any intrinsic value. Is there such a thing as morality-for-morality's-sake? Seems not. There is only an instrumental value to morality. We act morally to get something in return, in life or after death.

DEMETRA: But I don't think that that is what Socrates is saying in the myth of Er. I'm not even convinced that the reincarnation story is a relevant point. If we recall the high standard that Glaucon and Adeimantus set—namely, the moral person will be judged to be immoral by humans and by the gods regardless of what she says or does—then Socrates is now telling us that rewards and punishments are immaterial to what happens when we die. We must still make choices based on our character. The moral life is best because the soul remains in harmony, regardless of punishments and rewards here or in the hereafter. Any choice is a good choice when the soul is balanced and the target is the Good.

    The myth of Er reinforces what we already know and have established throughout this dialogue this evening: We can choose best, given the conditions under which we live, if we operate with a balanced soul led by reason in harmony with emotions and desires. Then we judge accordingly. So, we choose that which we judge to be good, whether the choice is one that we live with or is one that we make even if in the next moment we'll be dead. Stay in harmony by choosing as wisely as we can by properly balancing the three parts of the soul.

HERMIAS: Something else to notice: Perhaps more important than the life Odysseus chooses is the manner by which he chooses. He used his diverse experiences of suffering as a reminder to take his time and look hard before choosing. There are more lives available, Er tells us, than souls to choose, and so Odysseus still has choices among diverse lives. This reminds me, as I argued earlier tonight, that diversity is important and must be part of any healthy city with more than three rigid classes.

DEMETRA: Diversity in ways of living and thinking, yes, Hermias, I agree. But the message for us tonight, and not just in the myth of Er, is about the importance of philosophy. Odysseus didn't choose that way. He took his time, true enough. Yet he doesn't choose out of virtue or philosophy. He chooses as a reaction to the kind of life he led earlier and the results found in the afterlife from living that life. He wants the opposite of the life that he had just lived. He is acting out of instinct and thus chooses poorly—the very kind of story of heroes that Socrates had banished from the fevered city early in the dialogue.

KYDES: So, Socrates is telling us about the weakness of this Greek hero. For Odysseus, as for almost every soul in Er's tale, choices are about seeking rewards of some sort in the next life.

DEMETRA: That's how the story might appear to Glaucon and Adeimantus. But beneath that story is one about making the right choices, wise choices, those arrived at through philosophy. Odysseus might get lucky and be born in the healthy city, as Socrates described it. Then his quiet, private life might well lead him to philosophy and the paramount concern with the state of his soul.

As for political rule, the hierarchy to pay attention to isn't that of the city; it's that of the soul. Clearly for Socrates—and, I'm guessing, for Plato—one whose soul is in harmony, whose reason rules over the appetites with the help of emotions, is a better person, a more moral person, than someone whose soul is in disharmony. The balanced, harmonious, or moral souls, those with the greatest depth manifested in their souls, bear some responsibility, have some sense of obligation, to educate those who are unbalanced and help them turn their souls toward the Good.

KYDES: Perhaps the message of this evening's dialogue isn't really about the structure of the moral city. Nevertheless, it raises that issue. So, following you, Deme, what if the moral person can educate, can help turn each captured soul, each prisoner in the cave? What if all persons could come to know the Forms and thereby be moral and good? Would the city they lived in be a democracy?

HERMIAS: How and why would they agree to live in any other kind of city? The moral person is self-ruling. If all persons were self-ruling, then each would rule himself and would be working with self-ruling others. Would that not be a democracy?

KYDES: But they aren't all self-ruling at the same time. All the citizens might be, as Deme said, souls of gold, but they would come to know the Forms and the Good at different times and to different degrees. Would we not want the best to rule as the rest move up the Divided Line?

HERMIAS: An aristocracy, eh? The constitution would then have to be a mixed constitution—part aristocracy, part democracy—for the citizens, even as they are learning and growing, aren't going to be without the ability to exercise their self-rule to whatever extent possible.

KYDES: And provided the aristocracy doesn't degenerate into an oligarchy.

DEMETRA: Here, again, is the necessary emphasis on education, philosophy, and virtue. Citizens strive to find a compatible political life to match and engender the harmony of their souls. Certainly, in this life, we are still searching.

This talk about judgment has got me thinking. Early in the discussion tonight, Socrates describes the healthy city and asks the question that has been our focus all night—where does morality enter into the city? We provided, I think, some solid responses to that. But now I think that morality must already be present if Socrates judges the city to be healthy. By asking the question, he is simply reinforcing that morality is already there. It has to be if this is a healthy city, because creating and maintaining a healthy constitution is itself good. This is why he calls it *"the true city"* (372e5).

HERMIAS: Deme raises a good point. Why did Socrates declare that city to be the healthy and true city? We already pointed out that he hadn't said anything about education or philosophy. He hadn't said anything about how the city is governed. Are we to glean where morality in that city lies from what he did say? I think maybe we are.

Here's something that Socrates said about the healthy city that we've already commented on, but it deserves another look. Recall that in the healthy city the residents bear no more children than their resources permit "*lest they fall into either poverty or war*" (372c1). The residents don't want either poverty or war. Both bring hardship and heartache.

But what keeps the residents from both? What keeps them within the boundaries of their resources? It must be a philosophy, an outlook, that values virtues over material goods—that is, that values moderation over luxury, contentment over avarice, fairness over dominance, generosity over miserliness. All of that is grounded by education over natural inclination, however that is understood or determined.

KYDES: The organization and governing of the city are important, because the city is the environment in which philosophical education takes place. Where do morality and virtue come into the city? They must arise within the very structures of the city itself. The rituals, norms, practices, and institutions of the city reflect its values and morality.

HERMIAS: This is the point that we argued earlier, but I agree, Kydes, that it bears repeating. And this one as well: Every city must have politics of some kind, for important decisions about the city's welfare and the welfare of those in it have to be made. Who will make those decisions and how?

KYDES: As we said, it won't only be philosopher kings or philosopher queens, which might be appropriate for the fevered city. Not, however, for ours. Underlying the foundation of our city's politics is philosophical education. Every citizen participates in that education, both as a lifelong student and also as an exemplar—teaching by the example of his or her life. The whole city is a school, a *paideia*, and every moment is a learning opportunity.

HERMIAS: And every citizen should also participate in governing. The politics will therefore be democratic. The politics serves to exercise, reinforce, and reflect education throughout the city. The aim of education whether of the city or of the individual is, I think, the same: to establish and maintain an ordered and balanced soul and to find inner harmony. What I think differs among the people is the level of judgment expressed at different periods in their lives. Wherever you find yourself on the

Divided Line, however far up or far down, you use reasoned judgment in deciding how to act.

KYDES: It sounds as if being angry, for example, is never appropriate. That would show internal disorder, no?

HERMIAS: I don't think so. The aim, again, is to order and balance the soul. The two are not the same. An ordered soul shows reason controlling emotions and appetites, but the balance among them depends on the situation one is facing.

DEMETRA: Maybe this example will help, Kydes. Your physical balance is different when you stand on one leg instead of two. You might have to shift your weight, adjust your arms, and move your torso to maintain your balance. The same is true of the parts of the soul. When someone says or does something that angers you, you must judge what response is most appropriate. First, you recognize the emotion that has overtaken you and the immediate response that ensues. But you need to take a moment to judge, using reason, what is the most appropriate response. In one situation a firm verbal response might be appropriate; in another, remaining silent might be the best answer.

KYDES: Never a quick slap?

DEMETRA (laughing): Not a quick slap if it follows a snap judgment. That, I think, would unbalance the soul and leave it, however fleetingly, disordered. Bear in mind that, as Hermias said, wherever you are on the Divided Line, the principle is the same: Do not harm others, for in harming others, you also harm yourself by losing your soul's order and balance.

KYDES: The answer, then, to "Why be moral?" is the same: Acting morally exercises and preserves your inner harmony, which we earlier described as the health of the soul. Socrates said, *"no city or individual can be happy except by living in company with wisdom under the guidance of morality"* (335d5–6). Wise judgment rules the soul, and morality is the mechanism for maintaining order and balance—harmony—in our soul.

What is different, depending on one's position on the Divided Line and thus one's level of philosophical understanding and use of dialectical thinking, is the quality of one's judgment. You judge according to your reading of the situation, the persons and actions involved, and what you discern at the time to be the possible consequences of your response. Someone says something that makes you angry. Your first response is to slap him. But upon reflection, taking into account what you know about this person, what circumstances might have led him to say what he's just said, and the current situation he now finds himself in, you decide what is best is not to act on your immediate emotion and desire, but instead to walk away.

HERMIAS: That sounds very mature, Kydes. I'd like to see you exercise that wise judgment the next time one of the young wrestlers steps on your foot.

PLATO: Now at the end of our evening's discussion, can we say to Glaucon and Adeimantus that morality in and of itself is better than immorality?

HERMIAS: I believe that we can, given what we've been saying this evening, and as Deme just mentioned, that morality is both the cause and consequence of harmony within the soul.

KYDES: Explain what you mean, Hermias.

HERMIAS: Well, when you try to act morally—act according to what you know and think is right at that time—then you build harmony in your soul. Your intention, thinking, and action bring greater harmony within. Each moral action adds to that harmony, like adding more voices and parts to a song.

KYDES: So, thinking and acting morally increases or causes more harmony?

HERMIAS: I think that that is right. And as a result of that inner harmony, your actions almost naturally lead to moral consequences or results.

KYDES: But that still makes morality instrumental. We act morally to get or express or preserve something—in this case, that "something" is inner harmony.

HERMIAS: That is always true, Kydes. We can agree, for example, that health is good. We want to be healthy. We can then always ask, "Why?" "Why be healthy? What does it bring us?" At that point, we've lost the idea that health is good in and of itself.

KYDES: We know plenty of people who choose behaviors that they know, and that we know, aren't good for their health. They do it because the pleasure of the act—say, gluttony—supersedes the desire for health.

HERMIAS: Yes, but they know that what they are doing is unhealthy and not good for them. They can't help themselves because they are driven in this instance by their appetites, which have overwhelmed their reason. They are out of balance; they have lost their harmony. They know that in the long run they are hurting themselves.

KYDES: Even so, they don't stop.

DEMETRA: Perhaps if we look at a fuller context for Plato's question, we'll have a clearer answer. The challenge to Socrates from Adeimantus and Glaucon was to demonstrate that it is better to be moral even when you have a reputation for immorality and even when immorality will bring you great wealth and acclaim. Thus, why be moral when it costs you wealth and comfort and the respect of your community? The answer, it seems to me, is that inner harmony is the greatest reward. Inner harmony, as the sign of order and balance, brings us as close to divinity as humans can be ... or so said Socrates. It is that inner harmony that both brings us to and reflects the Forms and the Good. We act, therefore, to maintain and perhaps augment that inner harmony, regardless of how our actions are perceived by others.

PLATO: Are you saying, Demetra, that someone who has this inner harmony, who *"consorts with what is divine and ordered and thereby becomes as divine and ordered as a human being can be"* (501c6–8) can do no other?

KYDES: What are you asking, Plato?

PLATO: Socrates tells us, *"A god's mind is nourished by intelligence [noēsis] and pure knowledge, as is the mind of any soul who is concerned to take in what is appropriate to it."*[1] What is appropriate to such a person might well be, as you all have pointed out, where that person is on the Divided Line. Through dialectic this soul can develop the mind of a god, *"delighting in seeing what is real and knowing what is true."*[2]

So, *"only a philosopher's mind grows wings"* and can see as a god's mind sees. The philosopher *"is the only one who is perfect as perfect can be."*[3] Thus, I ask you: Being as perfect as perfect can be, can this philosopher do harm? In other words, I am asking whether a moral person

---

1. Plato, *Phaedrus*, 247d1–4.
2. Plato, *Phaedrus*, 247d1–4.
3. Plato, *Phaedrus*, 249c7.

would not act immorally or could not act immorally? Does a moral person have no choice but to act morally? Does consorting with the divine eliminate choice in how we act? We can do no other.

HERMIAS: Well, *"as perfect as perfect can be"* doesn't mean that we are perfect, as gods might be perfect. We are still humans. It seems to me that as long as we have bodies, as long as our souls are encased within a physical body and we live in this world, we will always have choices to make. In that sense, then, a moral person would choose to act morally, but is the choice always clear? For example, let's say that a doctor is faced with saving the life either of the pregnant mother or of the *embryon*, the young one, that she is carrying. The doctor cannot save both. So, acting either way will result in the death of one of them. There will be harm done either way.

KYDES: The doctor can't prevent the death of one of them. He isn't killing one of them. It just means that one of them will die.

HERMIAS: But he must make a choice. Through his act, he will save one and lose the other. How does the moral man choose? Which action preserves his inner harmony, or which action results from his inner harmony?

DEMETRA: I don't think that his inner harmony produces one action or the other. I think that his harmony leads him in this case to make the best decision, which must involve taking into account as many of the variables in the case as he can muster—for instance, deliberating with the pregnant woman and with her family, considering the current health of both the *embryon* and the mother, trying to discover what might be the source of this medical emergency, perhaps consulting with other doctors. Then, having taken such considerations into account, the doctor makes his decision. The moral aspect here is that the doctor realizes that the decision isn't his alone. All of those involved in this case must participate to some extent.

HERMIAS: The doctor recognizes that whichever action he undertakes, he leaves undone what should also be done.

KYDES: Meaning what, exactly?

HERMIAS: Meaning that the doctor recognizes that both should be saved, but that both can't be saved. In saving one, which he must do, he harms the other, who himself or herself should be saved as well. He balances the action in the full view of that consequence. That, I think, is how a moral man would act, and that act would express and maintain his inner harmony.

PLATO: Socrates does say that we might call unjust or immoral any action that destroys this inner harmony (443e6). But recall from even earlier in our conversation tonight what Socrates said, *"Surely nothing good is ever harmful, is it?"* (394b3).

KYDES: Notice that Socrates is raising this as a question. He's not declaring that something good can never cause harm. Hermias's example shows that, no?

DEMETRA: In a dilemma such as the one Hermias introduced, harm is unavoidable. As Hermias said, it is the recognition that harm is unavoidable that is moral and that the other choice—to save the other life—is also something that should be done. But we can't do both.

KYDES: The doctor knows that leaving undone what must also be done causes him harm, too. Making a choice that causes harm can unbalance his order and harmony. So, the doctor would seek to minimize harm to maintain his inner harmony, though some harm is, as we said, unavoidable.

DEMETRA: That's a good reminder, Kydes. For a moral person, harming another also harms oneself, because it unbalances the internal order. But, again, in deciding, one takes all the steps necessary to act from a position where the soul is balanced and in harmony. The action then reflects this deliberation. Perhaps that minimizes harm or offsets the harm caused.

So, it isn't only the decision itself that is in play for the moral person. It is also how she makes that decision. Moral harmony involves looking at the situation or dilemma from a perspective of all persons involved. How should anyone in this situation, given their own perspective, decide the outcome? This would be a process that transcended time and place and person, a position that should be universally applicable to anyone taking into account all of the salient factors of the case.

HERMIAS: You aren't suggesting that the moral dilemma ceases to be situational?

DEMETRA: On the contrary, it is definitely situational, but every situation calls for a principled response in full recognition of all the factors at play. The best decision, it seems to me, is one that is made after considering the perspectives of all those who face the dilemma. What might they decide and how should they decide? Indeed, how would anyone acting rationally decide this case? What are the moral principles involved for anyone, regardless of social status or even time and location, facing this dilemma?

HERMIAS: In other words, other persons facing a similar situation but at a different time and in a different place could accept the reasons behind your decision and might themselves make the same decision.

DEMETRA: Yes. It is the principles that underlie the decision-making, more than the actual decision itself, that are paramount. For example, the principle that each woman in this situation has the right to be heard and to have her circumstances, her situation, taken into account. No decision can proceed without her input.

HERMIAS: So, while the decision procedures are all the same for all persons at all times, the decision itself might be different. As you said, circumstances change. Perhaps a city has a law against abortion. That could change the calculus. But what doesn't change is how the decision is made—that is, the decision procedure involved, including the standard of rationality. So, there are universal procedures—that is, a framework in which reasoned discourse, or dialectic, can take place—involving moral principles. Using that framework or procedure, persons can agree to accept an outcome, even as they continue to disagree with it in substance. In other words, there is a universal procedure for evaluating and adjudicating moral claims, but there is not a universal moral code of outcomes.

DEMETRA: That seems right. Though not held in common, the decisions were made in common. Making them in common helps us come to hold them in common.

We cannot predict what decisions people will make, but we can argue that the procedures that they use should rely on presenting arguments—reasons and evidence—that persons can accept as sound and good. In the future, more evidence and other reasons might come to light that could alter the decision, but not the decision procedure, the mode of argument, itself.

Principled thinking of this sort reinforces the significance of our inner harmony. Principles need to be interpreted according to our own experience, knowledge, and judgment. Experiences of the Forms bring forth knowledge of Truth, Reality, Beauty, and Morality. That knowledge informs our judgments, as the strength of our inner harmony is both the cause for and the consequence of knowing the Forms. As we grow in knowledge, our inner harmony draws in more transcendent light, which bolsters that harmony and results in better judgments and actions. Therefore, the more we know the Forms, the more we "dip our cloth" in the dye of transcendence and the more that that transcendence sticks.

KYDES: Oh, don't tell me, Deme: *Yogastha Kuru Karmani*?

DEMETRA (smiling): Precisely, Kydes. Establish yourself in Being and then perform judgment and action. In the *Symposium*, what is it that Diotima tells Socrates? Only when we know the Forms is it possible then to give birth within our souls and in our lives not to images of virtue, but to true virtue.[4]

HERMIAS: Socrates says that to rule, a philosopher needs after seeing the sun—that is, knowing the Forms—an additional fifteen years of education and experience (540a3). To rule what? Here I agree with Deme—to rule oneself, to rule one's soul. That is because they need time and experience to establish Being in their lives, to integrate Being in their lives, and thereby achieve lasting inner harmony and act rightly. Then they take their inner light out into the world.

KYDES: In that way, make the invisible visible.

PLATO: Let me remind you of something that Socrates said in the *Republic* that we touched on earlier, which has relevance and perhaps added meaning given where we are now in the conversation:

> "And in truth, morality is, it seems, something . . . concerned with what is inside; with himself, really, and the things that are his own. . . . [H]e regulates well what is really his own, rules himself, puts himself in order, becomes his own friend, and harmonizes the three elements together, just as if they were literally the three defining notes of an octave—lowest, highest, and middle—as well as any others that may be in between. He binds together all of these and, from having been many, becomes entirely one, temperate

---

4. Plato, *Symposium*, 212a5–6.

Inner Harmony Through the Transcendent Light

and harmonious. Then and only then should he turn to action, whether it is to do something concerning the acquisition of wealth or concerning the care of his body, or even something political, or concerning private contracts. In all these areas, he considers and calls moral and fine the action that preserves this inner harmony and helps achieve it, and calls it so, and regards as wisdom the knowledge that oversees such actions. And he regards the action that destroys this harmony as immoral, and calls it so, and regards the belief that oversees it as ignorance." (442d8–444a1)

HERMIAS: Remember also what Socrates said in the *Timaeus*: "*No one is willingly evil. A man becomes evil, rather, as a result of one or another corrupt condition of his body and an uneducated upbringing.*"[5] Educate the citizens in philosophy and help bring them up the Divided Line to the transcendental light. In this way, corruption will be rooted out and internal harmony can be completed. Thereby one will not become or do evil.

KYDES: And this from Socrates in the *Gorgias*: "*He who has learnt what is moral is a moral man.*"[6] What is "learnt" in this context? It is experience and knowledge of the Good.

Socrates asks Gorgias: "*Isn't a man who has learned what is moral a moral man, too?*" To this proposition, Gorgias agrees. Then Socrates adds: "*And a moral man does moral things?*" Here, too, Gorgias agrees.[7] Therefore, I think we can conclude that to know morality at this transcendental level is to be moral.

We did not appreciate earlier what Socrates said about morality and inner harmony, because we ourselves did not have the knowledge and experience that we have gleaned tonight. We did not have enough, or much, perspective on transcendence and the Good. For example, it seems that the philosopher cannot achieve inner harmony outside the cave. Yet, remaining in the transcendent light does not permit him to integrate the elements of his soul or, if we follow Deme's line of inquiry, does not permit him to integrate those ideas still chained up within him. He abandons all of that if he continues to commune with the Good. He must establish Being by integrating the transcendent light into the actions required of everyday life. He has seen the light; now he must bring it into his life and our lives.

---

5. Plato, *Timaeus*, 86d–e.
6. Plato, *Gorgias*, 460c–d.
7. Plato, *Gorgias*, 460b9–12.

HERMIAS: As we also learned tonight, since the Good is *"the cause of all that is correct and beautiful in anything and controls and provides truth and understanding"* (517c4–5), then it follows, it seems to me, that being established in Being and acting from the Good guides us to act morally. We move up the Divided Line as best we can, and we bring the knowledge that we learn there into our everyday lives. From however high we get, even if it isn't all the way to the transcendent, we try to order and balance—to harmonize—our souls to the best of our knowledge and ability.

KYDES: Recall this from what Plato read tonight from the *Tao Te Ching*:

> *If* [persons] *could remain centered on the Good*
> *All things would be in harmony.*
> *All people would be at peace,*
> *And the law would be written in their hearts.*[8]

Could there be a better description of the true and happy city?

HERMIAS: And of the true and happy soul.

DEMETRA: But right now, speaking of transcendence and the Good raises another aspect that I am hesitant to bring up.

PLATO: Hesitant? Why, Demetra?

DEMETRA: I don't know enough to say anything about it.

PLATO: You are simply raising the issue; you aren't declaiming for or against it.

DEMETRA: Very well. Just keep in mind that I'm tentative about all that I'll say. In the transcendent light outside the cave, when one can know the Forms and the Good, we also can know that we are part of one Soul, that we are really one Soul. It isn't simply that we share this Soul; we are this Soul. As such, then to harm anyone is to harm ourselves, since we are all one. How could I act unjustly toward another when that other is really myself?

HERMIAS: Haven't we already covered this idea, Deme, in talking about how harm to another causes harm to ourselves?

DEMETRA: In terms of harm, yes, Hermias, we have.

KYDES: Well, what other terms do you have in mind?

---

8. Lao Tzu, *Tao Te Ching* (trans. Mitchell), verse 32.

DEMETRA: Love. Our universal connection, our mystical connection as one Soul, takes us beyond wishing not to harm another and into loving one another as we love ourselves. We want everyone to prosper and grow just as we want to prosper and grow ourselves. We want only the best for them. We want to see them elevated, and we want to help them attain whatever they strive for. Yet we do not accept anything they wish to do or approve of everything they have said and done. Sometimes we have to apply tough love in the form of criticism and opposition. That, too, is love.

We could say that this love, this *agape*, is what brings the philosopher back to the cave. Love for all humanity, and not just fellow city-dwellers, is actually an expression of self-love and a reaching out to others with whom we share this one Soul. This is universal love, love in full openness to another and without expectation of love returned. Thus, the person described by Glaucon and Adeimantus who is thought to be immoral but who is truly moral feels no resentment to those who judge her. Instead, she feels love and compassion for those others, for she and they are aspects of the same, one Self. One acts morally, one does good, not to garner rewards, even of a good reputation. One acts to help and serve others, because it is the right thing to do, regardless of how they judge you. Anyone's suffering is also my own suffering. This rests, again, on the strength of our inner harmony.

KYDES: So, we all dissolve into one soup of self-love.

DEMETRA: I wouldn't put it that way. Maybe the better metaphor is that we are all ocean waves. Each wave thinks that it is a wave and fears ceasing to be an individual, distinct wave at all. But the wave's true being is water. Wave or no wave, a distinct individual or one Universal Soul, it doesn't matter. The form is unimportant. The wave is always water now and forever.

So, like the wave, the boundaries that separate us into separate selves dissolve. We remain as individuals; we continue to function as harmonious selves. But we recognize that our essence, our true Being, is sharing in the unbounded oneness of Love and Self. It is not "self-love"; it is "Self-Love." See?

KYDES: No, I don't. Right now, I only see the need to sleep.

HERMIAS: Don't we all.

KYDES: I wonder how Xanthippe liked the story.

HERMIAS: Socrates's wife? That Xanthippe?

KYDES: You know of another? Yes, that Xanthippe. After all, she started this tale by confronting her husband about where he had been all night. Then ensued the longest, and perhaps the greatest, excuse for staying out all night that I have ever heard.

HERMIAS: How far into the story was Socrates before she threw up her hands in disgust and walked away?

KYDES: Maybe he gave her the shorter version?

HERMIAS: Can there be a shorter version to the tale we heard tonight?

DEMETRA: Surely you could summarize Homer's *Iliad*, couldn't you? You could say that the poem is about the Greeks gathering to fight the Trojans to return Helen to Menelaus and then build from there by adding highlights and lessons as needed or requested.

KYDES: All right, Deme. Let's say that you wander by Socrates's house as he and Xanthippe face each other on the threshold. Xanthippe says, "Wait, Deme. You were with Socrates last night. What did you learn from his story. And don't go jabbering on and on, as he is doing. Give me your highlights and lessons."

DEMETRA: Well, I would say this:

All things emanate from the Good. Though the Good is beyond words and logic, beyond any description whatsoever, we can know It. Through dialectic, and through various methods practiced in the Far East, we can come to know the Good—the true nature of Reality, of Being, Truth, Beauty, Goodness, and all the Virtues.

Knowing the Good also awakens us to our own true nature. That nature is as the Universal Soul—eternal, unchanging, and perfect. We are not simply one with or connected to all things; through this Universal Soul, we are all things and beyond all things. We are the spaciousness in which any form arises. This spaciousness is simultaneously everything and nothing (no-thing). Yet it has intrinsic qualities. Among those are peace and happiness and guiding light. This light, above all, orients us toward expressing the right and the good in all that we do.

We bring this knowledge, this transcendent light, into our souls, to increase the light already within our souls. The brightness, the magnificence, of transcendent light is like sunlight when compared with the fire inside the cave of our souls. We bring this light into our cave not once but multiple times. Each time it increases the illumination within our souls, harmonizing its three parts. With this knowledge and illumination, we return to our everyday lives to bring our inner harmony out into the world to let this light of our souls shine forth in every thought, word, and deed.

We know—we don't hypothesize or believe—that all persons have light within them, but need their inner fire to be enhanced. That is done through exercising dialectic. So those who see the fire in every soul sense a duty to help others increase their fire and help bring them to the transcendent light. We call them philosophers.

It is the philosopher who translates the Good by trying to bring the transcendent to the earthly realm through images, metaphors, arguments, and, well, *elenchus* or dialectic. The philosopher both integrates the Good into his own life and educates others on how to know the Forms and the Good to enrich their own lives. Therefore, the principal duty of the philosopher is to teach persons to look after their souls above all else, to cultivate and activate a balanced and ordered soul—a soul in harmony.

However far up the Divided Line one travels, wherever she lands on the Divided Line, she must try to balance and order the three parts of the soul to maintain and express harmony. Only at the highest level, however, can the soul know the Forms and the Good and come as close as we can in human form to true Being. Living life established in Being leads to a fundamental shift in how we perceive the world: It is alive; it is one; it is perfect.

From this perspective, the answer to the question "Why be moral?" is that that is the only way to activate, develop, and preserve one's soulful or spiritual health—that is, one's inner harmony. Moral thought and behavior are how we give others and ourselves the concern and respect all deserve. We do so by exercising universal moral principles that pertain to all persons at all times and in all places. This exercise minimizes harm to others and to ourselves and maximizes benefits for both. After all, what are you, what am I, but equal expressions of the Good and equal manifestations of the Universal Soul?

Finally, since development of our souls is our most cherished value, providing an education in dialectic for all citizens is society's most important function. Only a city that provides and promotes such education for all—that is, a democratic city as an aristocracy of everyone—can be a worthwhile or moral or beautiful city.

Why democratic? Because it is a sign of poor education to be forced to live under a morality imposed by others (405b1–4). To avoid living under imposed rule, a person must be individually self-ruling, or autonomous, and collectively self-ruling or a democratic participant. So, both collectively and individually, we must deliberate about the rules, roles, norms, and laws that we follow. That honors individual and communal autonomy and requires the freedom to develop and express our own thinking, as well as the political freedom to participate in making the rules and laws. Dialectical education and democracy empower the people and enable the pursuit by everyone of the highest levels of morality that they can attain.

How did I do, Kydes?

KYDES (with a prolonged yawn): Quite well, I think. (Another yawn.) Thank you for that, Deme. Your speech could have gotten us all to bed much faster, I'm certain of that.

HERMIAS: But without the nuance or experience of dialectic. In short, without the growth brought forth tonight.

KYDES: I'll assess that in the morning.

DEMETRA: And probably for the rest of our lives.

At this point, smiling, Plato rose from his couch. The yawning now among the trio was incessant. As dawn broke, servants arrived to clear the urns, wine cups, table coverings, and the tables themselves. Plato said, "Let us pull your couches deeper into the grove. The sun will soon be up, and the thick olive branches will provide shade to help you sleep. Get your rest now before you venture into the hot sun." The trio was too tired to question, let alone argue.

With the couches now deep in the olive grove and the trio already wrapped in their blankets, Plato headed down to the river. There he stripped off his clothes and waded into the cool water, where he sat for several minutes. After a full immersion, he exited the water and lay naked for a time on a smooth boulder. Eyes closed, bathed in the fresh rays of the newborn sun, Plato rested in the ocean of ever-present silence.

A sudden shiver, and his mind began to swim back to thoughts about the night's conversation. He had been right in thinking that these three students could offer a lively, and trenchant, discussion of the dialogue. Plato could use their comments, questions, and insights as a guide for revising the dialogue and for reordering the books that constituted it. "Constitute," "constitution." That could be the title, *Politéia* or "Constitution," a term that applied both to the city and to the individual.

Then Plato rose. Caring not at all about his appearance, he put on his robes once more and headed back toward the Academy, thinking to eat for the first time since yesterday's midday.

On the way back, Plato thought more about these three students. He would gauge over the coming weeks how immersed in Being his charges were. He did not think at this point that any of them were established fully in Being. Established fully in Being, the person remains unattached to activity and to the vicissitudes of life. Unfettered in any act, the person lives in eternal freedom. Establishment in Being cannot then be disturbed, let alone broken, by any activity whatsoever, not even torture, humiliation, and death. The philosopher now and forever lives an existence of eternal, unchanging Being. That existence brings both a sense of unbounded freedom and a sense of abiding happiness. Radiance within matches radiance without. The flow of transcendent light within now brings an abundance of bliss, which is no other than calm joy.

Of course, desires and ideas of all sorts will continue to arise in the philosopher. The mind does not cease to yearn or distract or dream. But these desires and ideas are like water flowing into a tranquil sea. So, returning to the cave is not a threat, for those in the cave cannot disturb or corrupt this freedom or bliss.

When we know the Forms, then all thoughts and motions of ours are aligned with the divine and thus aligned and in harmony with the universe, because there is no separation between what we are, think, feel, and do and the universe itself. And this, as Socrates said, is "*that most excellent life offered to humankind by the gods, both now and forevermore*,"[9] because that excellent life is the divine and happy life.

How do we grasp the Forms, the "thing-in-itself"—that which each thing essentially is and which provides this transcendent light? We do, as Socrates said in the *Phaedo*, "*through thought alone . . . without any sense perception, using pure thought alone.*"[10]

These three were not yet fully established in Being, that was clear, and that realization was no disappointment. Yet were they far enough along to understand what "thought alone" is? Contemplation is that kind

---

9. Plato, *Timaeus*, 90d.
10. Plato, *Phaedo*, 65e3-10.

of thought—"*observing things in themselves with the soul by itself.*"[11] That simply means going quiet and becoming still. "*When the soul investigates by itself it passes into the realm of what is pure, ever existing, immortal and unchanging. Here is the eye of the soul, unattached to and undisturbed by the body and the mind, remaining in silence and stillness with what is pure.*"[12]

Plato thought that their reactions and responses to the evening's discussion showed that they might well be far enough along. And yet, Plato considered for a time, whether these three could also benefit now from drinking a *kukeon* mixed with some *ergot*, a natural-growing fungus, one of whose properties was a psychoactive ingredient that induced revelatory and mystical experiences. This was part of the Eleusinian Mysteries that Plato had referenced earlier in the night.

On the other hand, maybe a different approach or a complementary approach would be better? Chanting *OM*, they had learned tonight, was one form of contemplative practice. So, too, as Plato knew, was simply sitting in silence and remaining still. As Ladmon told Plato, those living in *Seres* and *Sinae* practiced something called *zhǐguǎn dǎzuò*, which translates as "just sitting" or "nothing but sitting." A more accommodating method, related to "just sitting," was to sit and follow one's breath, returning to the breath whenever the sitter became aware of drifting into thoughts or of focusing on some discomfort in the body. Finally, one of Plato's favorite contemplative methods was to ponder a proposition or question—an unanswerable puzzle—such as "How can that which is nothing be that which is everything?" or simply repeating the question, "Who is asking?" or its correlate, "Who am I?"[13] Was this not the essence of dialectic, in this instance an internal dialectic?

Plato would observe these three students over the next several weeks and months to determine what they each needed for their next educational steps. He wanted them remembering not backward to memories of past indiscretions or to roads poorly or well taken; he wanted them remembering forward to recall their timeless, eternal natures—that which they were now, had always been, and would always be. He was confident from their responses tonight that dialectic itself had taken sufficient hold

---

11. Plato, *Phaedo*, 66e1–2.
12. Plato, *Phaedo*, 79d1–4.
13. In the Zen Buddhist tradition, the practice of "just sitting," also known as "silent illumination," is called *shikantaza*; contemplating an unanswerable puzzle is the use in Zen of the *kōan*, which itself is the Japanese word for the Chinese *gong'an*.

in them to guide their lives. But had the Good's transcendent light taken sufficient hold within them that it could never be lost? If so, then they were now awake and always would be, even when they slept. And Plato smiled.

Bibliography

Aristotle. *Nichomachean Ethics*. New York: Oxford University Press, 1998.
———. *The Politics*. New York: Cambridge University Press, 1988.
Bloom, Allan. "The Education of Democratic Man: *Emile*." *Daedalus* 107.3 (1978) 135–53.
Bussanich, John. "Socrates the Mystic." In *Traditions of Platonism: Essays in Honour of John Dillon*, edited by John J. Cleary, 29–51. Farndon, UK: Ashgate, 1999.
Eisenstadt, S. N., ed. *The Origins and Diversity of Axial Age Civilizations*. Albany: State University of New York Press, 1986.
Graeber, David, and David Wengrow. *The Dawn of Everything: A New History of Humanity*. New York: Farrar, Straus and Giroux, 2021.
Harte, Verity. "Review of *Plato's Philosophy of Mathematics*." *Journal of Hellenistic Studies* 118 (1998) 227.
Hesiod. *Theogony*. Perseus Digital Library. https://www.perseus.tufts.edu/hopper/text?doc=Hes.+Th.+132 .
Jaspers, Karl. *The Origin and the Goal of History*. Translated by M. Bullock. New Haven, CT: Yale University Press, 1953.
Lao Tzu. *Tao Te Ching*. Translated by Robert Henricks. New York: Modern Library, 1989.
———. *Tao Te Ching*. Translated by Stephen Mitchell. New York: HarperCollins, 1991.
———. *Tao Te Ching*. Translated by Victor H. Mair. New York: Bantam, 1998.
———. *Tao Te Ching: A Book About the Way and the Power of the Way*. Translated by Ursula K. Le Guin. Boston: Shambhala, 1997.
Muraresku, Brian C. *The Immortality Key*. New York: St. Martin's, 2020.
Plato. *Plato Complete Works*. Edited by John M. Cooper. Indianapolis: Hackett, 1997.
———. *Republic*. Translated by Robin Waterfield. New York: Oxford University Press, 1993.
———. *Republic*. Translated by Chris Emlyn-Jones and William Preddy. Loeb 237. Cambridge, MA: Harvard University Press, 2013.
Prabhavananda. *The Upanishads*. Translated by Frederick Manchester. Hollywood, CA: Vedanta, 1947.
Rama. *Māndūkya Upanishad: Enlightenment Without God*. Honesdale, PA: Himalayan International Institute of Yogic Science and Philosophy, 1982.
Reeve, C. D. C. *Plato's Republic*. Translated and introduction by C. D. C. Reeve. https://123philosophy.files.wordpress.com/2018/12/Plato-Republic.pdf.
Rosen, Stanley. *Plato's Republic*. New Haven, CT: Yale University Press, 2005.

Rousseau, Jean-Jacque. *Emile or On Education*. Translated by Allan Bloom. New York: Basic, 1979.

Sophocles. *Antigone* and *Oedipus the King*. Translated by Peter D. Arnott. Wheeling, IL: Harlan Davidson, 1960.

Strauss, Leo. *The City and Man*. Chicago: Rand McNally, 1964.

Thucydides. *The Landmark Thucydides*. Edited by Robert B. Strassler. New York: Simon & Schuster/Touchstone, 1996.

Turner, Vernon Kitabu. "A Mind Like Water." Interviewed by Simeon Alev. *What Is Enlightenment?* Spring/Summer (1999) 116–29, 161–65. https://s3.eu-central-1.amazonaws.com/wieoldissues/wie_en_weboptimized/EN_issue_15.pdf.

Whitehead, Alfred North. *Process and Reality: An Essay in Cosmology*. New York: Free, 1985.

Yount, David. *Plato and Plotinus on Mysticism, Epistemology, and Ethics*. London: Bloomsbury Academic, 2017.

———. *Plotinus the Platonist*. London: Bloomsbury Academic, 2016.

Zimbardo, Philip. *The Lucifer Effect*. New York: Random House, 2007.

www.ingramcontent.com/pod-product-compliance
Lightning Source LLC
Chambersburg PA
CBHW031351230426
43670CB00006B/499